# Intersectional Identities of Twice-Exceptional Teens

The teen years can be turbulent for all students, but particularly so for those who are twice exceptional from traditionally underserved, minority populations. Focusing on the voices and stories of twice-exceptional students, this book explores the interconnectedness between teens' social identities and their twice exceptionality.

Each chapter focuses on a different underserved population and is written by an expert member of that population. Designed to help practicing educators better understand and serve their students, this book describes what it is like for these students navigating multiple social identities, illuminates areas of social emotional concern and common coping mechanisms, and offers suggestions for ways in which educators can provide much-needed support to address these needs.

Teachers, counsellors, psychologists, and gifted and special education specialists will find this book an invaluable resource for ensuring that their classrooms are bastions of success for these unique learners.

**C. Matthew Fugate** is Provost of the Bridges Graduate School of Cognitive Diversity in Education. He has presented on topics including the social-emotional needs of twice-exceptional students, culturally responsive teaching, and creativity. He is active in the National Association for Gifted Children and the Texas Association for Gifted and Talented. Matthew was named one of *Variations Magazine*'s "22 People to Watch" in the neurodiversity movement.

**Wendy A. Behrens** serves as the Gifted Education Consultant for the Minnesota Department of Education, where she focuses on developing an equitable infrastructure to support gifted, talented, and high-potential learners. Her expertise encompasses policy development, advocacy, service models and teacher training, all aimed at fostering educational excellence and inclusivity.

# Intersectional Identities of Twice-Exceptional Teens

## How Diverse Identities Affect the Social and Academic Experience

Edited by
C. Matthew Fugate and
Wendy A. Behrens

NEW YORK AND LONDON

Designed cover image: Getty Images

First published 2026
by Routledge
605 Third Avenue, New York, NY 10158

and by Routledge
4 Park Square, Milton Park, Abingdon, Oxon, OX14 4RN

*Routledge is an imprint of the Taylor & Francis Group, an informa business*

© 2026 selection and editorial matter, Matthew Fugate and Wendy Behrens; individual chapters, the contributors

The right of C. Matthew Fugate and Wendy Behrens to be identified as the authors of the editorial material, and of the authors for their individual chapters, has been asserted in accordance with sections 77 and 78 of the Copyright, Designs and Patents Act 1988.

All rights reserved. No part of this book may be reprinted or reproduced or utilised in any form or by any electronic, mechanical, or other means, now known or hereafter invented, including photocopying and recording, or in any information storage or retrieval system, without permission in writing from the publishers.

*Trademark notice*: Product or corporate names may be trademarks or registered trademarks, and are used only for identification and explanation without intent to infringe.

ISBN: 978-1-032-77725-2 (hbk)
ISBN: 978-1-032-77663-7 (pbk)
ISBN: 978-1-003-48451-6 (ebk)

DOI: 10.4324/9781003484516

Typeset in Aptos
by Deanta Global Publishing Services, Chennai, India

Access the Support Material: www.routledge.com/9781032776637

This book is dedicated to all the cultural warriors who came before us and to those who continue to fight the good fight.

# Contents

| | |
|---|---|
| ACKNOWLEDGMENTS | XI |
| FROM THE EDITORS | XIII |
| FOREWORD<br>Lisa Jobe and Susan Baum | XV |

### CHAPTER 1
*2e Learners—What Are We Talking About?* ......... 1
Eleonoor van Gerven

### CHAPTER 2
*Intersectionality and Identity Formation* ......... 25
Joy Lawson Davis and Carlita R.B. Cotton

### CHAPTER 3
*Living a Counterstory: Adolescence, Identity, and Growing Up Gifted and Unwhite* ......... 41
Angela M. Novak

### CHAPTER 4
*The Brilliant Intersection: Understanding Black Students Who Are Gifted, Exceptional, and Navigating Economic Barriers* ......... 55
Gilman W. Whiting

### CHAPTER 5
*Brillantes y Valientes: To Be Twice-Exceptional, Latinx/Hispanic, and Adolescent* ......... 77
Alexandra Vuyk and Maureen Montanía

### CHAPTER 6
*From Cultural Nuances to Educational Needs: Understanding and Supporting Asian American Twice-Exceptional Adolescents* ......... 101
Tiffany Chaiko and Enyi Jen

## CHAPTER 7
*The Intersectionality of Native American and Twice-Exceptional Identities*    121
Shana Lusk and Anne Gray

## CHAPTER 8
*Building Identity, Brick by Brick: Being Twice Exceptional and Transgender*    143
Orla Dunne

## CHAPTER 9
*Students on the Move*    165
Cecelia Boswell

## CHAPTER 10
*Exploring the Academic and Social Implications of Being a 2e Military-Connected Teen*    171
Kathryn Davis and Georgia McKeown

## CHAPTER 11
*Considerations for Serving Twice-Exceptional Homeless and High-Mobility Students*    199
Yvette R. Robinson

## CHAPTER 12
*How Diverse Identities Affect the Social and Academic Experience*    221
Debra A. Troxclair

## CHAPTER 13
*Depression and Suicidal Behaviors among Twice-Exceptional Secondary Students*    239
Jennifer Riedl Cross and Tracy L. Cross

FINAL THOUGHTS FROM THE EDITORS    263

APPENDIX A: SOCIAL IDENTITY WHEEL    265

APPENDIX B: SELECTED INTERSECTIONALITY RESOURCES    267

APPENDIX C: CULTURAL RECOGNITION: PRACTICAL TOOLS FOR EDUCATORS    269

APPENDIX D: EMOTIONAL AND PSYCHOLOGICAL PROFILES OF HIGHLY GIFTED STUDENTS    273

## Contents

EDITOR BIOS 279

GUEST AUTHOR BIOS 281

# Acknowledgments

This book is the result of countless conversations, deep reflection, and the generosity of those who were willing to share their lived truths. We are profoundly grateful to the twice-exceptional adolescents whose voices fill these pages. Your courage, vulnerability, and insight have shaped this work in ways words can hardly capture. Thank you for trusting us with your stories.

We extend our deepest appreciation to the guest authors who contributed their expertise and passion. Your perspectives brought richness and depth to this project, and we are honored to have your voices alongside those of the students, families, and educators whose lives you have touched in innumerable ways through your work.

A special thank-you to our dear friend and frequent collaborator Cecelia Boswell, whose enduring commitment to gifted and twice-exceptional learners from all walks of life continues to inspire and guide our work in the field. This book was born from your vision and encouragement, and we are deeply thankful for your influence.

We are also sincerely grateful to our editors at Routledge, Quinn Cowen and Rebecca Collazo, for their belief in this project and their unwavering support from the very beginning. Your guidance and encouragement have meant the world to us.

And finally, to our husbands—thank you for your patience, steadiness, and understanding as we once again disappeared into the long and winding process of writing. Your love and support made this work possible.

*Matt and Wendy*

# From the Editors

Symbolizing the transformation from adolescence to adulthood, our butterfly captures the unique journey of twice-exceptional learners. It represents beauty, strength, and resilience through challenges. Like a caterpillar unaware of its remarkable metamorphosis, teenagers face struggles that shape their identity. For twice-exceptional learners, this journey includes extraordinary gifts and obstacles.

The chrysalis stage reflects the intense growth of young adulthood—a time of self-discovery, perseverance, and preparation. For twice-exceptional learners, this period is marked by navigating both their extraordinary abilities and the challenges these bring, requiring resilience and adaptability. When the butterfly emerges, vibrant and ready to soar, it embodies the triumph of embracing adulthood, celebrating the unique strengths and individuality of these remarkable learners. This metaphor reminds us that transformation, though challenging, is a journey of empowerment and growth.

Adolescence is a challenging time for any young person, but for 2e teens—students who are gifted while also facing significant learning differences—the journey can be especially complex. This complexity is magnified for 2e adolescents from traditionally underserved and marginalized communities, who must navigate the intersections of race, ethnicity, gender identity, socioeconomic status, and other overlapping social identities.

This book delves into the lived experiences of these remarkable students, exploring their common social-emotional struggles and highlighting coping mechanisms and strategies that support their success. It also offers practical

## From the Editors

recommendations for educators to create classrooms that truly recognize, value, and nurture the diverse talents and potential of 2e learners.

We hope this work feels both personal and insightful as we invite you to engage with the authentic stories and voices of twice-exceptional adolescents. Expert contributors from each community share powerful narratives that showcase not only the exceptional creativity, resilience, innovative thinking, and rich cultural perspectives these students bring, but also the unique challenges they face—such as systemic bias, misunderstandings of their learning profiles, feelings of isolation, and a lack of emotional support.

We are deeply grateful for the bravery and honesty of the students and scholars who contributed their stories and wisdom. Through their perspectives, we aim to inspire educators and allies to create affirming educational environments in which every twice-exceptional learner can thrive.

And when the butterfly finally emerges, vibrant and ready to take flight, it symbolizes the individual's readiness to embrace adulthood—finding freedom, navigating responsibilities, celebrating their own distinctive gifts and talents.

*Matt and Wendy*

Intersectional Identities of **TWICE-EXCEPTIONAL TEENS**

How Diverse Identities Affect the Social and Academic Experience

**C. Matthew Fugate** and **Wendy A. Behrens**

A **Prufrock Press** Book

# Foreword

## Lisa Jobe and Susan Baum

*"I'm very many things to very many people in such a way that really, none of them sees the full perspective of who I am."*

*Brandon, 18*

*"I am just simply Maddie."*

*Maddie, 16*

In the heart of Studio City, California sits Bridges Academy (www.bridges .edu), a groundbreaking school where twice-exceptional students thrive in a strength-based, interest-focused learning environment. Here, 2e learners—those with both gifted abilities and learning differences often defined as disabilities (Al-Hroub, 2020; Baum et al., 2017)—discover acceptance and understanding, frequently after struggling in other school environments because of the intersection of their social identities and their learning differences. We invited four Bridges high-school teens to join us for a discussion exploring social identity in 2e adolescents. As we engaged with these adolescents, they appeared relaxed and self-assured, brimming with confidence and eager to share their journeys of self-discovery.

Adolescence is a pivotal time for cognitive as well as social-emotional learning and growth (Dunkel & Harbke, 2017). Developing self-identity in adolescence is complicated for teenagers as they struggle with questions such as, "Who am I?";

"Where do I fit in society?"; "What are my core values?"; "What is my purpose?" Teens are bombarded at school, at home, and on social media with messaging that influences how they perceive their appearance, gender, sexual orientation, race, socioeconomic status, and other aspects of who they are. Erickson (1968) described this adolescent stage as a time of crisis: identity versus role confusion.

Erickson's groundbreaking theory of psychosocial development identified eight developmental life stages during which individuals face significant conflicts that become "a necessary turning point, a crucial moment, when development must move one way or another, marshaling resources of growth, recovery, and further differentiation" (Erickson, 1968, p. 16). Adolescence becomes a critical turning point in the development of identity formation, separating teens' own roles from those around them. Individuals gradually build a sense of self-identity, recognize where they fit in with society, and begin planning future pathways (Erickson,1968). Adolescents going through this process are said to be in an "identity crisis," often experiencing confusion and anxiety as they struggle in their search to define who they are as individuals (Shaffer, 2009). This identity formation is said to be the most essential challenge of adolescence (Erikson, 1968).

Many researchers have built on Erickson's identity formation research with regard to adolescents (e.g., see Mishra, 2023). For example, Nagaoka et al., (2015) describe integrated identity as

> a sense of internal consistency of who one is across time and across multiple social identities (e.g., race/ethnicity, profession, culture, gender, religion). An integrated identity serves as an internal framework for making choices and provides a stable base from which one can act in the world.
>
> *(para. 7)*

Adolescents who are different from their peers often have more complex social identities. Gifted and talented children may, for example, adapt their behaviors to conform to societal and educational norms of their age-mates. When it comes to 2e adolescents, the intersectionality of social identities connected to their social and academic experiences becomes even more complex. For this reason, when asked to write this forward, we felt compelled to share the voices of 2e teens as they work through their identity development.

## *Identity Formation*

*Maddie, a 16-year-old sophomore at Bridges whose pronouns are they/them, bounded up the stairs to meet us, the rainbow strands in their hair highlighting their bouncing blond ponytail. As we walked to the lounge where we were gathering*

## Foreword

*with the students, they described the "incredible" concert they had attended the night before, referring to the lemon-yellow concert tee they were wearing. Once in the lounge, they quickly made themself comfortable on the couch, continuing to chat about their myriad creative interests.*

*A knock on the door caused Maddie to pause, then break into a huge smile as David, a popular senior, walked in and shook our hands. David, an 18-year-old Black teenager sporting a baseball cap, showed a mature confidence reflected in his warm smile as he took a chair next to Maddie. David started telling us about his upcoming college plans, including Maddie in the conversation.*

*A moment later, Adam, another 16-year-old sophomore, rushed through the door, a whirlwind of energy. He apologized for being late, explaining that he had changed into a more "professional" shirt for the occasion. He enthusiastically greeted each of his peers as he dropped onto the couch on Maddie's other side. Our fourth learner could not make the group discussion, so we began.*

Identity development in 2e adolescents—those with both gifted abilities and learning disabilities—creates intersecting layers of identity. For example, Dole (2001) studied twice-exceptional college students' self-identities, discovering both contextual and personal influences that shape these processes.

Contextual influences include support systems such as family members, teachers, mentors, and friends, as well as extracurricular activities, jobs, and community service. Important personal influences include self-knowledge, self-acceptance, and self-advocacy. Dole (2001) described identity formation in 2e learners as an ongoing circular process:

> Like a spider that is advancing or receding, yet continuously developing, it [begins] with self-knowledge, not only of their learning disabilities, but also of their learning abilities, talents, and strength. Knowledge of self [is] ongoing and [leads] to self-acceptance and self-advocacy, not necessarily in that order."
>
> *(p. 122)*

Additional research of this population by Wang and Neihart (2015) found that 2e students who are academically successful hold positive self-concepts that influence their learning outcomes. The identification of their unique strengths is critical to achieving their goals. These adolescents' parents, teachers, and peers have positively influenced their development of self-efficacy. Conversely, earlier experiences can also have devastating impacts on self-identity—or at least until countervailing experiences reset the messaging (e.g., see Duyar et al., 2023).

Further complicating the study of 2e adolescent identities is the intersectionality of other personal and cultural factors. Robinson's Triple Identity Theory (2017) provides an understanding of the complexities of identity formation.

## Foreword

Developed by John Howard Robinson, the theory posits that individuals have three identities: personal identity, social identity, and collective identity. The theory recognizes the dynamic nature of identity, highlighting that identities are not fixed and can change based on experiences, interactions, and societal influences. Understanding this flexibility is crucial to supporting identity development across diverse cultural contexts and in addressing issues related to identity formation, identity conflict, and identity negotiation. It is with this awareness we began our discussion with the students.

## Student Voices

As the teens settled in, we began the conversation by sharing a copy of "The Social Identity Wheel," a handout depicting 11 different categories of social identities (Pabdoo, n.d.) (Appendix A) and asking for their general thoughts about what the biggest factors shaping teens' social identities are in today's culture. Very quickly, they unanimously agreed that gender identity and sexual orientation, along with a general "coolness factor"—whether others want to be around you—have the biggest impact on how teens want to be seen. They also noted that autism, LGTBQ+, and neurodivergence often overlap among their school peers, pushing these issues to the forefront of social identity.

From this point, the teens eagerly shared the experiences that have shaped their unique identities.

### Maddie

Maddie's bubbly, creative social identity was immediately apparent from the moment we met them. We quickly learned that they love the stage, are "passionate" about art, and danced for many years. As we talked, they also shared their heightened anxiety, as well as their autistic diagnosis and their self-identity as a lesbian. Maddie identified the intersectionalities of their age, race, mental health, and twice-exceptionality as identities they think about the most. Comparatively, they suggested their identities with regard to gender, sex, socio-economic status, and race have the greatest effect on their social identity.

Maddie described significant school trauma in their elementary years, despite being identified as highly gifted at an early age. With Hashimoto's disease, they were often bullied for their weight, which created intense anxiety to the point that they hid under classroom desks. They changed schools often and were in and out of hospitals with mental health challenges including suspected obsessive-compulsive disorder, bipolar disorder, and eating disorders. They recalled that "I [truly] thought I was going crazy," until they found a lifeline in their autism diagnosis—which was originally dismissed by therapists because "I make great eye contact." Maddie went on to describe how much "easier" their life had become since the diagnosis, as they were able to get an individualized education program and their family "then knew how to parent me." While they said they had many friends, their family signifies the core of their social identity, and they became animated describing how much they and their mom have in common. At the same time, they relate to their Slovakian ancestry and greatly respect their father, who grew up in abject poverty.

While Maddie identifies with their gifted abilities as well as their learning challenges, they would describe themselves as a mediocre student whose academics are plagued by continuing anxieties. Nonetheless, they have strong self-efficacy and hope to become a medical examiner, describing their detailed plans through medical school that they have already been thinking through.

## David

David is a socially popular senior, co-captain of the golf team, and excited to be heading to a state university in the fall to study entertainment writing. He lit up when describing his passion, game scripting. In fact, he wrote his college essay about how he had found his identity through fictional characters. He presents as a mature, confident young man, contrasting with the trauma he described as a younger student with attention deficit hyperactivity disorder (ADHD):

> *I had a pretty big struggle ... there was never really a school that I fit in. I would move around from school to school like multiple times a year ... there was bullying ... I didn't do classes well [sic], couldn't focus. The teachers didn't get it. I even suffered physical abuse at one school ... [Without Bridges], I probably would have just thought that I just can't do school. It's just not for me. But I can do school. And I proved it [here].*

David expressed that as a Black teen with ADHD, race is still an important identifier for him. Though now a popular senior, he initially struggled at the school, where there are few other Black students, because:

> *... it is important to have people that look like you and can relate to your struggles around you. There's a thing with black people, like, we already have enough against us. So, ADHD people are kind of scared to get the help that they need when they're Black, because they don't want to add that extra pressure of having ADHD or having autism or something like that onto it. I think that's a problem because people need help from others.*

David also described other layers of his social identity. His parents, and then his friends, have influenced his core identity. While popular, he still harbors fears that others might reject his friendship, likely rooted in the social messaging he received in his early schooling. He feels a strong connection to his ancestry, particularly the background and struggles of his Japanese grandmother. Similarly, he is close to his grandfather, a renowned scholar. David described his grandfather as his biggest supporter, but at the same time recalled the self-doubts he had experienced in the past compared to the high academic legacy in his family.

While David does not identify with his giftedness because he "doesn't see [him]self as someone special," he did share that it is nice to hear others comment on how good he is at something, particularly when doubts or anxieties creep in.

## Adam

Adam is a vivacious sophomore, a student leader who is passionate about art and entertainment. He shared that as a gay and autistic teen, he identifies most strongly with his neurodivergence and sexual orientation. Adam described how he occasionally masks around others, particularly during times of high stress, while trying to put others' needs before his own. Adam socially identifies less with giftedness than with the term "neurodivergent," but lights up when discussing his passions. He noted that he was identified as autistic at a very early age and underwent significant speech therapy and frequent school changes long before he was identified as gifted. Interestingly, he framed his school success in terms of how he treats others with respect and is recognized for that kindness.

As for the other 2e teens, family is highly important to Adam. His twin brother, who is not 2e, attends a separate high school, yet they are extremely close. Adam spoke proudly of his mother, who raised their family on her own while running a small business; and his grandfather is also important in his life. Adam also connects heavily with his Jewish heritage. This family connection interweaves with his career focus in the entertainment industry: he mentioned that his family have been in the business for what will be six generations.

## Brandon

Brandon, an exceptionally gifted autistic senior, shared his journey in self-identity with us in a separate conversation. When we handed him "The Social Identity Wheel" (Pabdoo, n.d.), he merely glanced at it, explaining as he set it down that it doesn't work that way for him. Choosing his words very precisely, he began to describe how he views his social identity. First, he explained, "I'm very many things to very many people in such a way that, really, none of them sees the full perspective of who I am." His teachers, for example, assumed that he was most enthusiastic about humanities subjects such as literature, history, and art because he was the most outspoken in those conversations. "In reality, I was fascinated with science and mathematics, and I was using that as a lens to view it through," he explained.

He paused to bring a visual to mind, then described his core self-identity as a hanging mobile, such as one that might be hung over a nursery crib. His foundational identity, which holds everything else together and motivates all his actions, is his Christian faith. The rotating threads hanging from the foundation are all aspects of his personality, possibilities, competing thoughts—all tied to the anchor.

Unlike the others, Brandon was homeschooled until high school, yet he still faced identity crises in his academic pursuits. He described how his identity had been fully equated with his academics, but that he was always haunted by wanting to do more, even suffering "existential crises" by always having more to learn. It was only by discovering the "finiteness of life" that he was able to rectify that need.

A voracious reader, he described how characters in a novel are just as impactful as real-life peers; that what he reads becomes real: "I've lived thousands of lives, hundreds of thousands of lives through everything I've read. And so, I feel very old, although I am very young." The purpose of school itself was just to "learn social skills." Yet, with these social experiences, he said, "I am a more complete human being because of it." These social identities, even if not fully understood, have helped him develop his own self-identity.

Brandon shared snapshots of how his social identities have affected him. For example, he contrasted how he must balance "the love of learning" with "actually navigating the [school] reputation you want." He described how his leadership persona had developed as he worked through Eagle rank in Scouts and with exceptional mentors on his robotics team. He, too, credited his family as being the foundation of his social identity, sharing the sacrifices they made to be able to travel extensively and study together.

As for his peers, Brandon's self-efficacy is well developed, particularly when sharing his passions. He became more animated talking about his love of learning, his job after graduation with NASA, and his personal writing, demonstrating more social connection through his eye contact and body language, learning forward in earnestness. What Brandon seeks, perhaps more than the others, is to be fully understood. Just before he raced off for class, we asked him why he loves to write. For such a complex young personality, his explanation was remarkably simple: "I'm trying to leave a footprint on the collective human imagination."

# Intersectionality and the Experiences of Twice-Exceptional Adolescents

Just in this small sample of 2e adolescents, we see how many different layers of social identity have been interwoven from their experiences, and how this affects them as students and as individuals. As we see with each of these remarkable teens, 2e adolescents have their own unique tapestry of interwoven identities, best understood through their individual lived experiences. While each individual tapestry is a unique work of art, common themes emerge when we examine the lived experiences which have guided each thread. By examining these themes through a collection of vignettes, the authors of this book are adding significant contributions to understanding and supporting twice-exceptional adolescents.

Understanding the intersectional factors shaping adolescent identity, particularly for 2e minoritized students, is crucial, as they may bring unique challenges to the learning experience (Hunter et al., 2024). Recognizing the unique experiences of 2e learners and the self-identities that these experiences form is crucial to eradicating systemic barriers and other inequities. Doing so also enables our educators and other stakeholders to implement tailored instructional strategies in which each aspect of their identities is valued. By supporting each aspect of our learners' identities, we foster positive learning environments where these students thrive, where their unique perspectives contribute to the whole, and where all benefit from shared learning experiences.

# References

Al-Hroub, A. (2020) Use of the Jordanian WISC-III for twice-exceptional identification. *International Journal for Talent Development and Creativity, 8*, 121-144. https://doi.org/10.7202/1076752ar

Baum, S., Schader, R., & Owen, S. (2017) *To be gifted and learning disabled: Strength-based strategies for helping twice-exceptional students with LD, ADHD, ASD, and more.* (3rd Ed.). Prufrock Press. https://doi.org/10.4324/9781003239147

Dole, S. (2001) Reconciling contradictions: Identity formation in individuals with giftedness and learning disabilities. *Journal for the Education of the Gifted, 25*(2), 103-137. https://doi.org/10.1177/016235320102500202

Dunkel, C. S. & Harbke, C. (2017) A review of measures of Erikson's stages of psychosocial development: Evidence for a general factor. *Journal of Adult Development, 24*(1), 58-76. https://doi.org/10.1007/s10804-016-9247-4

Duyar, S. N., Özkaya, C., & Akdeniz, H. (2023) A systematic review of the factors affecting twice-exceptional students' social and emotional development. *Gifted and Talented International, 38*(2), 177-189. https://doi.org/10.1080/15332276.2023.2245861

Erickson, E. H. (1968) *Identity: Youth and crisis.* Norton.

Gross, M. U. (1998) The "me" behind the mask: Intellectually gifted students and the search for identity. *Roeper Review, 20*(3), 167-174. https://doi.org/10.1080/02783199809553885

Gross, M. U. M. (1993). *Exceptionally gifted children.* Routledge.

Hunter, W., Rath, S., Barnes, K., Hilliard, L., White, C. L., & McGiffert-Sandoval, D. (2024) "Take me to the bridge": Transitional support for minoritized twice-exceptional Learners. *TEACHING Exceptional Children, 0*(0). https://doi.org/10.1177/00400599241239332

Mishra, A. (2023). The Pursuit of Eriksonian fidelity in education for the gifted: A literature review exploring its interpersonal and intrapersonal determinants. *SENG Journal: Exploring the Psychology of Giftedness, 2*(2), 43-56. https://doi.org/https://doi.org/10.25774/b34m-jq42

Nagaoka, J., Farrington, C. A., Ehrlich, S. B., & Heath, R. D. (2015) Foundations for young adult success: A developmental framework. The University of Chicago Consortium on Chicago School Research. https://consortium.uchicago.edu/sites/default/files/2019- 01/Exec_Summary_YAS_Framework.pdf

Pabdoo. (n.d.). *Social Identity Wheel.* https://sites.lsa.umich.edu/equitable-teaching/social-identity-wheel/

Porter, L. (2020). *Gifted young children: A guide for teachers and parents.* Routledge.

Robinson, S. A. (2017). Phoenix rising: An autoethnographic account of a gifted Black male with dyslexia. *Journal for the Education of the Gifted, 40*(2), 135-151. https://doi.org/10.1177/0162353217701021

Shaffer, D. R. (2009). *Social and personality development (6th ed.).* Wadsworth/Cengage Learning.

# Chapter 1

# 2e Learners—What Are We Talking About?

Eleonoor van Gerven

*Tommie is nine years old. He is gifted and diagnosed with ADHD and autism. Tommie attends a special class for twice-exceptional learners. Looking at Tommie's strengths and barriers in the context of the need for change, we see that his strengths are mostly academically focused. His challenges relate to his executive skills. In his group, there are four other students, all with different problems. Tommie has meltdowns several times a day. There is a pattern that can be distinguished in these meltdowns. It starts with Tommie being restless. He says loudly that he is stupid and will not master the new skills. He smashes his hand on the table, throws his book into the classroom and runs off, and hides behind the coat racks in the hall. His meltdowns occur when he must do regular classroom assignments with time limits or unclear instructions, or experiences consecutive failures without the feeling of progress. Due to his problems with self-regulation, self-actualization is difficult for Tommie.*

*Tommie's educational needs clarify how individual factors might unintentionally influence his problems. His problems with his executive skills, his weak central coherency, and his persistent problems with social communication and interaction prevent him from being successful. Combined with the emphasis on high results, the educational context stimulates low self-esteem.*

*Tommie's challenges are less severe when he can do his project work for history and geography, when he is encouraged to do research, and when the teacher allows him to spontaneously relate what he has discovered and what he knows afterwards. These golden moments are characterized by his teacher structuring the learning process and setting specific, measurable, achievable, relevant, and timebound educational objectives. Structuring his environment decreases stress. Letting him work by himself more often makes interaction at other times less stressful. Whenever his parents point out small successes, Tommie shows that he is eager to learn.*

This chapter lays out a crucial framework for comprehending the concept of twice-exceptional learners. We start by defining "twice-exceptionality" and exploring what makes a definition effective. Then, we delve into the benefits of shifting from a label-based approach to one based on educational needs. By considering the opportunities that stem from characteristics of giftedness and the barriers associated with learning or developmental disabilities, we can adopt a more positive approach to supporting twice-exceptional learners.

## Defining "Twice-Exceptionality"

International theory on twice-exceptionality defines "twice-exceptional learners" as both identified as gifted and diagnosed as having a learning or developmental disability (Baska & VanTassel-Baska, 2018; Baum et al., 2017; Fugate et al., 2020; Hughes, 2011; Maddocks, 2018; Reis et al., 2014). However, the co-occurrence of giftedness with a disability is not always acknowledged in educational practice (Reis et al., 2014). For students who are both gifted and hampered by a learning or developmental disability, this has significant consequences. It may result in them not receiving an appropriate education (Trail, 2022). In some schools, they are excluded from interventions aimed at gifted students; in others, based on their giftedness, they are not offered support in the domain or domains affected. A significant reason for the lack of recognition in educational practice is that there are unruly preconceptions about what giftedness is and how it should manifest itself in everyday life (Assouline et al., 2008). Giftedness is often still seen as a synonym for high achievement and an optimal capacity for self-regulation (Bakx et al., 2021). This misconception increases the likelihood of misdiagnosis. Students who also have a learning or developmental disability are not recognized because they do not perform commensurate with the expectation that fits the described view of giftedness. Further, because of the disability, they may experience difficulties in self-regulation and the application of executive skills, so they do not distinguish themselves positively from other students in that area either. Therefore, their education is often based on the perspective of the perceived learning and/or developmental disability rather than on their giftedness (Fugate et al., 2020). An integrated approach to the combination of their giftedness and the learning and/or developmental disability is hardly applied (Weterings-Helmons, 2023).

The definition with which we opened this section seems unambiguous, but this is not true. First, there is no universal definition of "giftedness" (Dai & Chen, 2014); and second, the concept of disability is widely varied.

> ### Definition of "Giftedness"
>
> #### *Based on the Gifted Child Paradigm*
>
> Giftedness is asynchronous development in which advanced cognitive abilities and heightened intensity converge in the creation of inner experiences and heightened awareness that are qualitatively different from the norm. This asynchronicity increases as intellectual abilities increase. The uniqueness of the gifted makes them particularly vulnerable, requiring adjustments in parenting, teaching, and supervision to allow for optimal development. (Kreger-Silverman, 2013, p. 44)
>
> #### *Based on the Talent Development Paradigm*
>
> Subotnik et al. (2011) are the best-known exponents of talent development thinking. They defined "giftedness" as:
>
> - a normative concept, which therefore reflects the norms and values of society;
> - demonstrable in the form of achieved excellence;
> - domain specific;
> - the result of interacting biological, pedagogical, psychological, and psychosocial factors; and
> - relative not only to the average but also to the top performance in the domain of action.
>
> #### *Based on the Differentiation Paradigm*
>
> In this view, giftedness is seen as a concept that describes an educational need, temporary or otherwise. "Giftedness" is described as an educational situation in which a student in one or more domains is so far ahead of other students in their development that there are educational needs for which the regular supply cannot provide appropriate guidance, or cannot do so adequately (Peters, Matthews, McBee, & McCoach, 2014). Thus, in this view, the word "giftedness" refers not so much to the child's aptitude but to a specific educational need that becomes apparent depending on the context in which a student functions (Borland, 2012). "Giftedness," therefore, refers to a temporary status with only one message: "I need more than I am getting now to continue to develop."

Reis et al. (2014) wrote a review article exploring possible tools to provide a good definition of what should be understood by the concept of twice-exceptional learners. The idea behind this was that if this definition is sharp, misdiagnoses and/or missed diagnoses can be prevented. The biggest takeaway is that the authors emphatically stated that working with lists of "characteristic behaviors and symptoms" can be misleading if they are not interpreted within the context in which the behavior occurs. This warning is in line with the development whereby the influence of the learner's ecology is becoming more evident in education (Bronfenbrenner, 1979; van Meersbergen & de Vries, 2017; Weterings-Helmons, 2023; Ziegler & Stoeger, 2017).

---

**Definition of "Dyslexia"**

Dyslexia is a disorder characterized by a persistent problem with learning and applying reading and/or spelling accurately and/or fluently at the word level that is not the result of environmental factors and/or physical, neurological, or general intellectual disability:

- The skill level in reading at word level and/or spelling is significantly below what is required of the individual given their age and circumstances (criterion of retardation).
- The problem in learning and applying word-level reading and/or spelling persists even when adequate remedial instruction and practice are provided (criterion of didactic resistance). The interventions must be at least related to Level of Care 3—that is, they have taken place at school but outside the context of regular (Level of Care 1) or extended (Level of Care 2) instruction in the classroom.

Students with dyslexia have difficulty with:

- reading and/or spelling at word level in Dutch (sound-sign pairings, spelling conventions);
- reading texts quickly and accurately (decoding) in all subjects; and
- spelling quickly and accurately (encoding) functional writing in all subjects.

(American Psychiatric Association, 2014) (de Jong, et al., 2016) (van Viersen, de Bree, Wijnekus, van den Boer, & de Jong, 2016) (Verhoeven, de Jong, & Wijnen, 2014)

### *Definition of "Dyscalculia"*

Dyscalculia is a disorder characterized by persistent problems with learning and fluent and/or accurate recall and/or application of arithmetic/mathematical knowledge (facts/rulings):

- There is a significant arithmetic deficit relative to age and/or educational peers, which hinders that person in daily life (criterion of severity).
- There is a significant arithmetic deficit relative to that which may be expected based on that person's individual cognitive development (criterion of retardation).
- There is a persistent arithmetic problem that is resistant to specialized help (criterion of didactic resistance).

Students with dyscalculia have problems with one or more of the following aspects (van Luit H., 2018):

- Declarative knowledge: Issues with remembering and recalling math facts (automation deficit).
- Procedural knowledge: Errors in executing step-by-step plans/calculating procedures.
- Visual-spatial knowledge: Problems with understanding and notation space (placing numbers on number line, digits in large numbers, geometry).
- Number knowledge: Lack of understanding of number systems and insufficient knowledge of the place value of numbers.

(van Luit, Bloemert, Ganzinga, & Mönch, 2014; van Luit H., 2018)

### *Definition of "Autism Spectrum Disorder"*

Autism is a spectrum disorder. By this is meant that the degree to which symptoms occur may vary from case to case, making each case unique. Autism spectrum disorder (ASD) is characterized by persistent deficits in social communication and interaction and limited, repetitive patterns of behavior, interests, or activities.

Students with characteristics of autism have problems with one or more of the following aspects:

- Persistent deficits in social communication and interaction:
  - Lack of social-emotional reciprocity.
  - Problems in nonverbal communication.

- Problems in developing, maintaining, and understanding relationships.
- Restricted, repetitive patterns of behavior, interests, or activities:
  - Stereotyped or repetitive motor movements; placing objects according to fixed patterns; compulsively repeating words or phrases; using idiosyncratic expressions.
  - Stubborn adherence to existing routines; inability to be flexible.
  - Very limited or abnormal interests with extremely high intensity and focus.
  - Hyper or hyposensitivity to sensory stimuli.

(American Psychiatric Association, 2014; American Psychiatric Association, 2014)

### *Definition of "Attention Deficit Hyperactivity Disorder"*

Attention deficit hyperactivity disorder (ADHD) is a neurobiological developmental disorder that occurs among approximately 5% of all children. It is characterized by "a persistent pattern of inattention and/or hyperactivity-impulsivity that impairs functioning or development."
The *Diagnostic and Statistical Manual of Mental Orders*, Fifth Edition (DSM-5) describes six classification characteristics of ADHD:

- inattention;
- hyperactivity and impulsivity;
- symptoms observed before age 12;
- symptoms present in two or more areas;
- symptoms that interfere with school, social, or occupational functioning; and
- symptoms that do not occur in the course of a mental disorder and cannot be better explained by another mental disorder.

Not every child with ADHD shows the same behavioral characteristics to the same degree. Three types of ADHD may be distinguished:

- Type 1: Children who are primarily hindered by a high degree of inattention. In this case, they are also referred to as "ADD" instead of "ADHD."
- Type 2: Children who are primarily hindered by a high degree of hyperactivity.
- Type 3: Children who are hindered by both high inattention and high hyperactivity and impulsivity.

(American Psychological Association, 2013)

Moreover, according to Reis et al. (2014), the definition of "twice-exceptionality" must describe the interaction between the different characteristics of giftedness and the characteristics of the learning or developmental disability. A definition that does not describe this interaction does not help recognize and guide twice-exceptional students. The interaction between giftedness and, for example, autism leads to different behaviors than the interaction between giftedness and dyslexia or dyscalculia. From this perspective, the general definition of "twice-exceptionality" should always be supplemented by a description of the interaction of giftedness and the characteristics of the specific disability that hinders the student. Theoretically, this leads to a wide range of sub-definitions, making this specification practical but equally complex.

The notion of twice-exceptionality differs from that of comorbidity. With comorbidity, there are two co-occurring disabilities in a person. This is substantially different from twice-exceptionality. Giftedness is not a disability. Therefore, the coexistence of giftedness and a learning or developmental disability is not a valid reason to use the term "comorbidity."[1] However, co-occurring disabilities among twice-exceptional students can exist. In that case, there are always two or more coinciding classified disabilities, while the student is also gifted. These cases can be referred to as "multi-exceptional."

## Recognition Without Labels

The implication of co-occurring disabilities is that traditional instruments for recognizing giftedness and/or a learning and developmental disability are not reliable because of the interaction between the characteristics of giftedness and those of the disability. Some characteristics of giftedness come into sharper focus; others are suppressed. The same is true of the characteristics of a learning and/or developmental disability. In this regard, several studies highlight that behaviors may be observed in twice-exceptional students that are observed neither in students who are gifted only nor in students of average intelligence who are hindered by a disability (Costis, 2016; Fugate, 2020; Hughes, 2011).

In international literature, there is a strong emphasis on formal diagnostics to inform appropriate action. However, this is easier said than done. Not all schools have the financial resources to contract psychologists who can conduct the necessary testing to obtain a diagnosis. In addition, identifying twice-exceptional students requires specific knowledge regarding the interpretation of the test results. The lack of such knowledge may lead to an incorrect interpretation of these findings.

As a result, parents sometimes consult a professional who can explain why their child is not developing in a manner commensurate with being gifted.

However, few parents have the financial means to do so. This presents a dilemma in terms of inequality of opportunity in education. These consultations often mark the beginning of a long search for appropriate and feasible support in the current field of education. Therefore, it would be preferable if, in daily educational practice, the term "twice-exceptionality" was interpreted as having both "characteristics of giftedness and characteristics of a learning or developmental disability" (van Gerven, 2024).

This brings us back to Reis et al.'s (2014) suggestion that a definition of the concept of twice-exceptionality offers guidance only if the interaction between the characteristics of giftedness and the specific barriers the student faces are explicitly described. The takeaway from this is that there is no such thing as "the profile" of a particular type of twice-exceptional learner (Maddocks, 2018), or that one cannot add twice-exceptional learners as an additional category to generic profiles of giftedness, as some scholars have done (Betts & Neihart, 2010). Thinking in terms of such profiles is an outgrowth of so-called "medical model" thinking, which is far removed from an approach based on change and solution-focused thinking. A change and solution-oriented approach is based on the need for change (van Gerven, 2021), and not on a diagnosis framed by the DSM-5. This increases the group of twice-exceptional students compared to all students who are screened through psychological testing. Fewer students are excluded because the margins of description become very wide. The other side of the coin is that this way of doing things also allows for more attention to be paid to learners who need more support in their development but who otherwise would still be excluded from appropriate education.

## Moving Away from a Strength and Challenges Approach

During the past ten to 15 years, thinking about students' strengths and challenges has become a very popular approach in education. This has had its benefits, as it has made us understand that profiles are unique and that every learner may excel in different domains. We have also come to an understanding that some gifted students excel in only one domain and not in all, and that this has consequences for the curriculum offered and for how teachers select and apply their pedagogical and didactical strategies. However, at this point, we would like to highlight that there is also a downside to thinking in terms of strengths and challenges.

The expectation of how learners develop is based on a normative concept of what we define as "average" (Ronksley-Pavia, 2015). This perspective determines our thinking in terms of "advantaged," "behind" or "at grade level" (Oliver,

1996). Teachers' pedagogical and didactic actions are based on this premise (Bakx et al., 2021). Within a strength-challenge approach, there is always a strong side opposite a weak side (Burger-Veltmeijer & Minnaert, 2016), such as excelling in math but achieving an average level in language arts; or having high developmental potential in psychomotor skills but not such great potential in the academic domains. The norm for what is considered average or at grade level may refer to an intrapersonal or interpersonal norm. An "intrapersonal norm" refers to the examples given. An "interpersonal norm" refers to a situation in which we compare the learner with other members of their age group.

If the learner deviates from the norm—whether intrapersonal or interpersonal—their achievements are perceived as either advanced or behind and referred to as "strengths" or "challenges," respectively. This comes with the risk that those who do not meet that norm may be perceived by others from a deficit-focused perspective, which may lead to neglect or denial of developmental potential (Baum et al., 2017; Trail, 2022; van Gerven, 2024).

Moving away from thinking about strengths and challenges implies the need for different terminology. As talent development is essential to the strategy, "talent" replaces "strength." This is interpreted as a learner's intrapersonal capital for developing knowledge and skills in a specific domain that, supported by an appropriate educational context, can result in excellence (Gagné, 2010). Talent can be the interplay between human capital and ecological influences. "Challenge" refers to an intrapersonal notion in the learner's functioning. However, as this is also a normative concept defined by what is considered average, it does not align with current educational paradigms based on inclusion. It is therefore better to replace "challenge" with "barriers." Barriers to learning are raised by the interplay between the learner's traits and their ecological system and, therefore, are always extrapersonal factors.

> ### Gifted or Disabled? How Society Defines Us
>
> Consider a society in which livelihoods depend on hunting and gathering. John, growing up in this context, possesses strong motor and executive skills. His proficiency in these areas leads to his identification as gifted. While he experiences challenges in reading and writing, these skills are of little importance in his society, posing no hindrance to his success.
>
> Kadir is John's friend. While Kadir has good executive skills, his psychomotor skills are minimal. Kadir stands out because when the tribal elders teach him, he never meets the set goals. Kadir is, therefore, identified as a child with a learning disability. Now, Kadir happens to be very good at reading and writing. These skills are offered marginally because the children

> of this society will seldom use them later. The skills thus will not help these children become self-sufficient in the future. Kadir's limited developmental potential in the psychomotor domain is a significant barrier.
>
> If both boys grew up in a society in which academic skills were essential for self-sufficiency, the roles might be reversed: John might be the student with the learning disability, while Kadir might be the gifted student.

2e learners show high developmental potential in domains unaffected by their disability (Baum et al., 2017; Reis et al., 2014; Trail, 2022; Webb, et al., 2016). Within these domains, they can experience accelerated and deepened development if intrapersonal variability is recognized and accepted. Thus, in this approach, developmental potential is not used as a compensatory tool to overcome barriers and tackle challenges but is linked to its own existence. At the end of this chapter, we will discuss some of the practical consequences of this specific lens for education.

## Misdiagnoses and Missed Diagnoses

From the moment one assumes that specific behavior can be observed, the interpretation of the observed behavior might become biased (Bryman, 2012; Kallenberg et al., 2007). This comes with the risk that one only sees what one expects to see, instead of being entirely objective both during the observation and when interpreting the results. Therefore, it is important to keep in mind that recognizing twice-exceptional students can be complicated in three ways (Baum et al., 2017; Hughes, 2011; Webb, et al., 2016). First, there are students whose giftedness masks their disability. In their behavior, characteristics of giftedness can be recognized. However, their school performance falls short of the environment's expectations based on the observed characteristics of giftedness. Unfortunately, because of their ability to compensate, their performance is often still at or around the group average; the difficulties are often attributed to a lack of challenge. As a result, these students are often mistakenly labeled as underachievers.

Second, there are students for whom their disability masks their giftedness. They experience so many challenges that it is not recognized that they are also gifted and have high developmental potential in domains that are not affected by the traits of their disability. A student's learning and/or behavioral difficulties can be so significant that they may overshadow their giftedness. These characteristics help us "recognize" the student, albeit not entirely for the right reason.

Third, there are students whose giftedness and challenges mask each other. These are gifted students with a learning or developmental disability whose giftedness and difficulties cancel each other out, so the student appears to be an "average" student.

## The Uniqueness of Profiles

If you have a group of 100 students with an IQ of 130 or higher, you may say that all of them are capable of gifted-level achievement. That gives you a framework for defining your target group. But if you view those students as individuals, you will see that each of them has a very distinct intelligence profile. Relative to an average IQ of 100, each of these students has personal talents and will experience barriers, creating all kinds of challenges. This so-called "intrapersonal profile" influences their development. However, as human development always takes place in interaction with the environment, this intrapersonal profile will be influenced by various catalysts (e.g., parents, school, peers, interests in the culture in which they are raised, political climate). The interaction between all these factors translates the learner's potential into achievements (and/or lack of achievements) (Gagné, 2010). Although these students have similar IQs in common, they are indeed 100 different students. Now imagine that these students also have a learning or developmental disability. Then, we may formally consider these students to be twice exceptional. However, anyone who delves into the DSM-5 will immediately observe that very different core difficulties are described for each disability. Again, we see differences among our 100 students that are related to their specific learning or developmental disability. In turn, each specific disability has its own possible "generic" needs profile that will fit the individual student to a greater or lesser degree (van Gerven & Weterings, 2014). For example, one student with dyslexia may experience more difficulties decoding information, while another may experience more difficulties encoding information. They are both hindered by dyslexia, but each has distinct educational needs (Maddocks, 2018). The same applies to students with dyscalculia, ADHD, or ASD (Fugate et al., 2020).

The intersection of the characteristics of giftedness and challenge forms the basis of a unique needs profile. Consequently, one gifted student with dyslexia may be appropriately supported if allowed to read complex texts with text recognition software. In contrast, another gifted student with dyslexia may feel better supported if the texts are slightly less complicated, enabling them to read independently without assistance and, therefore, perceive themselves less as an exception to the group.

Therefore, every suggestion for support can be appropriate, but whether it is appropriate can only be determined in the specific context of the educational situation. Thus, no known interventions are appropriate for all twice-exceptional learners; nor are there known interventions that will be a perfect match only for students with a specific twice-exceptional profile (Lee & Olenchak, 2014).

The third complicating factor is the influence of the learner's ecology (Bakxet al., 2021; Bronfenbrenner, 1979; van Gerven, 2024; Ziegler & Stoeger, 2017). The learner's primary educational ecology consists of actors (e.g., parents, teacher, peers) and factors (e.g., learning environment, curriculum). These (f)actors not only are sources of information from which much can be learned but also are actively involved in how the learner develops. As a result, the individual profile of the learner – where the intersection between abilities and challenges reveals an initial need – can be strongly influenced by that ecology.

Imagine you have a gifted student with autism. Imagine that the school focuses on developing social constructivist learning and collaboration, which is seen as a prerequisite for the constructivist didactics deployed. It could be that, based on the intersection of giftedness and autism, the learner could work at a high academic level, come up with creative solutions to complex situations related to learning content, and show great passion for the subjects offered, but could nevertheless fail to achieve optimal development because the emphasis on the social aspect of the learning process overshadows their chances of doing so.

If you focus only on the learner's characteristics, you might be inclined to set educational goals based on those characteristics (the learner must learn to articulate their thoughts in a way that ensures others understand them and to provide space for others' ideas in the learning process). However, if you adopt an ecological perspective, you might also conclude that for a twice-exceptional learner with autism, the pedagogies matching a social constructivist approach will never be a meaningful response leading to optimal learning results. In this example, it is likely that a different approach, not focused on "fixing what appears to be broken," might provide a more meaningful educational response to the learner's needs.

## Paradoxical Needs

The combination of talent and challenges leads to paradoxical, and more intense, needs (Costis, 2016; Hughes, 2011; Trail, 2022). The disability can not only mask but also amplify characteristics of giftedness. The same is true of giftedness: it can not only mask the characteristics of the disability but equally reinforce them (Reis et al., 2014; Webb, et al., 2016). For example, consider a learner with highly developed verbal skills who likes to think critically but leaves little room for another person's opinion. This learner will not shy away from making their opinion clear. The other person may feel overwhelmed or sidelined, which may reduce opportunities for cooperation. The verbal abilities of the student in this example reinforce other personality traits, which can lead to awkward social situations in practice.

Now imagine you are dealing with a gifted student with characteristics of ADHD. This student also shows a high degree of creativity and flexibility but strays from the heart of the matter. The result might be that the student never turns in their work on time or at all. The teacher might have the impression that the student is running out of time or needs more time and thus might offer the student an extension. The deadline is postponed, and the teacher proposes a new date for when the project is due. By removing the time pressure, the student no longer experiences the much-needed incentives that were there before. The result is that the learner can focus even less and strays even further from the intended end goal. Their creativity and flexibility lead to chaos in both thought and action. They may benefit more from regular check-ins with the teacher to keep them on task, allowing for continuous progress. In a large project, this learner would be helped by clearly defined time blocks within which a defined task must be accomplished. The requirements of the task can be determined in advance in consultation with the learner, making the chances of success visible to the learner. For this learner, the paradox is that more time leads to an even longer process, with more room to wander and potentially greater chaos in thinking. Structured time helps them channel their creativity and flexibility, increasing their chances of success.

When working with twice-exceptional students, tailored educational responses offer significant opportunities to address the educational needs fueled by apparent contradictions and mutual reinforcements (van Gerven, 2024). In some cases, one can also make the contradiction and/or reinforcement the greatest opportunity for student success, provided you are aware that this requires a specific support structure.

# Disability or Difficulty?

Foley Nicpon et al. (2011) found that some twice-exceptional students experience distress from the diagnosis of learning and/or developmental differences. On the other hand, the authors mentioned in the same article that a diagnosis can also help to further address the highly differentiated needs of these students. A learning disability always involves a predisposed impediment to learning that reveals itself to be resistant to remediation despite good educational provision and the use of appropriate pedagogical-didactic strategies (Weterings-Helmons, 2023). Thus, before speaking of a disability, one must first determine the persistence of the difficulties. A learning difficulty occurs when the pedagogical-didactical responses during the educational process do not sufficiently match the student's needs (Weterings-Helmons, 2023). The educational environment does not function optimally for the student, causing their progress to stagnate. As soon as the educational environment is optimized (e.g., different pedagogical approach, different support), difficulties in the learning process can be overcome.

## How Can You Recognize the Distinction Between Child and Environmental Factors?

Figure 1.1 depicts the process teachers can use to reduce incidents of misdiagnosis. They begin by determining the persistence of the presenting difficulties—in other words, they try to distinguish between difficulties that exist primarily because of child factors and those that exist primarily because of environmental factors. The teacher can do this by examining the extent to which the impeding factor(s) are changeable. After thoroughly exploring the situation, they develop an educational response plan that will be deployed for three consecutive periods of six to eight weeks, setting realistic goals and involving all educational partners in this process (van Gerven, 2024). During the first period, everyone involved must get used to the fact that things will be different than before. After this first period, one cannot expect the difficulties to be solved. However, one can expect that everyone involved will be used to the new situation and the new approach. During the second six-week period, the new approach should start to produce improvements.

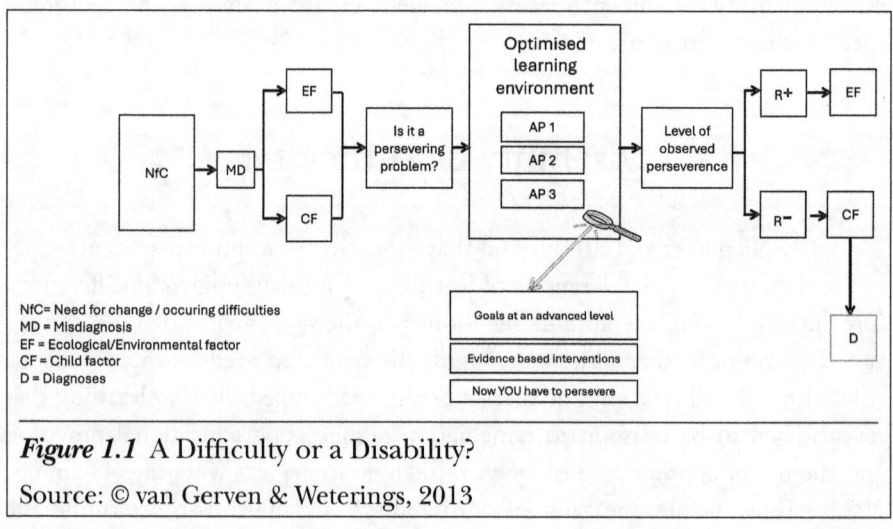

*Figure 1.1* A Difficulty or a Disability?
Source: © van Gerven & Weterings, 2013

## 2e Learners—What Are We Talking About?

If improvements are observed after six weeks, the teacher can continue and maybe even tweak the plan in small ways. If they still do not see any improvements, all educational partners must consider whether psychological testing is necessary. In the meantime, the teacher will continue with their initiated intervention plan. The psychologist can use the results of the pre-diagnostic stage to understand which interventions have been applied to exclude environmental factors as the cause of the student's difficulties. The difference between a learning difficulty and a learning disability can only be revealed if the teacher intervenes systematically and in a structured way with the help of a well-thought-out support plan and monitors both the process and the result.

Figures 1.2 and 1.3 depict two different situations. Figure 1.2 involves a gifted student whose learning outcomes fall short of expectations. Performance is situated in the small triangle on the model's left side. By optimizing the learning environment, adjusting the curriculum, and adapting pedagogical-didactic strategies, the results shift to the right side of the model. Thus, the student seems receptive to a different approach, indicating that the need for change is not resistant to remediation. The impediments are changeable. This in turn supports the assumption that it is unlikely to be a learning disability. If, over time, the outcomes continue to fall short of expectations, the teacher can revisit the approach. If the difficulties persist and progress is limited, conducting a psychological assessment to identify the cause of the stagnation is advisable.

Figure 1.3 concerns a gifted student, where we see that adjustments in guidance, curriculum, and educational environment show only a small degree of

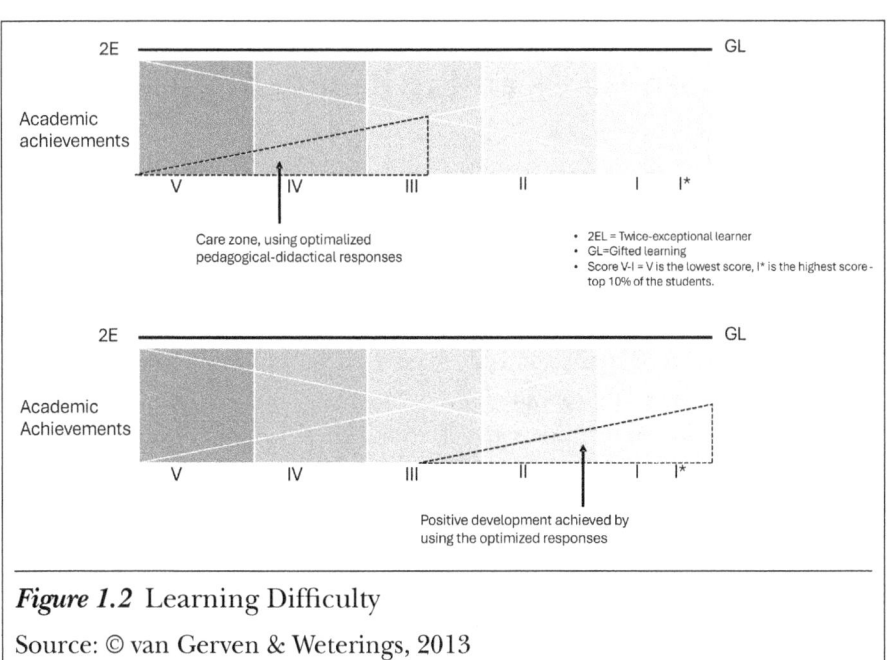

*Figure 1.2* Learning Difficulty
Source: © van Gerven & Weterings, 2013

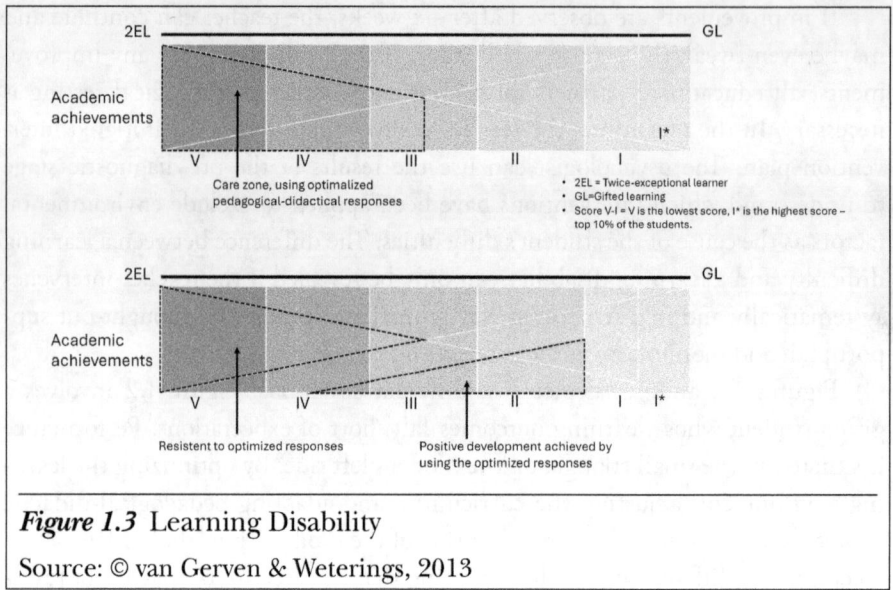

**Figure 1.3** Learning Disability
Source: © van Gerven & Weterings, 2013

improvement. This part shows a shift to the right in the model. Only a small degree of changeability in the hindering factor(s) can be seen. However, we also see in this model that a large portion of performance is unaffected by the different strategies. So there are child factors at play that show themselves to be resistant to remediation and where there must be respect for the delimitation implied by the disability.

## Misdiagnosis as an Environmental Factor

In distinguishing between a child factor and an environmental factor, both past and future interventions must be considered. In cases where an environmental factor causes the difficulties, it could be that the didactic approach applied in the past unintentionally led to the emergence of the difficulties, also known as a "misdidactic."

A misdidactic is a situation in which you use a pedagogical-didactic approach that may be considered appropriate for a large group of students but that does not adequately stimulate and support the developmental potential of a specific student in the way that their educational needs require (Weterings-Helmons, 2023). This can occur when you rely on generic assumptions regarding what is considered "good" education for "all gifted learners" and do not target interventions to the individual learner. Consider this example: "gifted learners like problem-based learning in an autonomous and self-regulated context." This assumption may be correct for many gifted students, but there are exceptions to the rule. Some gifted students may benefit from learning experiences with more direction or when offered more scaffolding, resulting in less emphasis on self-regulation. Another assumption that can lead to misdiagnosis may be: "gifted students are good at math." This holds true for many gifted students; however, individual discrepancies within intelligence profiles make some gifted students an exception to this rule. Suppose a student excels in language arts but, based on total IQ, is offered compacting and enrichment in mathematics because school materials for that subject are available, while no materials are available for language arts. This may result in gaps in mathematical knowledge and skills and insufficient challenge in the student's primary talent domain.

Compacting is a widely used strategy for teaching gifted students. It aims to offer regular learning content that matches the learning characteristics of the gifted student in the domain of their talent. There are different ways to compact the curriculum (Drent & van Gerven, 2012). What is important, however, is that the subject didactics of the domain in which compacting is done are held onto. In mathematics, for example, understanding the grade-level standards is required when considering compacting. Four elements should be considered: (1) developing an understanding of the right concepts; (2) developing an understanding of the desired strategies; (3) being able to apply the right strategy at an appropriate pace; and (4) being able to use what has been learned flexibly (i.e., being able to use the knowledge and skills in a different context than that in which they have been offered). If one of these elements is skipped, gaps in knowledge and skills can arise (Weterings-Helmons, 2017). These four elements can also be recognized in other subject areas. Therefore, when compacting, it is important to ensure that the student works in their zone of proximal development, and that the compacting is done in a way that ensures these core elements remain recognizable and balanced in the curriculum.

If only the learner's giftedness is considered, it may result in skipping too much curriculum content, offering too many enriching tasks, or placing too great a demand on the regulation skills of the student. Underachievement is often attributed to this scenario. In response, even more complex material is offered, learning steps become larger, and the student develops increasing gaps in knowledge and skills due to overestimation. The assumption is that the student will become motivated as the task complexity increases or aligns primarily with their interests (Weterings-Helmons, 2017). All concerned become disappointed when they discover that results fall short of expectations even in the student's favorite interest areas. Doubts arise about the pupil's possible giftedness because the disability always remains out of the picture: "The student is apparently not as smart as we thought."

If only the disability is seen, it is likely that the "deficit of the pupil as a result of the disability" will be the focus for interventions (van Gerven, 2021).

Consequently, little or no attention is paid to the domains in which the student could excel because their development potential there is not hindered by the disability. Subsequently, the student experiences frustration in one of two ways: either they experience limited development in the domains affected by the disability or their talent in other domains is directly frustrated and an appropriate piece of the curriculum is omitted (Foley-Nicpon et al., 2020).

A third form of misdidactic occurs when a student's giftedness and disability are acknowledged but addressed separately. For example, a student needing extra reading practice may be given simplified texts, disregarding their advanced comprehension skills. Learning a difficult skill outside one's strengths requires perseverance, but if the content is far below their intellectual potential, motivation is likely to decline. Conversely, a student might explore a topic of interest and present on it but struggle with organizing information due to executive functioning challenges. Without sufficient support, they risk becoming overwhelmed, leading to subpar outcomes and frustration. This disconnect arises when expectations for self-direction exceed what is reasonable given the student's learning or developmental disability.

## When Two Worlds Collide

In the international literature on twice-exceptional students, several authors describe these students as experiencing a clash, as it were, between two worlds (Baum., 2017; Trail, 2022). On the one hand, their developmental potential seems able to take them very far. At the same time, they experience strong limitations in the domains affected by their disability. This intrapersonal discrepancy can lead to confusion for some of these students. However, there is insufficient empirical evidence to support that this is true for all twice-exceptional learners. Many studies on twice-exceptional learners that have been conducted and reported are based on single case studies or studies among very limited research groups (Hughes & Troxclair, 2019). What is clear is that in each case, different learner characteristics can reinforce and/or hinder each other. Consider the previously mentioned example of a learner who strongly holds their beliefs and has difficulty empathizing with another person's point of view. The result may lead to social problems, especially if the twice-exceptional learner in question is less focused on receiving social cues and does not know when enough is enough. In other scenarios, limited flexibility can be an advantage when combined with an ability to think logically; lines of thought need to be developed in a domain such as IT. The mutual interaction of the two characteristics yields gains at that time. Baum et al. (2017) used the metaphor of mixing yellow (strengths) and blue (challenges) to create green (twice-exceptionality), emphasizing that the whole is greater than the sum of its parts. From a solution-focused perspective, attempting to separate "yellow" and "blue" is unproductive; instead, the focus should be on the "green."

## Teaching Them to Embrace Their Challenges

For 2e learners, each barrier represents a challenge; and educational partners (e.g., teachers, parents) are paramount in teaching these learners how to embrace their challenges and find opportunities to enable their talents to flourish. Giftedness may never lead to the assumption that, because of their talents, twice-exceptional learners automatically know how to overcome their challenges and nurture their talents in a way that allows them to become self-actualizing individuals. Research by van Gerven (2024) suggests that where teachers and parents start thinking of the learner's potential in terms of strengths and challenges, a significant pitfall is focusing on what is regarded as the "challenge" as something that is broken and needs fixing, while their strengths disappear into the background. Responding meaningfully to the educational needs of twice-exceptional learners and teaching them how to embrace their challenges require that we address them from a holistic perspective. These learners need stimulation not only in the domain of their talents, but also in the domain of their experienced challenges. They need remediation in a way that helps them deal with their difficulties; and they need compensation as concrete support from the ecological system to overcome barriers. Finally, educational partners need to respect that there are limitations inherent to the learner's specific disability. These limitations may lead to a need to exempt them either temporarily or maybe even permanently from specific tasks. There is no list of ready-to-use interventions that will work out well for all of them. The most important thing we can do is give the learner a voice and listen to what they have to say (Den Otter, 2023). Learning to embrace both talents and challenges does not imply that students never have to do things they do not want to do; but it does imply that we can discuss with them what the circumstances and conditions are to realize their full potential and send out the message, "It is okay to be green."

## *Revisiting Tommie*

*Tommie works three times a week on a regular assignment and twice a week on an enrichment task. He can play music to stay focused. There is a rubric for the objectives. The tasks are divided into four stages. The teacher helps to identify process stages and supports Tommie in his time management. At home, his parents discuss his emotions during the learning process.*

*After eight weeks, Tommie's meltdowns are limited to twice a week. He needs the time-in spot once or twice a day. The regular assignments are all finished on time. His success rate for the regular tasks is 100%. However, none of his enrichment tasks is finished within the deadline. In week five, Tommie decides to ignore his enrichment tasks altogether.*

*During the evaluation meeting, the educational partners decide that the plan needs to be tweaked. Therefore, some changes are made. Tommie explains that he could not work on his enrichment tasks as he considers the playlist only fit for his regular coursework. His inability to approach this part of the plan more flexibly has prevented him from proceeding. Tommie now has two different playlists: one for each type of task. The instruction on the enrichment tasks becomes more unidirectional and the teacher now supports his time management on these tasks more stringently.*

*At the end of the intervention cycle, Tommie is more in control of his emotions. He can use the time-in spot as a timely vent to cool down. His work on language is of high quality and is almost always done within the time limits. If he knows what to do and how to do it, he no longer experiences time limits as stressful. Although coping with failure remains difficult for him, Tommie feels rewarded positively for his efforts and can attribute success and failure in a more balanced way.*

## Final Thoughts

In this chapter, we described, through various terms, the frameworks for what we see as a workable definition of the concept of twice-exceptional learners. In doing so, we distinguished between child and environmental factors. We distinguished between the terms "learning difficulties" and "learning disability"—a distinction determined by the persistence of the perceived impairment and whether the impairment shows itself to be truly resistant to remediation. It was discussed that the interaction between child and environmental factors plays a role in what is observed, and observations are always made in a particular context. Therefore, they are subject to the influences of those contexts, and behavior that is prohibitive in one situation can be an advantage in another. The sum of the characteristics of giftedness and the characteristics of learning or developmental disabilities is greater than the sum of their parts. Substantially different behaviors emerge from a different context than if the student is "only" gifted or "only" hindered by a learning or developmental disability.

## Things to Consider

- Traditional labels like "gifted" or "disabled" often fail to capture the nuanced needs of twice-exceptional learners. Instead, educators should adopt a flexible, needs-based approach that focuses on the intersection of talents and barriers rather than rigid diagnostic categories.
- A student's behavior and learning needs must be understood within their broader environment—family, classroom culture, teaching strategies, etc. What appears as a challenge in one context may be a strength in another.
- The strength-challenge binary can reinforce deficit thinking. Shifting to "talents" and "barriers" emphasizes potential and removes normative comparisons, encouraging more inclusive and individualized educational planning.

## For Discussion

- How does the interaction between child and environmental factors influence the way twice-exceptional learners are perceived and supported?
- What is the key distinction between learning difficulties and learning disabilities, and why is this distinction important in identifying twice-exceptional learners?
- How can the same behavior be seen as a challenge in one context but an advantage in another when considering twice-exceptional learners?

## Note

1 From this point in the text, we will no longer use the term "co-morbidity" but only refer to this as "co-occurring disabilities."

## References

APA. (2013). *Diagnostic and statistical manual of mental disorders,* (5th ed.). American Pscyhological Association.

Assouline, S., Foley Nicpon, M., Collangelo, N., & O'Brien, M. (2008). *The paradox of giftedness and autism.* University of Iowa College of Education. http://www2.education.uiowa.edu/belinblank/pdfs/pip.pdf

Bakx, A., van Gerven, E., & Weterings-Helmons, A. (2021). *Hoe dan?! Pakkend onderwijs voor begaafde leerlingen.* Pica.

Baska, A. & VanTassel-Baska, J. (2018). *Interventions that work with special populations in gifted education.* Prufrock Press.

Baum, S., Schader, R., & Owen, S. (2017). *To be gifted and learning disabled.* (3rd ed.). Prufrock Press.

Betts, G. & Neihart, M. (2010). Revised profiles of the gifted and talented. http://talentstimuleren.nl/thema/stimulerend signaleren/publicatie/269-revised-profiles-of-the-gifted-and-talented

Borland, J. (2012). You can't teach an old dogmatist new tricks. Dogmatism and gifted education. In D. Ambrose, R. Sternberg, & B. Sriraman (eds.), *Confronting dogmatism in gifted education* (pp. 11-24). Routledge.

Bronfenbrenner, U. (1979). *The ecology of human development: Experiments by nature and design.* Harvard University Press.

Bryman, A. (2012). *Social research methods* (4th ed.). Oxford University Press.

Burger-Veltmeijer, A. & Minnaert, A. (2016). De waarde van de Sterkte en Zwakte Heuristiek in diagnostiek bij het vermoeden van hoogbegaafdheid. *Tijdschrift voor orthopedagogiek, 55*(7-8), 160-174.

Cauffman, L. & van Dijk, D. (2009). *Handboek oplossingsgericht werken in het onderwijs.* Coutinho.

Costis, P. (2016). *Seeing the paradigm: Education professionals' advocacy for the gifted student with Autism Spectrum Disorder.* Dissertations, Theses, and Masters Projects. Paper 1463428512. doi:http://dx.doi.org/10.21220/W4201B

Cross, T. (2004). *On the social and emotional lives of gifted children: Issues and factors in their psychological development.* Prufrock Press.

Csikszentmihalyi, M. (1999). *De weg naar Flow.* Boom.

Dai, D. & Chen, F. (2014). *Paradigms of gifted education. A guide to theory-based practice-focused research.* Prufrock Press.

Dawson, P. & Guare, R. (2009). *Smart but scattered.* The Guildford Press.

Den Otter, M. (2023). Het belang van voicing. In E. Van Gerven (ed.), *De gids 2.0. Over begaafdheid in het PO en VO* (pp. 99-114). Leuker.nu.

Drent, S. & van Gerven, E. (2012). *Passend onderwijs voor begaafde leerlingen.* Koninklijke van Gorcum.

Foley Nicpon, M., Assouline, S., Schuller, P., & Amend, E. (2011). Gifted and talented students on the Autism Spectrum: Best practices for fostering talent and accomodating concerns. In J. Castellano & A. Dawn Frazier (eds.), *Special populations in gifted education* (pp. 227-248). Prufrock Press.

Foley-Nicpon, M., Cederberg, C., & Wienkes, C. (2020). Autism spectrum disorders and high ability. In *Critical issues and practical issues in gifted education. A survey of current research on giftedness and talent development* (pp. 61-75). Prufrock Press.

Fugate, C. M., Behrens, W. A., & Boswell C. (2020). *Understanding twice-exceptional learners: Connecting research to practice.* Prufrock Press.

Gagné, F. (2010). *Building gifts into talents: Brief overview of the DMGT 2.0.* Université du Québec à Montréal.

Hughes, C. (2011). Twice exceptional children: Twice the challanges, twice the joys. In J. Castellano & A. Dawn Frazier (eds.), *Special populations in gifted educations* (pp. 153-174). Prufrock Press.

Hughes, C. & Troxclair, D. (2019). *2E literature content analyses.* Nashville, WCGTC Conference.

Kallenberg, T., Koster, B., Onstenk, J., & Scheepsma, W. (2007). *Ontwikkeling door onderzoek. Een handreiking voor leraren.* Thieme/Meulenhoff.

Kreger-Silverman, L. (2013). *Giftedness 101.* Springer Publishing Company.

Lee, K. & Olenchak, F. (2014). Individuals with a gifted/attention deficit/hyperactivity disorder diagnosis: identification, performance, outcomes and interventions. *Gifted Education International*, 1-15.

Maddocks, D. (2018). The identification and performance of gifted students with learning disability diagnoses: A comparison of differentiated diagnostic criteria. *Gifted Child Quarterly, 62*, 175-192. doi:10.1177/0016986217752096

McCoach, D., Siegle, D., & DaVia Rubenstein, L. (2020). Pay attention to inattention: exploring ADHD symptoms in a sample of underachieving gifted students. *Gifted Child Quarterly, 64*(2), 100-116. doi:10.117/0016986219901320

Oliver, M. (1996). *Understanding disability: From theory to practice.* London: Macmillan Press.

Peters, S., Matthews, M., McBee, M., & McCoach, D. (2014). *Beyond gifted education: Designing and implementing advanced academic programs.* Prufrock Press.

Reis, S., Baum, S., & Burke, E. (2014). An operational definition of twice-exceptional learners: Implications and applications. *Gifted Child Quarterly, 58*(3), 217-230.

Ronksley-Pavia, M. (2015). A model of twice-exceptionality: Explaining and defining the apparent paradoxal combination of disability and giftedness in childhood. *Journal for the Education of the Gifted, 38*(3), pp. 295-318. doi:10.1177/0162353215592499

Subotnik, R., Olszewski-Kubilus, P., & Worrel, F. (2011). Rethinking giftedness and gifted education: A proposed direction forward based on psychological science. *Psychological Science in the Public Interest, 12*(1), 3-54.

Trail, B. (2022). *Twice exceptional gifted children. Understanding, teaching and counselling gifted students.* Routledge.

Van Gerven, E. (2016). *Addressing the needs of twice-exceptional students in the classroom.* Slim Educatief BV.

Van Gerven, E. (2017). Begaafde leerlingen met een autismespectrum stoornis. In E. Van Gerven (ed.), *De Gids. Over begaafdheid in het basisonderwijs* (pp. 199-224). Leuker.nu.

Van Gerven, E. (2021). *Raising the bar. The competencies of specialists in gifted education.* Leuker.nu.

Van Gerven, E. (2024). Treasure hunting for golden moments: A systemic, solution-focused approach for addressing the needs of 2e learners. *Journal for the Education of the Gifted, 47*(1), 54-83.

Van Gerven, E., & Weterings, A. (2014). 1+1=3. Begaafde leerlingen met een leer- en/of ontwikkelingsstoornis. *Opleiding Specialist Begaafd & Speciaal.* Slim! Educatief.

Van Luit, J., Bloemert, J., Ganzinga, E., & Mönch, M. (2014). *Protocol Dyscalculie: Diagnostiek voor gedragsdeskundigen (protocol DDG).* Graviant Educatieve Uitgaven.

Van Meersbergen, E. & de Vries, P. (2017). *Handelingsgericht werken in passend onderwijs.* Perspectief uitgevers.

Webb, J., Amend, E., Beljan, P., Webb, N., Kuzujanakis, M., Olenchak, F., & Goerss, J. (2016). *Misdiagnosis and dual diagnoses of gifted children and adults* (2 ed.). Great Potential Press.

Weterings-Helmons, A. (2017). Begaafde leerlingen met ernstige reken en wiskunde problemen en dyscalculie. In E. Van Gerven (ed.), *De Gids. over begaafde leerlingen in het basisonderwijs* (pp. 255-278). Leuker.nu.

Weterings-Helmons, A. (2023). Dubbel bijzondere leerlingen. In E. Van Gerven (ed.), *De gids 2.0. Over begaafdheid in het PO en VO* (pp. 231-254). Leuker.nu.

Ziegler, A. & Stoeger, H. (2017). Systemic gifted education: A theoretical introduction. *Gifted Child Quarterly, 61*(3), pp. 183-193. doi:10.1177/0016 986217705713

# Chapter 2

# Intersectionality and Identity Formation

Joy Lawson Davis and
Carlita R.B. Cotton

## Intersectionality and Identity Formation

> We are more than meets the eye, so much more, day in and day out we shift and change to stay afloat, to belong, to be seen, to hide, to be quiet, to roar, to float, to soar.
>
> *Joy Lawson Davis, May 8, 2024*

The theory of intersectionality was first framed by legal scholar Kimberlé Crenshaw (1996), while she was a graduate student in law school. Initially, intersectionality—a social theory—was described as the interaction and accumulated effects of varied social constructs that pose discrimination and barriers interactively and consistently in one's daily existence. This was the theory as discussed in Crenshaw's earliest works as she grappled with the barriers and discriminations that she experienced as a Black female law student in the late twentieth century. In a later interview in 2020, Crenshaw defined "intersectionality" as "a lens, a prism, for seeing the way in which various forms of inequality often operate together and exacerbate each other" (Steinmetz, 2020, para. 1).

As educators and advocates for equity, diversity, inclusion, and belonging, utilizing the intersectionality theory gives us a more fluid and powerful method to describe the multiple "worlds" that impact our students' lives. The concept was first framed based on what were perceived as, and in reality were, the disadvantages or inequalities that functioned interactively as Crenshaw experienced her own multiple social constructs and contexts daily. The identities that she initially drew attention to were race, gender, and position as a student of law who happened to be a Black female. Together, these social identities were a source of painful discrimination and were barriers as she studied, researched, and made an impact in a field in which she was a double minority: female and Black. At times, we can only imagine she simultaneously felt invisible, ignored, seen as "less than" and as not important in the grand scheme of her life as a legal student.

> **The Evolution of Intersectionality**
>
> On a personal note, I (Dr. Davis) can remember having those same emotions as a graduate student at one of the nation's oldest and most prestigious universities. I was alone on campus, and in most of my classes the "only one." I fought hard in class discussions to have my voice heard and listened to as I presented my views and analyses of the work being studied and responded to course assignments. Ironically, most of the research that I studied was also created by non-minority scholars. Thus, it was a lonesome experience in that I did not often "find myself" represented. Being a double minority, whose voice is often repressed and whose experience may be the subject of oppression, helps the individual to more clearly define their own multiple social identities and how they impact one's daily experiences. It was the depth of my feelings as a graduate student that sealed my vision to spend my career ensuring that other differently gifted students had a welcome space in high academic settings where their voices are heard and their needs met.

More recently, academics have also utilized the "intersectionality" framework to define the existence of the multiple identities and experiences of the students they serve—particularly those who are members of minoritized communities, those who may hold varied gender identities, those who may speak a language or derivations of a language different than the majority culture (who speak standard English), those who are considered twice exceptional, and others as well. There are many identities that we will explore in this chapter that repressed voices and oppressed communities are challenged by daily. We will discuss how the framework of intersectionality is well suited to create an understandable and enhanced description of the multiple social and psychosocial identities that interact as our students grow and develop. We will also offer resources and strategies to effectively enable students from our most discriminated communities to navigate the "multiple worlds" in which they live, breathe, and have their identities.

# Jamal

Jamal is an African American eighth grader who attends an urban private school. At 5'11, he is taller than most of his peers and is often mistaken for an older child—especially since he is an independent thinker who does not succumb to peer pressure. He prefers to spend time with adults instead of his classmates, because, in his words, "they are only interested in dating and dressing to impress." He enjoys listening to classical music and has often been called an "old soul" by his family and other adults.

At age three, Jamal began reading, to the amazement of his family, and he now reads at least six non-fiction books weekly. He is extremely affectionate, and his teachers have said his bearhugs are legendary. He greets most adults with hugs but rarely makes direct eye contact and sometimes rocks back and forth (stimming) as an anti-anxiety coping mechanism. He enjoys talking with his teachers and administrators but shies away from cultivating friendships with his classmates. Additionally, his awkwardness around his peers and perceived lack of interest in communicating with them have been described as "off-putting", "arrogant," and/or "rude." For this reason, he is often the target of verbal bullying for nonconformity with his peers' behavioral norms. His parents suggest that "he dances to a different drummer" and when asked, he will state that he does not care what others say or think about him.

Even though he is prone to perfectionism, which sometimes interferes with his ability to submit assignments on time, he excels in his academic classes. He struggled emotionally in music and gym classes and is now permitted to go to the school media center during gym and music periods, as accommodation. He uses his media center time to read and chat with the school librarian about religion, politics, and even his ongoing research on autism spectrum disorder (ASD). He was diagnosed as autistic in sixth grade and continues to struggle with understanding why he is considered neurodivergent, often asking his school counselor if she is "absolutely sure that is what I have." His parents have stated that they will have an IQ test administered to him once he is in high school, to support his inclusion in competitive extracurricular academic enrichment programs. They hope that if he has positive experiences with other similarly motivated peers, it will encourage him and help him understand that he is not alone.

Jamal is a 3e student: gifted and culturally diverse with an exceptional condition. Many schools are unprepared to work with 3e students, and Jamal did not thrive in the local public elementary school. Since transferring him to a smaller private school, his parents have been encouraged by the strides he is making and the extra support he is receiving. They added that since he has been at this new school, he has had no meltdowns and they haven't had to pick him up early due to panic attacks.

## An Interview with Jamal

**Q: What's it like to be 2e and African American?**

**A:** I'm still trying to understand ASD and why people think I have it. Is it because I'm a smart, big Black boy, as they say? Is it because I'm not interested in the same things as my classmates? Do you [the interviewer] see something different about me? I know you explained that "twice exceptional" means I am gifted and have a disability. Even my doctor said that. But I don't understand the disability piece; are you all sure that's what is going on with me?

**Q: What are your joys? Your challenges?**

**A:** I get joy from playing video games and reading books that make me think. I think I'm supposed to be a philosopher, or maybe a scientist. I also love listening to music—it calms me and makes me forget the mean things that I hear said about me daily. What I really wish would happen is for people to just leave me alone. I don't bother them, I don't care about them, I don't try to fit in with them—so why do they tease me? I used to want other kids to like me, but they would call me names like "Oreo" and say that I talked like a White boy. That used to hurt, but I don't care anymore. Now I just want to live my life and do what I want to do. I don't care about the latest sneakers, and I don't want a girlfriend until I'm older. I just want to be left alone to be me! What is so wrong with that?

**Q: What is/are your coping mechanism(s)?**

**A:** I think that being excused from gym and music class helps a lot. I get tired of people telling me that I should play football—I hate sports. I like to listen to music, but I don't want to play a musical instrument or sing. So, I cope by reading and avoiding being around a lot of people. I also cope by spending quiet time in my room and if I'm feeling too anxious at school, I can always go to Mrs. Naraine's [school counselor] office and just chill out. She has an impressive African American history book collection, and she allows me to freely borrow them and sit in the beanbag chair and read. She also doesn't mind me hugging her and doesn't judge me. She talks to me like I have good sense and a brain and that helps a lot. She gets me when I say that there's always more than one way to do something or think about something. She treats me like an adult because I can't stand to be talked down to like I'm stupid.

**Q: What gets you through the day?**

**A:** I'm grateful for my parents and grandparents because they accept me as I am and don't try to change me. I'm also grateful for people like you; I really love you, Auntie [pauses to give interviewer, who is not his aunt, a hug]. I also know that I'm smarter than my classmates, so I try to keep that in mind because they don't understand where I'm coming from and they're probably jealous of my intelligence.

**Q: What advice do you have for others?**

**A:** The teachers that I have now are better than my other school, but sometimes their rules don't work for me. I think they should let kids study what they want to study. I love science—why can't I have two periods of science every day? I think adults should ask us what we want to do and not always tell us what we have to do. They're not always right just because they're older.

# "Who Am I, Really?" Identity Formation

Social scientists, psychologists, and gifted education specialists define "identity formation" as a period when an individual begins to understand more clearly who they are and how their life is impacted or shaped by the many social identities that comprise their natural self (Cerezo et al, 2023; Hebert, 2021; Tormos, 2017; Whiting, 2022). These social identities include language (spoken at home, in the community, in school) and dialects; gender identity/sexual orientation; family/community/income/religion; neurodivergence type 1–general intellectual giftedness, domain-specific giftedness, high giftedness; neurodivergence type 2—learning disability, autism, behavior disorder, executive functioning disorder, other health impairments; peer relationships (positive and negative); and their own sense of self. Figure 2.1 depicts the intersectional identities discussed here. Note that the lines are imperfect to reflect the organic/fluid process of identity formation.

While we can label varied social identities, it is not an easy task to go through the process of shaping an identity or, as it is typically called, "identity formation." In a detailed chapter on identity formation, Hébert (2020) shared multiple identity formation theories as related to gifted adolescents. He described the early identity formation theory of Erikson, who indicated that identity formation is the most important challenge for adolescents, as it prepares them for adulthood. Crocetti et al (2023) discussed the vital role that families and significant others play in identity formation by being role models and showing their adolescent children "who they are" in an attempt to help them shape their own personal identity. Gifted learners, however, because of their enhanced intellectual and psychosocial capacities, are more apt to consider the multiple possibilities of who they are based on their interests, strengths, and views of the world.

*Figure 2.1* Intersectionalities and Identities: Navigating Multiple Worlds

Identities: gender identity; race/culture; language; interests; giftedness; other exceptional conditions; family/community; income; age; creativity.

### A Cinematic Example of Identity Formation

An interesting example comes to mind. In the movie *The Secret Life of Bees*, the young Black male beekeeper assistant, Zack, is dedicated to becoming a lawyer or maybe a star athlete. The movie is set in 1965—the same year that President Lyndon B. Johnson signed the Civil Rights Act. Zack makes friends with a White girl, who also assists with the bees, and takes her to the movies one afternoon. They sit together in the colored-only section (the balcony), and moments after leaving the theater, he is arrested and beaten by police. When he finally is released and returns home, he shares a conversation with his friend, telling her that he can no longer concern himself with his earlier dream; after the injustice that has happened to him, he must become "a foot soldier for justice." Thus, one traumatic/oppressive act changes the young Black male's view of his identity formation.

# Jamal's Intersectional Identity Formation

As a Black autistic teen who has high intellectual potential and is high functioning, Jamal appears to be struggling with his identity formation. He knows what he likes to do, yet he often feels like the school doesn't allow him to do the things that he likes best. He is also a bit confused about his label as "twice exceptional." He feels bullied at times; but at other times, he switches roles from being bullied to bullying his peers with his language, which is a characteristic of his autism. He can occasionally come across as very harsh, lacking feeling and concern for others. His high intelligence, however, leaves him a target of oppression by others—sometimes just because he's Black and smart.

One of the challenges for Jamal's parents, clinicians, and family support members is to help him improve his peer relationships and perhaps be more considerate of his peers, to increase positivity in their experiences. Utilizing communication strategies is recommended for Jamal. Simultaneously, however, it is important to engage all students and educators in being more empathetic and inclusive in their behavior toward Jamal. Danielian (2021) shared strategies that he suggests are necessary to shape more inclusive and inviting school cultures that ensure all participants (students, teachers, staff, specialists, and administrators) feel welcomed and belong. Most importantly, however, we believe that Jamal needs an educational setting in which he can focus on his strengths. Perhaps a strength-based assessment such as the Suite of Tools devised by the Strength-Based Assessment Lab at Bridges Graduate School of Cognitive Diversity in Education would be recommended for a student like Jamal (Rivera, 2024). This assessment could provide beneficial information for Jamal's family and educators now and in the future. As Jamal's comfort level in school improves, it is anticipated that his performance and sense of belonging will likewise improve.

# Intersectionality and Identity Formation: A Dynamic Force

When the two constructs of intersectionality and identity formation merge, the force of their interaction is not unlike colliding universes. The combination of intersectionality and identity formation (IIF) is such a dynamic force that it has the potential to create new understandings of impacted individuals and those within their community. Far too often, the shifting IIF construct is a source of pain, trauma, confusion, discrimination, and injustice that many learners in school experience on an internal and external level every day. Conversely, these dynamic interacting social identities can also be the source of new understandings about oneself, others, and the world we all share.

Being gifted and Black or Latino, or LGBTQ++, is often enough to create feelings of discrimination within the context of general society (Brown, 2021; Davis, 2024; Sedillo, 2017). Consider, then, the complexity and additive impact of the multiple challenges of being a gifted Black learner with one or more exceptional conditions and carrying with you the weight of these multiple identities—some that may be totally invisible to the community at large. The same holds true for a multi-identified gay, transexual, multilingual, or highly gifted rural area student and others for whom every experience and interaction hold the potential to be discriminatory, painful, or traumatic.

As indicated by Figure 2.1, among the intersectional constructs that we believe are important in the lives of 2e/3e learners are the impact of the family organization (e.g., single family, nuclear family, female-led household, intergenerational household, single father, parents of similar genders, biracial, multiracial); gender identity; neurodivergence; sense of self; language; and religion/spirituality.

As educators, we have a critical responsibility to better understand all the complex identities of our students, particularly those who are already burdened by societal barriers and norms that increase potential for discrimination and inequities. As educators working with 2e and 3e learners, we should be as knowledgeable about our students' psychosocial needs as we are of their intellectual needs. Understanding the multiple identities that individuals carry with them daily, we have not always been as sensitive to the intersectionality of these identities. Identity formation, then, includes the development of several psychological and environmental stages, personalities, and constructs that compose everyone's life (Davis, 2021).

## Navigating Multiple Complex and Intersecting Worlds

The many worlds that gifted and 2e/3e students navigate daily are complex and interactive. The very nature of being a gifted individual whose mind processes incoming information rapidly and differently; who is keenly sensitive to the emotions, conversations, and insights that they discover while engaged with others (whether that engagement is voluntary or forced); who has a thirst to learn and understand more intricate details about everything; who has the will and inner drive to move obstacles as they work toward the accomplishment of their goals—all of this and more makes being gifted anything but an easy ride. Couple their giftedness with an invisible handicap/disability/barrier to clearly understanding what they know "they know" and being the subject of ridicule and taunting by others who don't truly understand what it's like to live inside of a 2e or 3e self, and the slow process that it takes in some cases to create, discuss, or write about solutions to problems to which they have already the answers, and this makes for a challenging, complex life.

# Raising the Student Voice: Empowering 2e and 3e Learners

As we have discussed, twice-exceptional students are among those most underrepresented in gifted programs nationwide (Fugate et al, 2020), thus placing them at a grave disadvantage in schooling environments. Combine the disadvantages that emerge as twice-exceptional learners with those inequities that students of color face and we have a group for whom their identity becomes a major source of discrimination and inequity everywhere (Davis & Robinson, 2016; Ford et al, 2021; Fugate et al, 2020). In addition to academic research and theoretical analyses of twice-exceptionality, nonfiction writers are sharing compelling stories of their own experiences of being twice exceptional and Black in varied social contexts (Baraka, 2021; Brissett-Bailey, 2023).

Baraka's autobiographical story shares the emasculating effects of being a young Black male learner who struggled with undiagnosed dyslexia. His story is one shared by so many Black students across the nation, male and female. As an undiagnosed special needs student, he was a prime candidate for the school-to-prison pipeline (Baraka, 2021). Educators and advocates are seeking to change systems of communication in schools by being more cognizant of the power of student voices (Davis & Douglas, 2021). Empowering underrepresented students by enhancing their voice as self-advocates is a systemic strategy that has the potential to shift the paradigm in school environments by placing the **student at the nexus of decision-making** regarding services made available and matching student interest identity with instructional and support programs (see Figure 2.2).

Empowering scholars of color and those whose lives represent the challenges of intersectional identities (including twice exceptionality) provides a rich combination of anecdotal, qualitative research and educational practice strengthening the legitimacy of "voice." Hispanic scholars were among the first gifted education scholars to address the intersectional impact of culture, language differences, and giftedness (Castellano & Diaz, 2004). Research on cultural identity and identity formation suggests that Black students who hold a strong racial/cultural identity utilize that identity as a source of strength to enable and empower them as they face discrimination and inequities (Ford et al, 2021; Mayes & Moore, 2016; Robinson, 2016; Whiting, 2014).

In his ethnographic research describing his experiences as a gifted Black male with dyslexia, Robinson (2016) positioned himself among the first scholars of

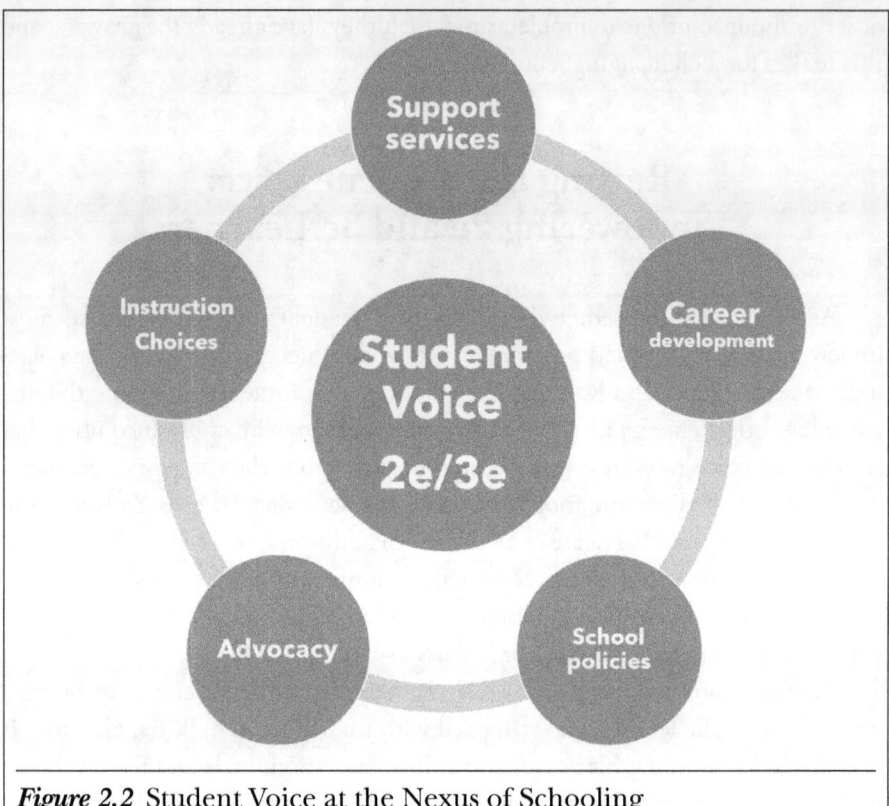

*Figure 2.2* Student Voice at the Nexus of Schooling

color to declare that being Black, having potential for giftedness, and being dyslexic was a specialized condition that should be noticed, studied, and provided for. Robinson's "triple identity theory" (gifted, Black male, with disability) was the first to elucidate the intersectional experiences that caused trauma in his earlier life. After meeting and being mentored by a linguistic scholar, Robinson developed a strong identity, enabling him to survive, thrive, and become a successful scholar (Robinson, 2016). Davis and Robinson (2018) drew increased attention to this "triple identity theory" by extending the definition of "twice exceptional" to become "thrice exceptional," denoting gifted learners who have other exceptional conditions and are culturally diverse, as illustrated in Figure 2.3. This new articulation of the unique needs of culturally diverse twice-exceptional learners is beginning to give much-needed attention to a group of 2e learners who have not received attention in research or practice (Davis, 2024).

As we have articulated throughout this chapter, it is critical that educators, allies, parents, and family members of exceptional, gifted learners understand the complexity and nuances of their important development of racial identities, given the multiple intersectional worlds that these students navigate daily. We believe they deserve the intentional attention of researchers, scholars, advocates,

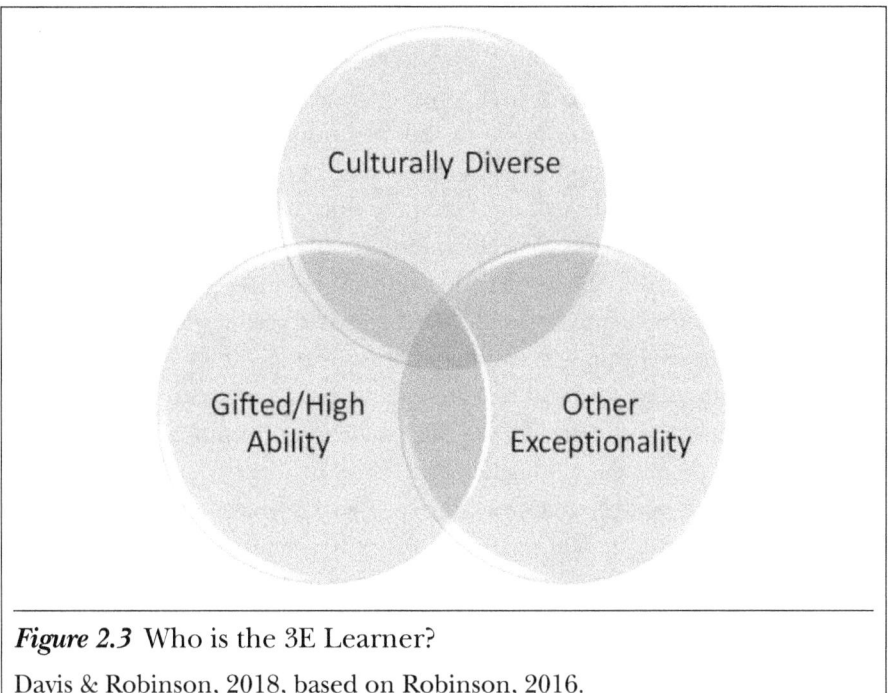

***Figure 2.3*** Who is the 3E Learner?
Davis & Robinson, 2018, based on Robinson, 2016.

educators, and others who understand that, without direct and specific attention regarding their specific cognitive, psychosocial, creative, and intellectual needs, we will continue to ignore, misrepresent, and marginalize these exceptional learners. This is needed today more than ever, as our individual liberties are being threatened by increasingly insensitive political norms that jeopardize our very humanity. The student profiled here, as well as countless others across the nation, and around the world, merit and require our immediate attention.

## Things to Consider

- It is imperative to consider the intersectionality of race, exceptionality, and cultural background when identifying and developing appropriate, individualized services for 2e/3e students to ensure that their unique identities and experiences are acknowledged and valued. By recognizing and addressing these factors, educators and policymakers can create more inclusive and supportive environments for all gifted students, regardless of their cultural backgrounds, family norms, language, gender identity, or other distinguishing features.

- 2e and 3e learners who express their gender identities may differ from many in their school community. As a result, there is sometimes a sense of *disclusion*—a lack of belonging that may become, like other disadvantages, traumatic and oppressive. It is vital that schools ensure that all personnel are fully trained in the norms of gender identity and sexual orientation, with access to all appropriate laws and rules of grammar that impact these learners. Parents and community members should also be invited into sessions to discuss these issues in a nonconfrontational manner.
- Identity plays a crucial role in shaping a student's sense of self and their place in the world. For gifted students with cultural differences and learning exceptionalities, the issue of identity mismatch can have profound implications for their social and emotional wellbeing. When a student is identified as gifted but does not see themselves reflected in that identity, it can lead to feelings of isolation and alienation. Research by Collins (2018) highlighted the challenges faced by gifted students from culturally diverse backgrounds who may not have a reflective identity that aligns with their gifted identification. This mismatch can create a disconnect between how they are perceived by others and how they see themselves, leading to a sense of not belonging or being misunderstood.
- Addressing identity mismatch among gifted students with cultural exceptionalities requires a holistic approach that considers their cultural background, lived experiences, and social context. Educators and school administrators play a crucial role in creating inclusive environments where all students feel valued and understood. Thus, their understandings must be clear and absent of bias while they serve in the roles of trainers, mediators, or mentors supporting students, other educators, and families
- By recognizing and validating the diverse identities of 2e/3e students, schools can help foster a sense of belonging and empowerment. The practices and norms of an inclusive school environment are critical to ensure a sense of belonging for 2e/3e students (Danielian, 2021). This, in turn, can support 2e/3e students in realizing their full potential and thriving academically, socially, and emotionally.
- Another reality that warrants consideration by educators is the extra pressure to fit in that 3e students may experience within their own cultural groups. This can cause a gifted minority student to underachieve because they may not want to assimilate into the majority-dominated society. In fact, what will need to happen is a re-education

for all students—a concerted effort to show and convince minority students that they are not losing something (or losing themselves) but rather will gain more in the long run by "playing the school game."
- 3e individuals are also challenged by societal norms as they seek to develop their full identity as LGBTQ+ persons. A moving contribution in a comprehensive collection of essays written by Black scholars across multiple domains described the trauma experienced as a queer disabled person attempting to develop an identity and a sense of belonging throughout their adolescent years (Brown, 2021). In the tumultuous and confrontational environment of some communities across the nation, school administrators must remain vigilant in ensuring that all students feel a sense of belonging and safety in their school environment, all day, every day. To achieve this, the voices of students, educators, and specialists must be heard as programs are challenged, redesigned, and framed to create the best possible setting for our most vulnerable populations, including the 2e/3e LGBTQ+ populations.
- Another important consideration is the availability, expertise, and sense of responsibility of varied services providers. Guidance counselors, social workers, language specialists, exceptional education and gifted education specialists, and clinicians are all needed to improve service options and program models for the students we define in this chapter. The tragedy in many schools is the lack of support and availability of cultural competency trained guidance counselors (this includes training in support practices for youth in the following groups: Black, Indigenous, Hispanic, low socioeconomic status, LGBTQ+ youth, and multilingual learners). The willingness (or unwillingness) to collaborate, share expertise, share resources, and convene regularly can make the difference between "safe spaces" with effective, compassionate specialists serving 2e/3e learners and "in name only" programs, where students remain unserved and too often traumatized by their daily experiences. Bringing all stakeholders to the proverbial table to engage with others, assess the landscape, and receive the impassioned pleas of students and advocates is vital moving forward. Where such safe, healthy spaces exist, free of discriminatory behavior—without the use of inappropriate language and trauma-charged experiences—growth can occur and the potential for more neurodiverse students to realize their dreams can become a reality. See Appendix B for additional resources to learn more about intersectionality.

## For Discussion

- As an advocate for culturally diverse twice-exceptional learners, what steps can you take to build a stronger community for these learners who are often overlooked and misunderstood?
- Who might be some of the important allies that you can engage to assist in making a substantial and long-term impact on the lives of racially diverse learners?
- What steps can you take to ensure that 3e learners are empowered and have an audience that will listen to their concerns?
- What in-school and extracurricular enrichment experiences can you provide for 2e/3e learners?
- How can you inform, influence, and solicit local, state-level, and national legislators' advocacy on behalf of 2e/3e learners?

## References

Baraka, A. (2022). *Undiagnosed: The ugly side of dyslexia.* Simple Words Books.

Brissett-Bailey, M. (ed.) (2023). *Black, brilliant & dyslexic.* Jessica Kingsley Publishers.

Brown, K. (2021). We are human too: On Blackness, vulnerability, disability and the work ahead. In T. Burke & B. Brown (eds.). *You are your best thing: Vulnerability, shame resilience and the Black experience* (pp 79-86). Random House.

Castellano, J. A. & Diaz, E. (eds.) (2002). *Reaching new horizons: Gifted and talented education for culturally and linguistically diverse students.* Allyn & Bacon.

Cerezo A., Cummings M., Holmes M., & Williams C. (2020) Identity as resistance: Identity formation at the intersection of race, gender identity, and sexual orientation. *Psychology of Women Quarterly, 44*(1), 67-83. doi: 10.1177/0361684319875977

Collins, K. H. (2018). Confronting colorblind STEM talent development: Toward a contextual model for Black student STEM identity. *Journal of Advanced Academics, 29*(2), 143-168. https://doi.org/10.1177/1932202X18757958

Cotton, C. R. B., Davis, J. L., & Collins, K. H. (2022) See me! Recognizing and addressing the invisibility of gifted Black girls with other learning exceptionalities. In F. H. R. Piske, K. H. Collins & K. B. Arnstein (eds.) *Critical issues in servicing twice exceptional students: Socially, emotionally, and culturally framing exceptionalities* (pp. 171-181). Springer

Crenshaw, K. (1989) Demarginalizing the intersection of race and sex: A Black feminist critique of antidiscrimination doctrine, feminist theory and anti-racist politics. *University Chicago Legal Forum, 1*, 139-167. http://chicagounbound.uchicago.edu/uclf/vol1989/iss1/8

Crocetti, E., Albarello, F., Meeus, W., & Rubini, M. (2023). Identities: A developmental social-psychological perspective. *European Review of Social Psychology, 34*(1), 161-201. https://doi.org/10.1080/10463283.2022.2104987

Danielian, J. (2021). School climate change: Requiring understanding of our students and community. In M. Fugate, W. Behrens, C. Boswell, & J. L. Davis (eds). *Culturally responsive teaching in gifted education: Building cultural competence and serving diverse student populations.* Prufrock Press.

Davis, J. L. (2024, February). Intentionally opening the world of twice exceptionality for culturally diverse learners. *Teaching for High Potential*, pp. 1, 16.

Davis, J. L. & Douglas, D. O. (eds.) (2021). *Empowering underserved gifted learners: Perspectives from the field.* Free Spirit Publishing.

Davis, J. L. & Robinson, S. A. (2018) Being 3e: A new look at culturally diverse students with exceptional conditions: An examination of the issues and solutions for educators and families. In S. B. Kaufman (ed.) *Twice exceptional: Supporting and educating bright and creative students with learning difficulties.* Oxford University Press.

Davis, J. L. (in review). *Addressing the intellectual and psychosocial needs of Black gifted learners.* Education Sciences.

Ford, D. Y., Whiting, G. W., Fletcher, E. C., Moore, J. L., & Wright, B. L. (2021). I got this: Helping gifted and talented Black students advocate for themselves in the face of educational injustices. In J. L. Davis & D. Douglas (eds). *Empowering underrepresented gifted students: Perspectives from the field* (pp. 29-42). Free Spirit Publishing,

Fugate, C. M., Behrens, W., & Boswell, C. (2020). *Understanding twice exceptional learners: Connecting research to practice.* Prufrock Press.

Galbraith, J. & Delisle, J. (2022) *The gifted teen survival guide: Smart, sharp and ready for (almost) anything.* (5th Ed.). Prufrock Press.

Hérbert, T. (2020). *Understanding the social and emotional lives of gifted students* (2nd Ed.). Prufrock Press.

Robinson, S. A. (2016). Triple identity theory: A theoretical framework for understanding gifted Black males with dyslexia. *Urban Education Research and Policy Annuals, 4*(1), 147-158.

Sedillo, P. J. (2017). A response to the six social-emotional issues for G/LGBTQ students. In J. Danielian, C. M. Fugate & E. Fogarty (eds.) *Teaching gifted children: Success strategies for teaching high ability learners.* Prufrock Press.

Steinmetz, K. (2020) She coined the term "Intersectionality" over 30 years ago. Here's what it means to her today. *Time Magazine,* February 20. https://time.com/5786710/kimberle-crenshaw-intersectionality

Tormos, F. (2017) Intersectional solidarity. *Politics, Groups, and Identities,* 5(4), 707-720. https://doi.org/10.1080/21565503.2017.1385494

Whiting, G. W. (2014) Scholar identity model: Black male success in the K-12 context. In F. Bonner (ed.) *Building on resilience: Models and frameworks of Black male success across the P-20 pipeline* (pp 88-108). Stylus.

# Chapter 3

# Living a Counterstory

## Adolescence, Identity, and Growing Up Gifted and Unwhite

### Angela M. Novak

In her 2003 book *Building Community*, author, activist, and LGBTQ icon bell hooks wrote, "Dominator culture has tried to keep us all afraid, to make us choose safety instead of risk, sameness instead of diversity" (p. 196). It is in silence that we lose. hooks continued: "Moving through that fear, finding out what connects us, reveling in our differences; this is the process that brings us closer, that gives us a world of shared values, of meaningful community" (hooks, 2003, p. 196). In this chapter, the author presents meaningful counterstories—powerful voices of resistance and intercultural communication—to share how multi-exceptional and multiply marginalized teens experience social and academic life through their unique intersectional lenses.

## Cultural Intelligence

*The model minority stereotype [is] inherently deceptive, especially in an era of colorblindness where racism flourishes. Asian American academic achievement spawns attention, which is used to further marginalize other minorities. The model minority stereotype is false, hegemonic, and self-empowering for whites.*
Nicholas Hartlep, Korean-American Endowed
Chair in Education Studies, Berea College

Within socio-cultural and socio-historical cognitive developmental theory, cognition does not exist in a silo (Empson & Nabuzoka, 2010; Vygotsky, 1978). Giftedness, talent, and twice or thrice-exceptionality are interpreted through what Vygotsky (1978) would describe as "signs": the essential building blocks of mental functioning are language (verbal, written, non-verbal) or symbols. Definitions of "giftedness" vary (e.g., see Smedsrud, 2020 for an analysis), but this language reference is socio-linguistic. Not all languages have an exact translation for "gifted"—at least not one that refers to the construct at use in a local school district—but several studies have considered this topic.

Studies have revealed that in determining intelligence in school, conformity and respectful behavior were significant expectations among recent immigrants, while American-born parents valued autonomy. Parents of historically marginalized groups (non-White) rated non-cognitive skills such as motivation and social skills as desired outcomes; while parents of historically advantaged students (White) emphasized problem-solving, creativity, and verbal skills as preferred outcomes (Empson & Nabuzoka, 2010; Sternberg, 2004)—though this depended on the study conducted, the cultural group, and the location. Rural Kenyans balanced four domains of intelligence (based on the closest translation): problem solving or thinking, processing or initiative, respect or obedience, and ability or skills (Grigorenko et al., 2001); while in other African nations, harmony and intergroup relationship skills were valued as intelligence (Sternberg, 2004).

Okagaki and Sternberg (1993) studied parents' conceptions of education, noting differences between historically marginalized groups, with Latine parents emphasizing social skills and Asian immigrant parents focusing on cognitive skills. This research generalization—once expanded from the participants (Mexican immigrant and Mexican American, and immigrant families from Cambodia, Vietnam, and the Philippines) to Latine, Asian, or Asian American when cited in broader literature—is echoed in the model minority stereotype, and in Nicholas Hartlep's (2021) quote at the start of this section. The model minority myth obscures the diversity that exists among individuals (Hartlep, 2021), such as Taiwanese conceptions of intelligence, which stray from cognition and align with traditional Chinese philosophies of Confucianism and Taoism (Yang and Sternberg, 1997). "The Confucian perspective emphasizes the characteristic of benevolence and of doing what is right … the intelligent person spends a great deal of effort in learning, enjoys learning, and persists in life-long learning with a great deal of enthusiasm" (Sternberg, 2004, p. 334). In contrast, Taoism "emphasizes the importance of humility, freedom from conventional standards of judgment, and full knowledge of oneself as well as of external conditions" (Sternberg, 2004, p. 334). Within the Yup'ik Alaska Native population, elders hold the traditional knowledge of the people; a valued trait of the Yup'ik nation is showing respect for elders. One study of practical intelligence was measured through sea and river or land knowledge, and included items related to hunting or fishing, weather, game preparation, and herbs and berries. Thinking skills and problem-solving ability were also valued forms of intelligence (Grigorenko et al., 2004).

## Learning and Growth through Marginalized Identities

*What I'd like to share with people is that what we have to give to our children are values, not so much material, [but] a social conscience. You have to involve them at a very young age so they grow up knowing that this is something they can do that they have power to help people. And I think that's the biggest thing I gave my children.*

Dolores Huerta, Latina activist and Presidential Medal of Honor winner

During adolescence (i.e., aged ten to 15), according to social-cognitive development theory, youth begin to understand concepts of reciprocity: the idea that their racial/ethnic group members might have ideological views that differ from those of other racial/ethnic groups (Takriti, 2010). Exploring these differing views can cause dissonance, leading to learning and growth. Analogizing decolonialization and social justice, individual identities, and emotional and psychosocial growth through the film *The Shape of Water*, Grande (2020) describes myriad characters of different ethnic, cultural, (dis)ability, talent, gender, and sexual identities, acknowledging their awareness of the othering, marginalization, and limitations perpetuated by these differences. It was in their foe's oppressive belief systems that the characters found success; their marginalized intersectional identities rendered them invisible, able to operate unnoticed and in collectivity. As Dolores Huerta's (2016) words which started out this section reveal, values and social conscience were the powers that enabled their success. Grande shared a pivotal moment from the movie in which:

> [an] older, White male character was suddenly overcome with fear and doubt about putting his life on the line for "the other" and exclaimed, "But he's not even human!" And his friend responds, "And if we do nothing, neither are we."
>
> *(Grande 2020, p. 148)*

It was the characters alone that recognized the humanity in the decolonialized others and the power that they held.

In Nêhiyawak (Cree) teachings, there are four times, or milestones, in life: time of motion (birth); time of identity (ten years old); time of purpose (30 years old); and time of teaching (60 years old). Secondary students are in the time of identity; this is when they explore themselves as individuals, apart from their family, their peer group, or their nation/clan. This can be a heavy experience with reflection; during each time period, a gift is bestowed, and in the time of identity, children receive humor so that, alongside deep moments of introspection, they might also find relief. Each time period also has a giving/receiving continuum; during identity, children move from consistently receiving from their community in their childhood to learning to give back, while still receiving guidance, care, love, and support. At this older age, children learn more directly from the elders and engage in more direct shared experiences. A Cree child will prepare for isolation and introspection to receive a vision which will lead to stagnation or activity. If they don't finish this vision or reject it, they will experience a time of stagnation; otherwise, they take part in the community through activity (shared by Eddie Belrose, Cree Elder; Stone Brown, 2014). Like Huerta's (2016) inspirational words, this Cree way of knowing and being is steeped in social consciousness and giving back to the community.

## Identity Development

*Something is changing in this generation of Asian Americans. We are tired of being told that we don't experience racism, we are tired of being told to keep our heads down and not make trouble. We are tired of Asian American kids growing up and being asked where they're REALLY from, of having our eyes mocked, of being objectified as exotic or being told we're inherently unattractive … We are tired of being invisible, of being mistaken for our colleague or told our struggles aren't as real … Being an Asian American doesn't mean we don't experience poverty and racism. Being a 9-year NBA veteran doesn't protect me from being called "coronavirus" on the court. Being a man of faith doesn't mean I don't fight for justice, for myself and for others.*

Jeremy Lin, Taiwanese-American Harvard graduate and professional basketball player

In a call for educator activism, Valdez et al. described a "shared struggle for the right to get to feel human" (Valdez et al., 2018, p. 247). This centering of humanity calls for a cognitive and holistic model of identity development for talented youth. The Scholar Identity Model (SIM™) (Whiting, 2006) (Appendix C) is one such model, grounded in psychological and sociological research, set in pyramid formation with four pillars for support (see Figure 3.1).

# Identity and Growing Up Gifted and Unwhite

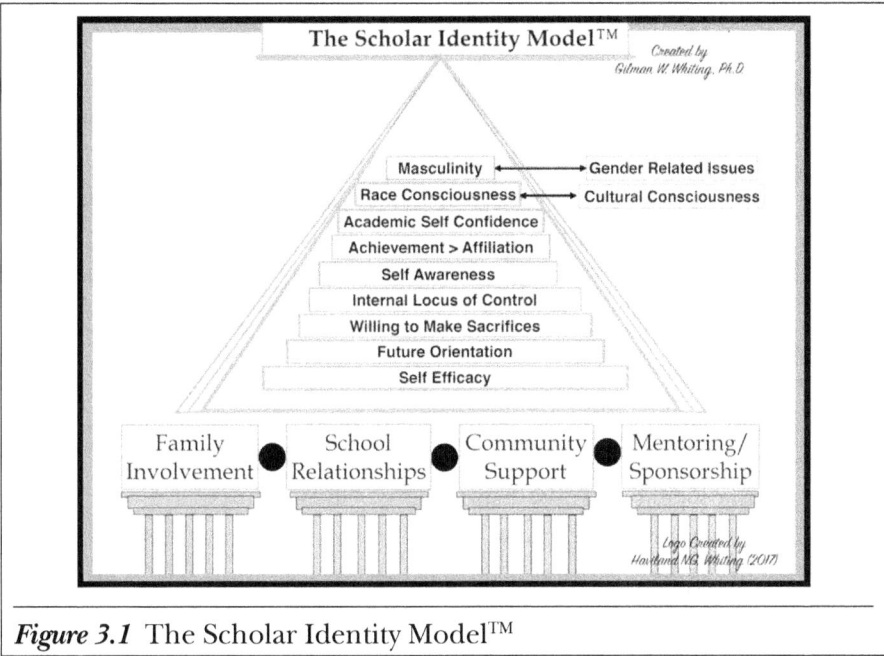

***Figure 3.1*** The Scholar Identity Model™

*Self-efficacy*—the belief in one's ability to be successful—is the base of the pyramid, the foundational strength. Having goals, hopes, and dreams anchored in the present while planning for what's next is the *future orientation* characteristic. *Willing to make sacrifices* can vary on the part of the individual, with the crucial component being an understanding that progress comes after struggle. The next level of the pyramid is the *internal locus of control*, or the belief that outcomes—whether positive or negative—are based on one's ability, effort, and/or preparation. This ties closely with a scholar's level of *self-awareness*: their ability to understand, and adapt to, their own strengths and weaknesses.

The next level, *achievement > affiliation*, refers to an internal focus on achievement. This may be through means such as goal setting and careful planning for high-quality work rather than over quantity of time and effort spent on work; friendships value the same quality over quantity model, and the need for achievement is strong compared to their desire for affiliation. Close to the top of the pyramid is *academic self-confidence*; scholars believe they are strong students and are at ease in academic settings. They are open and self-aware both of their ability and of the ongoing effort they need to put into maintaining their academic excellence.

The characteristics up until this point in the triangle may be common to many high-ability students, while the final two characteristics are more specific to marginalized communities (Whiting, 2006). At the *race consciousness and cultural consciousness* level, understanding a scholar's identity from a racial, ethnic, and/or cultural perspective is crucial. Blackness is honor, intelligence, beauty, joy, and greatness; scholars are demonstrating these expectations. Jeremy Lin's (2021) quote in the epigraph above speaks to this racial consciousness. His comments on invisibility and the erasure of racism calls are indicative of the model minority myth (Hartlep, 2021). Pre-existing notions of talented youth, along with the barrage of messages from family, school, and media regarding gender, may cause conflict for youth in sharing their gender identification or reflecting on it personally. Whiting's (2006) aspect of *gender-related issues* speaks to this potential for identity conflict of societal norms versus the self, regarding developing a scholar identity.

The bulk of SIM™ (the triangle) is internal: how students understand and believe in themselves as thinkers and doers within the classroom community. External forces are the four pillars that bolster the triangle: family involvement, school relationships, community support, and mentoring/sponsorship. While these pillars together create a foundation, if one was missing, the scholar's identity formation wouldn't crumple; even if two were not available due to place, funding, circumstances, etc., the scholar may be able to rearrange and adapt.

Embedded in a high school to capture youth voices around the model minority myth, Asian American researcher Stacey Lee found that among students whom she categorized as Asian American within the high-school community, they had four different race or cultural consciousness identities, as described by the SIM™. Most Korean students identified as such, while the remainder were split between three pan-ethnic or pan-Asian subgroups. The Asian subgroup consisted primarily of new immigrants (China, Hong Kong, Taiwan) or refugees (Laos, Cambodia, Vietnam). The self-identified Asian New Wave group were in recent groups of refugees (second or third), predominantly from China, Cambodia, or Vietnam. The final, and smallest, subgroup identified as Asian American were from a variety of the above ethnic groups. What distinguished this subset is that they saw themselves as having both Asian and American identities. Xuan said: "my culture is not all Asian and it's not all American. It's something entirely different. And it's not like some people say, that it's a mixture. It's like another whole different thing" (Lee, 1996, p. 44). Having a collective group identity is essential for organization movement, which emerges from connections rather than critical mass (Lee Boggs, 2011); but overreliance on a generalized, stereotyped, monolithic identity perpetuates racism, as in the model minority myth (Hartlep, 2021).

Thinking back to Knicks basketball player and Harvard graduate Jeremy Lin, a Boston-based Ben & Jerry's franchise created a locally available "Taste the Lin-Sanity" flavor to celebrate the local graduate's meteoric rise in 2012. The flavor contained lychee honey—while a popular flavor in Taiwan, this sweet swirl was not anything that Lin had previously (or since) made any public statements regarding. The second "honorific" flavoring was fortune cookie pieces. While popularized in American Chinese restaurants, *tsujiura senbei* originated in Kyoto, Japan (Lee, 2008), exemplifying the monolithic Asian cultural grouping perpetuated by the model minority myth. One student from Lee's study said:

> When I say I'm Asian American I feel like I establish a root for myself here. My parents think of themselves as Vietnamese because their roots are in Vietnam. Being Asian American is like a way to feel like I belong.
> *(Lee, 1996, p. 45).*

A both/and approach is crucial to dismantling the myth: balancing the importance of collective identity while concurrently learning about and welcoming individual differences, both within ethnicities and within people as human beings.

## Psychosocial Development

*I have never encountered any children in any group who are not geniuses. There is no mystery on how to teach them. The first thing you do is treat them like human beings and the second thing you do is love them.*
Asa G. Hilliard III, African American Fuller E. Calloway Professor of Urban Education, Georgia State University (until his homegoing, while leading a study group in Egypt)

The first Native American US poet laureate, Joy Harjo, powerfully recounts her ancestors' displacement in "Exile of Memory." In one short section, she tells the story of the children sent to boarding "school"—in reality, forced confinement for religious and cultural assimilation (see discussion questions; Harjo, 2019a). These schools actively and irrevocably harmed students and their families (Fear-Segal & Rose, 2016). Historically marginalized individuals are continually othered, oppressed, and physically and psychologically harmed through curriculum, schooling, media, and daily practices of micro- and macro-aggressions. Dr. Hilliard's quote above offers two simple suggestions to avoid this trend: love and humanity.

Understanding the psychosocial development of 2e and 3e learners requires moving beyond typical stages and theory taught in standard educational psychology courses—the same theories taught 30 years ago when I was an undergraduate—in which the psychologists' research sample was most likely male, monochromatic, and middle to upper class. Chicana activist and author Gloria Anzaldúa's collection of essays and poetry, *Borderlands/La Frontera: The New*

*Mestiza*, includes an anecdote that is all too common in today's classrooms. She was ostracized from her classmates and removed to the corner of the room for the crime of "'talking back' … when all I was trying to do was tell her how to pronounce my name. 'If you want to be American, speak American. If you don't like it, go back to Mexico where you belong'" (Anzaldúa, 1999, p. 61). In another incident, she tells of being punished with three smacks of a ruler after being caught speaking Spanish with friends during free time, demonstrating the inherent carcerality of her psychological development. When leading with love and humanity, it is beneficial to have a broader understanding of psychological and social development that considers all gender and sexual identities, as well as learners' race/ethnicities and cultures.

Sidney Stone Brown (2014), Siksika Nation, shares a Native American model of self-esteem that is presented in a circular shape; this allows an iterative process to revisit self-esteem throughout spiritual journeys, taken as they advance through adolescence and adulthood. The elements that are required for high self-esteem are situated in four cardinal directions. Starting with north and moving clockwise, the elements are (Clemens, 1986, as cited in Stone Brown, 2014): knowing (life philosophy or goals; future directions); having (connections to cultural heritage); being (uniqueness or special abilities); and doing (empowerment or a sense of capability or influence).

The triple quandary (TQ) framework highlights three psychosocial spinning plates that Black individuals continually balance in order to thrive in the White supremacist culture of American society: (1) mainstream (White/American) values of effort optimism, the democratization of equality, egalitarian-based conformity, possessive individualism, material wellbeing, and a person-to-object orientation; (2) the interconnected dimensions of social-cultural integrity valued within Black families/communities of communalism, verve, spirituality, harmony, oral tradition, movement, expressive individualism, affect, and a social time perspective; and (3) the lived experiences of being minoritized, which begets "adaptive and compensatory reactions, social perspectives, and defensive postures that help one to cope with the predicament created by the oppressive forces" (Boykin et al., 2023, p. 432). The TQ framework extends to other marginalized populations, with a goal of understanding learners' culture and applying this understanding to make the classroom a space of learning.

# Conclusion

*The Lakȟóta term Mitákuye Owás'iŋ is translated as all my relations, but it has a deeper meaning … [It] is a way of knowing and a reciprocal relationship to all living beings, spiritually, physically, and energetically, in this world and in the spirit world ... we must take the time to know the importance of each other's languages and traditional lifeways and also learn about and from other's histories.*

Alayna Eagle Shield, Húŋkpapȟa Lakȟóta,<br>Dakȟóta, and Sáhniš; co-founder of the Mní Wičhóni<br>Nakíčižiŋ Wóuŋspe (Defenders of the Water School)

As educators strive to contextualize students' intersectional identities and authentically integrate this knowledge into the social and academic experience, it will lead to positive outcomes. At the forefront of culturally sustaining pedagogy and equitable democratic education are three key tenets. (1) Truly see all individuals, recognize talents, and maintain an asset-minded approach in the teaching and learning community. (2) Equity is a natural embedded aspect of the democratic educational culture, with an open and honest dialogue encouraged with love and respect. (3) Social change requires not only recognition and awareness, but also intention and action. By embracing these principles, educators can create inclusive learning environments that empower all students to thrive academically, socially, and emotionally.

## Things to Consider

- Western definitions of "giftedness" need to include how different cultures conceptualize intelligence—emphasizing community, harmony, practical knowledge, or respect for elders over traditional academic metrics. Educators should critically reflect on how culturally biased definitions of "giftedness" shape who gets identified and supported.
- Gifted youth who are also part of historically marginalized racial, cultural, or linguistic groups often navigate conflicting expectations. Their identities—racial, cultural, linguistic, gendered—intersect in ways that affect their educational experiences, sometimes rendering them invisible or "othered" within systems not designed for them.
- The stereotype of Asian American academic success not only is inaccurate but also reinforces systems of racial inequity by dismissing real struggles and using one group's perceived "success" to justify the marginalization of others. Recognizing and disrupting this myth is essential for equitable support.

- Whiting's SIM™ emphasizes both internal traits (e.g., self-efficacy and race/cultural consciousness) and external supports (e.g., family, mentoring, community). Educators should prioritize holistic, identity-affirming strategies that help students see themselves as capable scholars, particularly those from underrepresented backgrounds.

## For Discussion

*All cultures and peoples turn to poetry during times of celebration, transformation and challenge—those times when ordinary language cannot carry meaning beyond our understanding. The road from childhood to adulthood is a precarious path, yet full of miracles. We need poetry as we navigate that archetypal journey.*

Joy Harjo, Mvskoke Nation, 23rd US poet laureate

- In the spirit of US Poet Laureate Joy Harjo's message, listen to her reading "Exile of Memory" (https://www.loc.gov/item/2020785224/) on the Library of Congress site. A transcript is available for accessibility, as is a copy of the poem. Discuss "I can feel our people still there. Most of our stories and songs have roots in that place. My poetry has roots in that place" (Harjo & Library of Congress, 2020, 7:45-7:53). Discuss the implications of historical place when teaching twice and thrice-exceptional learners, particularly with respect to community-driven and identity-affirming educational practices. Then discuss the implications of forced displacement (e.g., enslavement, forced removal of Native Americans from their ancestral lands, refugees and asylum seekers) on these same practices.
- How do different cultural perspectives on intelligence and giftedness shape the way students are identified and supported in educational settings? Consider using "Playground Elegy" by Clint Smith (2015) (https://www.stilljournal.net/clint-smith-poetry.php) to deepen your discussion of this question.
- In what ways do intersectional identities influence students' experiences of inclusion, marginalization, and academic success within the school system? Consider using "To Live in the Borderlands" by Gloria Anzaldúa (1999) (http://www.revistascisan.unam.mx/Voices/pdfs/7422.pdf) to deepen your discussion of this question.

- What role do educators play in challenging stereotypes, such as the model minority myth, and fostering an equitable learning environment for all students? Consider using "Not Your Model Minority" by Rosa Kim (2021) (https://bclawimpact.org/2021/02/15/not-your-model-minority/) to deepen your discussion of this question.

For greater accessibility, YouTube has videos of the Smith and Anzaldúa poems read aloud. Kim's poem has an audio recording of an introduction and the poem available on the site.

# References

Anzaldúa, G. (1999) *Borderlands/la frontera: The new mestiza* (5th ed.). aunt lute books.

Boykin, C. M., Coleman, S. T., Hurley, E. A., Tanksley, G. N., & Tyler, K. M. (2023) From triple quandary to talent quest. The past, present, and future of A. Wade Boykin's contributions to psychology. *American Psychologist. 78*(4), 428-440. https://doi.org/10.1037/amp0001116

Eagle Shield, A. (2020) Naǧí uŋkíčhopi (calling our spirits back) through language and culture from mitákuye owás'iŋ and beyond. In A. Eagle Shield, D. Paris, R. Paris, & T. San Pedro (eds.) *Education in movement spaces: Standing Rock to Chicago Freedom Square* (pp. 57-66). Routledge.

Empson, J. M. & Nabuzoka, D. (2010) Culture and cognitive development. In D. Nabuzoka & J. M. Empson (eds.) *Culture & psychological development* (pp. 142-177). Palgrave Macmillan.

Fear-Segal, J. & Rose, S. D. (eds.) (2016) *Carlisle Indian industrial school: Indigenous histories, memories, & reclamations.* University of Nebraska Press.

Grande, S. (2020) After-words of the otherwise. In A. Eagle Shield, D. Paris, R. Paris, & T. San Pedro (eds.) *Education in movement spaces: Standing Rock to Chicago Freedom Square* (pp.145-148). Routledge.

Grigorenko, E. L., Meier, E., Lipka, J., Mohatt, G., Yanez, E., & Sternberg, R. J. (2004) The relationship between academic and practical intelligence: A case study of the tacit knowledge of Native American Yup'ik people in Alaska. *Learning and Individual Differences, 14,* 183-207. https://doi.org/10.1016/j.lindif.2004.02.002

Grigorenko, E. L., Geissler, P. W., Prince, R., Okatcha, F., Nokes, C., Kenny, D. A., Bundy, D. A. & Sternberg, R. J. (2001) The organization of Luo conceptions of intelligence: A study of implicit theories in a Kenyan village. *International Journal of Behavior Development, 25*(4), 367-378. https://doi.org/10.1080/01650250042000348

Harjo, J. (2019a) *An American sunrise.* W. W. Norton & Co. "Exile of Memory" https://tile.loc.gov/storage-services/service/afc/afc2020004/afc2020004_24/afc2020004_24_ms01.pdf

Harjo, J. (2019b) Last word. *Library of Congress Magazine, 8*(6), 28. https://www.loc.gov/lcm/pdf/LCM_2019_1112.pdf?loclr=blogpoe

Harjo, J. & Library of Congress. (2020) *Joy Harjo reads and discusses Exile of Memory on August 5.* Library of Congress. https://www.loc.gov/item/2020785224/

Hartlep, N. D. (2021) *The model minority stereotype: Demystifying Asian American success* (2nd Ed.). Information Age Publishing.

hooks, b. (2003) *Teaching community: A pedagogy of hope.* Routledge.

Huerta, D. (2016) Writer's almanac with Garrison Keillor. Minnesota Public Radio, April 10. https://www.writersalmanac.org/index.html%3Fp=7827.html

Kim, R. (2021) Not your model minority. BC Law Impact, February 15. https://bclawimpact.org/2021/02/15/not-your-model-minority/

Lee Boggs, G. (2011) *The next American revolution: Sustainable activism for the twenty-first century.* University of California Press.

Lee, J. 8. (2008) *The fortune cookie chronicles: Adventures in the world of Chinese food.* Twelve.

Lee, S. J. (1996) *Unraveling the "model minority" stereotype: Listening to Asian American youth.* Teacher's College Press.

Lin, J. [@jlin7] (2021) *I know the model minority stereotype to be inherently deceptive, especially in an era of colorblindness where racism flourishes. Asian* [Photograph/Post]. Instagram, February 25. https://www.instagram.com/p/CLu9Qq0J9jA/?img_index=1

Okagaki, L. & Sternberg, R. J. (1993) Parental beliefs and children's school performance. *Child Development, 64*(1), 36-56. https://doi.org/10.2307/1131436

Smedsrud, J. (2020) Explaining the variations of definitions in gifted education. *Nordic Studies in Education*, 40(1), 79-97. https://doi.org/10.23865/nse.v40.2129

Smith, C. (2015) Four poems. *Still: The Journal, 17*(Poetry). https://www.stilljournal.net/clint-smith-poetry.php

Sternberg, R. J. (2004) Culture and intelligence. *American Psychologist, 59*(5), 325-338. https://doi.org/10.1037/0003-066X.59.5.325

Stone Brown, S. (2014) *Transformation beyond greed: Native self-actualization.* BookPatch.

Takriti, R. (2010) The development of cultural and ethnic identity. In D. Nabuzoka & J. M. Empson (eds.) *Culture & psychological development* (pp. 210-246). Palgrave Macmillan.

Yang, S. & Sternberg, R. J. (1997) Conceptions of intelligence in ancient Chinese philosophy. *Journal of Theoretical and Philosophical Psychology 17*(2), 101-119. https://doi.org/10.1037/h0091164

Valdez, C., Curammeng, E., Pour-Khorshid, F., Kohli, R., Nikundiwe, T., Picower, B., Shalaby, C., & Stovall, D. (2018) We are victorious: Educator activism as a shared struggle for human being. *The Educational Forum, 82*(3), 244-258. https://doi.org/10.1080/00131725.2018.1458932

Vygotsky, L. S. (1978) *Mind in society: The development of higher psychological processes.* Harvard University Press.

Whiting, G. (2006) From at risk to at promise: Developing scholar identities among Black Males. *The Journal of Secondary Gifted Education, 17*(4), 222-229.

Whiting, H. N. G. (2017) The Scholar Identity Model™. Graphic Representation. Used with Permission from Gilman W. Whiting.

# Chapter 4

# The Brilliant Intersection

## Understanding Black Students Who Are Gifted, Exceptional, and Navigating Economic Barriers[1]

### Gilman W. Whiting

Twenty years ago, I began documenting a child's socio-emotional educational experience. I wrote a short article entitled "May I take your order please? The transmission of whiteness: Subliminal factors that reinforce white supremacy, foster underachievement, and cause stress." I described a young Black girl whose intellectual gifts shone brightly before elementary school: at just eight years of age, she wrote a children's travel book. I predicted as she grew older, the very friends who once clamored and queued to have playdates and sleepovers, and who celebrated her achievements (by 17, she was a published poet), would turn against her—not because of any change in her abilities, but because of deeply rooted societal prejudices, bigotry, and racism that would begin to surface. These daily low dosages of what psychologist Dr. Chester M. Peirce coined "microaggressions" could gradually manifest as self-doubt. This article wasn't just academic theorizing; this was my daughter, and my prediction unfortunately proved prophetic—at least concerning the emergence of racial biases. Over time, we would observe that many of these same biases were held by those entrusted adults in her schools. She was a young, gifted, and Black female.

This anecdote isn't just about one creative Black child with gifts and talents. It's about the countless Black children whose gifts are overshadowed by what W. E. B. DuBois called "the veil": that peculiar sensation of always looking at oneself through the eyes of others. Today, for our gifted Black children who also have learning differences, this veil is especially burdensome. They aren't just seeing themselves through others' eyes but through a warped and distorted lens that often focuses on their challenges while missing their brilliant potential. This confusing feeling of believing you fit into a place or constantly trying to fit into a place where ultimately those whom you call friends are getting their daily, fortifying dosages of White supremacy ideology vexes the spirit. When Dr. Pierce and Dr. William H. Cosby advised the long-playing *Sesame Street*, they presented a vision of an integrated society in which children were happy and, in the words of Dr. Martin Luther King, Jr., judged by the content of their character. Racism's awakening, then, is ultimately concerning for all children.

### "Nobody Is Born a Bigot"

Decades ago, I recall crossing one of the many bridges that beat life into New York City. There was a giant billboard with an off-white background and two children were sitting, one Black, the other White, each wearing only a diaper. They appeared to be looking directly at you. The words above them read: "Nobody Is Born a Bigot." It was a simple yet powerful and accurate message to millions of travelers. But the sign also begs several questions: If nobody is born a bigot, and in that category we are well represented, when does bigotry emerge? How does it happen? Is its transmission intentional, vicarious learning, or unintentional, and like water, we drink it? Are we taught it in school, our communities, other communities, and mass media? We are all somewhat familiar with the outcome of segregation in America's schools with the 1954 *Brown v. Board of Education* ruling; this landmark decision was but one of the conversations around what was happening to Black students' psychological wellness in schools. Much of the conversation and controversy today around Black history being stripped from schools due to the alleged "harm" caused to white children for learning about historical events reopens the historical debate and will eventually add to the resegregation of schools and harm to Black children's mental health. The road to the *Brown* decision was not the only front on which people like Thurgood Marshall and his mentor Charles "The Man Who Killed Jim Crow" Hamilton Houston, and Drs. Kenneth Clark and Mammie Phipps-Clark, as well as luminaries like Dr. Martin D. Jenkins in the field of gifted education, helped pave the way. There were many others across the country who were working on the psychological state of children as well as adults.

*Table 4.1* Merton's Typology

|  | Non-discriminator | Discriminator |
| --- | --- | --- |
| Unprejudiced | Type 1: All-weather liberal | Type 2: Reluctant liberal |
| Prejudiced | Type 3: Timid bigot | Type 4: All-weather bigot |

In 1949, psychologist Robert K. Merton described how prejudice and discrimination can operate in Merton's Typology. In Merton's model, there are four types (see Table 4.1).

Type 1 is an unprejudiced/non-discriminator (all-weather liberal). This person thinks and acts with folks from a different race as they would a family member. They *actually* have Black friends; and if they are teachers, they believe, act, and bring out the best in all students. They know a child comes from a zip code where poverty, unemployment, or even crime may be proportionally higher than where they live or grew up but view those circumstances as an opportunity to pour in love and draw out excellence. They do not mollycoddle but push with the appropriate skill and pressure they would expect of a teacher teaching their child.

Type 2 is an unprejudiced/discriminator (reluctant liberal). This person thinks one way but acts in other, discriminatory, ways. They can often be found leading the class. In their mind, they are being fair and equitable, but their actions and behaviors lead to suspensions and expulsions. This person tells themselves, "I am being fair, but she needs better attendance to be included in gifted services. He needs to stop fidgeting and tapping his feet to be involved in advanced services. They come from the south side of town, where there is a lot of crime and unemployment. They likely would not be successful in an Advanced Placement (AP) or International Baccalaureate program." The teacher/administrator believes they are doing something good for the Black child.

Type 3 is a prejudiced/non-discriminator (timid bigot). This person, like Type 2, thinks one way but acts another. They appear welcoming in public, like the O'Jays' timeless classic backstabbers: "They smile in your face." There is an uncomfortable familiarity with this type of person. In their mind, they actively dislike you because of your race. This type of person is common in America's classrooms. Their actions appear welcoming, but their thoughts are clouded with dismissal (ignoring or downplaying students' experiences), devaluation (undervaluing their potential), diminishment (making them feel smaller or less significant), detachment (emotional disconnection). This person says to themselves, "I need this job, and I don't want to be known as a bigot, so I will be friendly." They may sometimes even use Black vernacular. The result for the student is similar to the Type 2 teacher.

Type 4 is a prejudiced/discriminator (all-weather bigot). This person walks it like they talk it. Their thoughts and actions align. In public, they openly display prejudgment (making assumptions about capabilities before giving a fair chance), presumption (automatically attributing behavioral issues to cultural background), and preconception (holding fixed negative beliefs that affect how they treat students); and in their minds, they are justified. These are mere misperception (seeing threats or defiance in normal childhood behaviors), misjudgment (wrongly interpreting cultural expressions or communication styles), and misconception (maintaining incorrect beliefs about intelligence or family values). This type of person should never be allowed to work with children—especially those from Black communities. But over the years, I have heard from superintendents, principals, assistant principals, and teachers about this guy who teaches math, this woman who runs gifted services, or this president of a gifted association who fits neatly into the Type 4 personality. They often display condescension (speaking down to students, assuming they can't understand), contempt (showing open scorn or disrespect for cultural differences), and callousness (displaying indifference to students' emotional needs or struggles). In their minds, they actively dislike you because of your race and will actively thwart all efforts for a child of a different race to succeed and fulfill their gifted potential.

Another psychological model was developed around the time of the *Brown* decision, which I believe is worth considering. In his 1954 book *The Nature of Prejudice*, Gordon Allport theorized five worsening levels of prejudice. I will only focus in depth on the first level:

- Antilocution—"speaking against" verbal abuse: For Black children who are gifted, have a disability, and come from a family with a low income, verbal microaggressions ring louder. Children and teachers regularly commenting on their ability, hair texture, skin color, or lack of finances to purchase markers of middle-classness make Black children not want to enter the room. "Placism" is equally demoralizing—as was the experience of gifted scholar and author Dr. Donna Y. Ford, who shared one of her childhood educational experiences with me. Upon entering an accelerated class, the only Black child was asked, "Are you lost?" Placism is the discriminatory assumption that certain individuals, particularly Black students, don't "belong" in specific academic spaces or advanced programs. It manifests when educators or others question the presence of Black students in advanced, gifted, or accelerated courses, implying they must be "lost" or "in the wrong place," despite their qualifications and right to be there. This is particularly harmful because:
  - it undermines the student's confidence and sense of belonging;
  - it reinforces false stereotypes about academic capabilities;

- it creates a hostile learning environment in which students must constantly justify their presence;
- it can discourage participation in advanced programs and academic achievement; and
- it can empower bullying and give a false sense of white supremacy.

Many may consider the question "Are you lost?" a typical and quite harmless one. However, it reveals biased expectations and prejudices. Feelings of not belonging to a child can cause doubt, fear, and resentment. As the field struggles to identify children with gifts and talents, it simultaneously pushes out Black high-achieving students.

- Avoidance: When identified as gifted, Black children with disabilities who live in poverty find themselves in increasingly empty spaces. As their academic talents emerge white families quietly transfer their children to "better schools," while administrators create invisible barriers through selective communication about advanced programs. A gifted Black child with dyslexia might never learn about the school's enrichment opportunities because newsletters "accidentally" don't reach certain homes, or meetings are scheduled when working parents can't attend. Modern redlining persists through selective zoning that clusters resources in predominantly white neighborhoods, while "school choice" becomes a euphemism for systematic abandonment.
- Discrimination: Today's legalized racism wears the mask of "objective" policies. Schools require private testing for gifted programs—tests costing hundreds of dollars that Medicaid won't cover. Individualized education program meetings are scheduled during work hours, forcing parents to choose between advocacy and employment. When Black children qualify for both gifted and special education services, they are often forced to choose one or the other, as if their brilliance and their challenges cannot coexist. The system creates paper trails of "reasonable" denials that amount to institutional betrayal.
- Physical attack: While less overt than historical violence, today's physical attacks manifest in the weaponization of school discipline. A gifted Black child's frustration with unchallenging work becomes labeled "defiance." Their disability-related behaviors are criminalized rather than supported. School resource officers are called for minor infractions, introducing talented Black children to the school-to-prison pipeline. Their bodies bear the stress of constant surveillance and the threat of physical restraint—violence dressed up as "security."
- Extermination: Modern extermination is the systematic destruction of potential. When schools fail to identify Black gifted children with

disabilities, they extinguish future scientists, artists, and leaders. Each time a child is pushed out of advanced programs through hostile environments, another light is dimmed. The slow death of dreams through chronic underservice and active discouragement isn't as visible as historical acts of genocide, but the impact on communities persists through generations. This "soft" extermination of intellectual potential maintains systemic inequities just as effectively as its historical counterparts.

Merton (1949), Allport (1954), and *Brown v. Board* (1954) are as salient today as they were during the eras of Jim Crow and the civil rights movement. The same stages of discrimination leading to identification in gifted and talent programs for 4e Black students are evident across the country (see Access Denied, 2019). These models are partly why the HOPE+ scale and the Scholar Identity Model™ (SIM™) are needed today.

## Seeing Jasmine

*The numbers danced in Jasmine's head as she sat in her seventh-grade math class, her body fidgeting and rocking slightly back and forth in her seat. Before Mr. Peters could finish writing the algebra problem, she had already solved it in her mind. But when she called out the answer—again—without raising her hand, she saw that familiar look of frustration cross his face.*

*"Jasmine," he sighed, "we've talked about this. You need to wait your turn."*

*He didn't know that Jasmine had spoken to her parents about Mr. Peters going days not calling on her when she does raise her hand. Frequently, other students are called on even if they don't have their hands raised. Her family told her to speak up. Later, in the teachers' lounge, Mr. Peters shook his head as he discussed Jasmine with her other teachers. "She's bright, sure, but that ADHD makes her impossible to manage. Maybe she should be moved to the regular math class where the pace is slower." Mr. Peters didn't know that Jasmine solved problems quickly because the numbers would slip away like water through her fingers if she didn't. Her rapid-fire responses weren't defiance—they were her way of catching brilliant solutions before her active mind moved on to the next challenge.*

This scene plays out in classrooms across America every day. Black students who are both gifted and dealing with learning differences—what educators call "twice-exceptional"—face a unique set of challenges. But many of these students are dealing with not just two but up to four exceptional circumstances that shape their educational experience.

> **Understanding Gifted 4e**
> - Excellence: Their intellectual gifts and talents.
> - Exceptionalities: Their learning differences or disabilities.
> - Ethnicity: The impact of their racial identity in educational spaces.
> - Economics: The influence of socioeconomic factors on their educational access and support.

When I walk into schools as a university professor and advocate for these students, I see what Carter G. Woodson described nearly a century ago in *The Miseducation of the Negro*—that is, a system that too often fails to recognize and nurture Black genius in all its forms. But I also see hope. I see teachers who are willing to learn, parents who are ready to advocate, and students who, despite every obstacle, continue to shine.

# Historical Context and Contemporary Reality

Special education in the United States has two distinct yet interconnected domains: students identified with disabilities and those identified as gifted. While the Education for All Handicapped Children Act of 1975 (IDEA, 1990) promised equitable access to education, today's data reveals a troubling pattern of racial inequality that has persisted and evolved. Black students face a paradoxical reality: they are disproportionately over-identified for disability categories while being systematically under-identified for gifted services.

Current data paints a stark picture. While Black students comprise 13.8% of the general student population, they represent 17.89% of students in the special education disability categories. Conversely, their representation in gifted programs stands at just 3.4% nationally, compared to 12.4% for Asian students and 7.7% for white students. This dual disparity reflects deeply rooted systemic issues in how schools interpret and respond to Black students' behaviors and abilities.

The same behaviors that might lead to gifted identification in white students—such as questioning authority, intellectual curiosity, or high energy—often result in disciplinary actions or disability labels for Black students. This disparate identification is evidenced by alarming disciplinary rates: 65 removals per 100 Black students with disabilities compared to 29 per 100 for all students with disabilities. These patterns of misidentification and harsh discipline often lead to a cycle where missed opportunities for gifted services result in disengagement, which then reinforces disability categorization and further exclusion from advanced learning opportunities.

While the 2004 reauthorization of IDEA aimed to address disproportionality, it has yet to stem these trends. Today's special education landscape reflects a system in which Black students are simultaneously overserved in restrictive environments and underserved in talent development programs—a manifestation of what scholars term the "4e framework": exceptional, excluded, expelled, and educated in restrictive settings. The data clearly shows several concerning disparities that connect to the 4E framework.

> **Understanding Special Education 4E**
>
> - Exceptional: Overrepresented in special education.
> - Excluded: Less time in needed classes.
> - Expelled: The long-term cumulative impact of missing school.
> - Educated: The long-term implications of drop-out and graduation.
>
> - Exceptional: Shows the overrepresentation of Black students in special education (17.89%) compared to their general population representation (13.8%).
> - Excluded: Demonstrates how Black students with disabilities spend less time in regular classrooms (59% vs. 64% for 80% or more of the day) and are more likely to be in a more restrictive environment.
> - Expelled: Highlights the dramatic disparity in disciplinary removals (65 per 100 Black students vs. 29 per 100 for all students with disabilities).
> - Educated: Shows the educational outcomes gap with lower graduation rates (66% vs 73%) and higher dropout rates (20% vs 16%).

# The Persistent Veil

I have taught, trained, and consulted within K-20 settings for over 30 years, and I have enjoyed working with young minds who challenge me and keep me sharp. New perspectives are reset and fashioned by current policies and politics year after year. With the changing socioeconomic and demographic landscape of America, what has held constant for Black students who received Government Assistance for Tuition Expenses services is the feeling of anxiety, a sense of never quite fitting in, and questioning their potential and value. Many of my students have gone on to become educators. I often ask them to imagine being constantly viewed as a problem to be solved rather than a gift to be nurtured. Their talent, as they all were talented, was obscured by a lack of self-efficacy and belonging. In 1903, W. E. B. DuBois wrote about "double consciousness," of "always looking at oneself through the eyes of others." Over a century later, our Black students—especially those who are both gifted and dealing with learning differences and financially stretched families—still live with this reality. When Carter G. Woodson wrote *The Miseducation of the Negro* in 1933, he cautioned us about an educational system that could make a person feel inferior despite their gifts. Today, in our post-COVID-19 classrooms, with states banning Black history and legislators attempting to erase the contributions of Black intellectuals from school curricula, Woodson's words ring with renewed urgency. As Dr. Ivory Toldson reminds us in *No BS (Bad Stats)*, the narrative about Black student achievement is too often written by those who neither understand nor believe in our children's potential.

---

**Understanding Historical Impact**

- The so-called "achievement gap" narrative often masks opportunity gaps.
- Historical prejudices shape current teacher perceptions
- Systemic barriers persist despite legal progress.
- Cultural wealth often needs to be recognized in traditional educational settings.

---

# Marcel's Story

*"You're too smart to be acting like this."*

*Marcel heard these words from his teachers so often they had lost their meaning. Sitting in his AP chemistry class at Central High, he could feel the weight of being the only Black male student in the room. His mind raced between the molecular structures on the board and the worry about his father, who had recently passed from COVID-19, and how he felt it was his responsibility to feed his family. The same quick intelligence that got him into AP classes made it impossible to sit still and focus on just one thing at a time.*

*His teacher saw the fidgeting, the distraction, the occasional outbursts. She recalled the numerous news broadcasts that paraded Black boys and men across her television screens all her life. She associated them with the sports and entertainment that were a significant part of her high school and college experiences. She recalled the stories family and friends had told her about the dangers of Black boys like Marcel. What she didn't see was the boy who taught himself complex gaming code at night, who helped his younger siblings with their homework, who understood chemical reactions at a level his peers couldn't touch. She didn't know that his attention deficit hyperactivity disorder (ADHD), presented as a behavior problem that was still undiagnosed, was both his greatest challenge and, when appropriately channeled, his greatest gift.*

This story illustrates what my research has consistently shown: our gifted Black students often navigate multiple worlds, identities, and challenges simultaneously. The same qualities that mark them as gifted can also be interpreted as problematic in traditional classroom settings.

## The 4E Framework in Action

Understanding how these four exceptional circumstances—excellence, exceptionalities, ethnicity, and economics—interact in real classrooms requires more than just theoretical knowledge. It demands a fundamental shift in how we see, interact with, and support our students.

---

**Recognizing the 4E Interaction**

- Excellence markers:
  - Creative problem-solving.
  - Advanced questioning.
  - Unique perspectives.
  - Rapid learning in areas of interest.
- Exceptionality considerations:
  - Learning differences as potential strengths.
  - Alternative expression of knowledge.
  - Need for multiple learning approaches.
  - Impact of processing differences.
- Ethnic identity impact:
  - Cultural communication styles.
  - Community knowledge and experiences.
  - Response to stereotypes.
  - Racial battle fatigue.

- Economic influences:
  - Access to resources.
  - Outside learning opportunities.
  - Family support capacity.
  - Stress impacts on learning.

Failing to consider all four elements risks missing crucial opportunities to support our students' growth and development. The SIM™ provides a framework for understanding how these elements interact and influence academic achievement. Our challenge isn't just about identifying twice-exceptional Black students—though that's certainly part of it. It's about how we miss many Black children with gifts and talents. It's about understanding how the 4Es interact, overlap, and influence one another. It's about recognizing that in this post-COVID-19, increasingly anti-Black political era, our children need us to see them fully, support them completely, and advocate for them tirelessly.

**The Power of Perception: Classroom Observation Guide for Hidden Gifts**

*Mathematics and Logic*

- Struggles with showing work but arrives at correct answers.
- Creates unique shortcuts for solving problems.
- Notices patterns others miss. Example: *Marcus couldn't follow the standard multiplication algorithm and created his system of breaking numbers down, demonstrating advanced number sense.*

*Language and Communication*

- May struggle with written expression but excels in oral storytelling.
- Code-switches effortlessly between different cultural contexts.
- Shows sophisticated humor and wordplay. Example: *Krsna's essays were basic, but her spoken word poetry demonstrated college-level metaphorical thinking.*

*Leadership and Social Intelligence*

- Organizes peers effectively during group work.
- Mediates conflicts naturally.

- Shows empathy and emotional intelligence. Example: *Devon was labeled "too talkative" but consistently helped peers understand complex concepts in ways teachers could not.*

### *Research Connections*

- Ford and Whiting's (2016) research reveals that teacher recommendations for gifted programs show significant bias against Black students who display behavioral differences.
- Toldson's (2019) work demonstrates how "behavior problems" often mask gifted traits in Black students.
- Robinson's (2020) studies establish that dyslexic students often develop advanced spatial and problem-solving abilities as compensation strategies.

## Understanding Exceptionalities in Context

*"Every time I enter my classroom,"* Dr. Shawn Robinson once shared, *"I remember what it felt like to be that Black boy with dyslexia who loved learning but hated reading—the one they said would never make it to college."* Today, as a Black man, gifted scholar, social entrepreneur, innovator, and advocate, his story reminds us that understanding learning differences in Black gifted students requires more than just knowledge of disabilities—it demands an understanding of possibility.

### Dr. Robinson's Framework

Drawing from his personal journey and research, Dr. Robinson offers these key insights:

### *Recognition Protocols*

- Look for areas of unexpected excellence.
- Document patterns of strength.
- Consider cultural context.
- Engage family perspectives.

### *Support Strategies*

- Build on cultural strengths.

> - Allow alternative demonstration methods.
> - Create success opportunities.
> - Develop advocacy skills.

## Different Learning Needs: The Symphony in David's Mind

*His pencil drumming on his thigh matched the complex polyrhythms playing in his head. David sat outside the principal's office, his leg bouncing and his mind racing through musical patterns, waiting for another discussion about his "disruptive behavior."*

*"But did you see his music theory work?" Mr. Rivera, the band director, argued in the staff meeting. "As only a sophomore, he's writing compositions our seniors can't understand."*

*"That's nice," the math teacher replied, "But he can't focus for five minutes in my class. He needs to be evaluated for some disability, maybe behavioral or ADHD." Both teachers were right, but they only saw part of the picture.*

> **Common Learning Differences in Gifted Students**
>
> - ADHD: Often masks mathematical or creative gifts.
> - Dyslexia: May coincide with advanced spatial reasoning.
> - Processing differences: Can indicate unique thinking patterns.
> - Emotional intensity: May signal deep intellectual engagement
>
> Understanding these learning differences requires what Dr. Ford calls "cultural competency plus"—seeing how learning differences manifest differently across cultural contexts.

## The Urban Education Landscape

Dr. Gloria Ladson-Billings reminds us that urban education isn't a problem to be solved but a promise to be fulfilled. Our 4e students in urban settings often develop what she calls "cultural excellence": the ability to navigate and excel in multiple worlds simultaneously.

## The Saturday Scholars

Something remarkable happens every Saturday morning at the Bishop Joseph Johnson Black Cultural Center. Twenty 4e students gather for the Ambassador Club, which includes a "Genius Hour." Created through a partnership between a university, local schools, and community organizations, this program understands that giftedness and learning differences aren't contradictions—they are complementary parts of these students' identities.

*"Here, I can be all of myself," explains Malik, a 15-year-old with profound mathematical gifts and anxiety. "During the week at school, teachers sometimes only see my anxiety. Here, they see everything I can be."*

*"My mom always said I was a born leader," shares Jayla, 14. "But at school, they call me 'disruptive' and 'too outspoken' when I try to help organize group projects or speak up about issues. At the Ambassador Youth Leadership program, they put me in charge of our social justice initiatives. They see what my family sees: a young activist, not a troublemaker."*

*"In my regular English class, teachers focused on my 'unfocused behavior' and kept trying to move me to the back of the room," says Devon, 16. "They never noticed I was finishing the reading assignments in minutes. My aunt, an English professor, recognized I was bored and gave me James Baldwin to read. Now, in the gifted program, my analysis of* Native Son *is being published in a youth literary journal. The difference? My new teachers read my work instead of just watching my movements."*

*"At my old school, the guidance counselor wanted to put me in special ed because I was always asking 'too many questions' in science," recalls Zaria, 13. "My grandmother took me to a Black Girls Code workshop, and now I'm developing an app about climate change in urban communities. My weekend STEM mentors understand that my questions aren't disruptive but a curiosity."*

*"When I get excited about historical connections, I talk with my hands and my voice gets louder," shares Marcus, 17. "White teachers used to send me to the office for being 'aggressive,' but my history teacher, Mr. Washington, recognized my passion. He helped me start a podcast about hidden Black history. Those teachers who labeled me 'difficult' asked me to use my podcast in their classes. Mr. Washington saw my enthusiasm as a gift, not a threat."*

# A Final Challenge: The Battle for Educational Equity in an Era of Resegregation

In conclusion, we must confront an uncomfortable truth: we again stand at a critical crossroads in American education. The progress made since *Brown v. Board of Education*—hard-fought, incomplete, but vital—faces unprecedented threats. Gentry and Whiting's (2019) research on the "missingness" of Black children in urban gifted education across the country reveals not just gaps but systematic exclusion. These existing disparities face even more significant challenges in our current political climate.

The proposed elimination of federal oversight in education, including the potential dismantling of the Department of Education, isn't just about administrative restructuring; it's about the possible erasure of accountability for equity in our schools. When W. E. B. DuBois proclaimed that "the problem of the twentieth century is the problem of the color line," he couldn't have known that we would be fighting to prevent that line from being redrawn with even starker consequences in the twenty-first century.

> **Clear and Present Dangers**
> - Resegregation through "local control."
> - Elimination of federal equity oversight.
> - Dismantling of diversity initiatives.
> - Reduction in civil rights enforcement.
> - Loss of data collection on racial disparities.

The threat to gifted education is particularly acute. Historically viewed as the domain of "elite" white wealthy students, gifted programs risk becoming even more exclusive, more segregated, and more inequitable. Without federal oversight states, I fear that states may eliminate equity requirements; districts may reduce identification efforts; resources may be redirected from diverse communities; and achievement gaps may widen irreparably.

Therefore, our charge moving forward as we work with 4e Black students takes on even greater urgency in this critical moment. We must do the following:

- Document and defend:
  - Maintain detailed records of student achievements.
  - Collect data on identification and outcomes.

- Build evidence-based cases for equity.
        - Create community accountability systems.
    - Organize and advocate:
        - Form parent-teacher-community coalitions.
        - Engage with local and state policymakers.
        - Build networks of support and resistance.
        - Develop alternative support structures.
    - Prepare and protect:
        - Strengthen existing programs.
        - Create independent support systems.
        - Develop community-based alternatives.
- Build resilient support networks.

Twenty years ago, my journey began with my daughter, a three-year-old Black gifted child. Today, she is 23, pursuing an advanced degree in Paris, France—a testament to the heights Black gifted minds can reach when given a chance to soar. Yet as we celebrate her achievements, we must confront a devastating truth about what's at stake for gifted Black lives in America. In 2019, another 23-year-old Black gifted soul, Elijah McClain, was walking home with a can of tea when someone called the police about a "suspicious" Black man looking "sketchy"—echoing the tragic 2012 case of Trayvon Martin, another young Black life cut short while walking home with tea and Skittles.

Elijah was extraordinary—a self-taught violinist, guitarist, and pianist who spent his free time playing music to abandoned cats at animal shelters. Dr. Michael Eric Dyson noted that he was "a sweet soul." But on that night, his gifts didn't matter. His humanity didn't matter. For 15 minutes, police knelt on his back as he pleaded for his life. When paramedics arrived, they injected him with ketamine. His last words haunt us still: "I can't breathe. I have my ID right here. My name is Elijah McClain … I'm just different, that's all … I'm not a bad person."

This is why our work cannot wait. Every time we fail to nurture, protect, and celebrate our gifted Black children and young adults, we risk losing another Elijah McClain—another brilliant mind, another gentle soul, another future that deserves to unfold. Their gifts are not just talents to be developed but lights that must be fiercely protected. The distance between a gifted Black child reaching Paris and a gifted Black adult dying on a suburban street should not exist in our America. Let Elijah's words—"I'm just different, that's all"—become not an apology but our battle cry. How many more gifted lights will we allow to be extinguished before we say, *"Enough!"*

We must speak up as educators, researchers, parents, and advocates. The struggle for educational equity isn't just about access to gifted programs; it's about the soul of American education. Every 4e Black student we identify, support, and champion becomes living proof of what is possible when we refuse to accept the redrawing of the color line in our schools. The Miseducation of America can lead to the final stage of psychologist Gordon Allport's theory of prejudice, which is extermination, which leads to rejection and death because instead of seeing exceptionally creative and talented people, we see the disability; we fear race, culture, and socioeconomics.

The question before us is how to serve our Black 4e students and protect their right to be served. The "missingness" of Black children in gifted education isn't an accident; it's a systemic failure that requires systemic solutions. And in this moment of potential retrenchment, our commitment to those solutions is more vital than ever.

Let us move forward with clear eyes about the challenges ahead and unwavering determination to ensure that our Black 4e students not only survive these challenging times but emerge stronger, more supported, and more celebrated than ever before. The color line of the twenty-first century must not be allowed to erase our children's brilliant potential. The future of equitable education hangs in the balance. What will you do to protect it?

## Things to Consider

- Black students who are gifted, have exceptionalities, and experience economic hardship face compounded barriers. Each "E" (excellence, exceptionality, ethnicity, economics) uniquely shapes their educational experiences and opportunities.
- Policies, teacher biases, and economic inequities often misidentify or overlook gifted Black students—particularly those with disabilities—leading to underrepresentation, exclusion, and even criminalization in educational spaces.
- Everyday experiences of racism, "placism," and deficit-based thinking impact the self-perception, motivation, and mental health of Black gifted students, often stunting their academic potential.

## For Discussion

- How do the four "Es" (excellence, exceptionality, ethnicity, economics) interact to shape the educational trajectory of Black students? In what ways might schools overlook these overlapping identities?
- What role does teacher bias—whether explicit or implicit—play in the under-identification of Black gifted students with exceptionalities?
- What strategies can schools implement to protect Black students' intellectual and emotional development in the face of systemic inequality and political retrenchment (e.g., curriculum bans, removal of equity offices)?

## Note

1  See Appendix C for a list of resources related to this chapter.

## References

Annamma, S. A., Ferri, B. A., & Connor, D. J. (2023) Disability critical race theory: Exploring the intersectional lineage, emergence, and potential futures of DisCrit in education. *Review of Research in Education*, 47(1), 105-143. https://doi.org/10.3102/0091732X231155673

Assouline, S. G., Foley-Nicpon, M., & Whiteman, C. (2020) Cognitive and psychosocial characteristics of gifted students with specific learning disabilities. *Gifted Child Quarterly*, 64(1), 3-23. https://doi.org/10.1177/0016986219890334

Belgrave, F. Z. & Allison, K. W. (2018) *African American psychology: From Africa to America* (4th ed.). SAGE Publications.

Bonner, F. A., II. (2014) *Building on resilience: Models and frameworks of Black male success across the P-20 pipeline.* Stylus Publishing.

Bonner, F. A. & Dickenson, T. S. (2021) Equity and excellence: African American gifted and talented students in a post-pandemic era. *Gifted Child Today*, 44(4), 194-200. https://doi.org/10.1177/10762175211035166

Borland, J. H. (2019) The gifted constitute 3% to 5% of the population: What does this mean and why does it matter? *Gifted Child Quarterly*, 63(2), 84-97. https://doi.org/10.1177/0016986219825738

Boykin, A. W. & Noguera, P. (2011) *Creating the opportunity to learn: Moving from research to practice to close the achievement gap.* ASCD.

Collins, K. M. & Ferri, B. A. (2022) Why Black girls with disabilities? An intersectional analysis of disproportionate referrals to special education. *Teachers College Record, 124*(2), 27-52. https://doi.org/10.1177/01614681221076877

Cordier, R., Speyer, R., Mahoney, N., Arnesen, A., Mjelve, L. H., & Nyborg, G. (2021) Effects of interventions for social anxiety and shyness in school-aged children: A systematic review and meta-analysis. *PLoS One, 16*(7), Article e0254117. https://doi.org/10.1371/journal.pone.0254117

Davis, J. L. (2016) *Bright, talented, & Black: A guide for families of African American gifted learners.* Great Potential Press.

DuBois, W. E. B. (2003) The souls of Black folk. *Modern Library.* (Original work published 1903.)

Ford, D. Y. (2023) *Multicultural gifted education: Theory, research, and practice* (3rd ed.). Prufrock Press.

Ford, D. Y. & Davis, J. L. (2019) Culturally responsive teaching and gifted education: Meeting the needs of diverse gifted students. *Gifted Child Today, 42*(1), 31-44.

Ford, D. Y. & Grantham, T. C. (2003) Providing access for culturally diverse gifted students: From deficit to dynamic thinking. *Theory Into Practice, 42*(3), 217-225. https://doi.org/10.1207/s15430421tip4203_8

Ford, D. Y. & Moore, J. L. (2020) Black gifted children need multiple supports: Building a research agenda that matters in schools. *Gifted Child Today, 43*(3), 172-183. https://doi.org/10.1177/1076217520915742

Ford, D. Y. & Whiting, G. W. (2016) Considering Fisher v. University of Texas–Austin: How gifted education affects access to elite colleges for Black and Hispanic students. *Gifted Child Today, 39*(2), 121-124.

Ford, D. Y. & Wright, B. L. (2021) *Recruiting and retaining Black students in gifted education: Ensuring excellence and equity.* Prufrock Press.

Ford, D. Y., Wright, B. L., & Trotman Scott, M. (2020) A matter of equity: Desegregating and integrating gifted and talented education for underrepresented students of color. *Multicultural Perspectives, 22*(1), 28-36.

Fugate, C. M., Behrens, W. A., Boswell, C., & Davis, J. L. (eds.). (2021) *Culturally responsive teaching in gifted education: Building cultural competence and serving diverse student populations.* Routledge.

Gentry, M. & Whiting, G. W. (2019) *Gifted education in the United States: Laws, access, equity, and missingness across the country by locale, Title I school status, and race.* Purdue University.

Gentry, M., Whiting, G., & Gray, A. M. (2024) Systemic inequities in identification and representation of Black youth with gifts and talents: Access, equity, and missingness in urban and other school locales. *Urban Education, 59*(6), 1730-1773. https://doi.org/10.1177/00420859221095000

Gershenson, S., Hansen, M., & Lindsay, C. A. (2021) *Teacher diversity and student success: Why racial representation matters in the classroom.* Harvard Education Press.

Givens, J. R. (2021) *Fugitive pedagogy: Carter G. Woodson and the art of Black teaching.* Harvard University Press.

Grantham, T. C. (2018) Equity in gifted education: Theories, practices and directions for the field. In S. I. Pfeiffer (ed.) *Handbook of giftedness in children* (pp. 235-253). Springer.

Grantham, T. C. & Ford, D. Y. (2021) Double whammy: How being Black and gifted can lead to racial isolation. *Gifted Child Today, 44*(1), 28-35. https://doi.org/10.1177/1076217520940736

Graves, S. L. & Brown Wright, L. (2021) Parent involvement and cultural capital: A review of disparities in assessment referrals. *Psychology in the Schools, 58*(8), 1517-1531.

Grissom, J. A. & Redding, C. (2016) Discretion and disproportionality: Explaining the underrepresentation of high-achieving students of color in gifted programs. *AERA Open, 2*(1), 1-25. https://doi.org/10.1177/2332858415622175

Grissom, J. A. & Redding, C. (2022) Discretion and disproportionality: Explaining the underrepresentation of high-achieving students of color in gifted programs. *Sociology of Education, 95*(2), 153-177.

Hamilton, R., McCoach, D. B., Tutwiler, M. S., & Siegle, D. (2021) The relationship between socioeconomic status and gifted program participation: A systematic review. *Journal for the Education of the Gifted, 44*(3), 234-263.

Harry, B. & Klingner, J. (2014) *Why are so many minority students in special education? Understanding race and disability in schools* (2nd ed.). Teachers College Press.

Hart, B. & Risley, T. R. (1995) *Meaningful differences in the everyday experience of young American children.* Paul H. Brookes Publishing.

Henfield, M. S. & Washington, A. R. (2012) "I want to do the right thing but what is it?": White teachers' experiences with Black students. *The Journal of Negro Education, 81*(2), 148-161.

Howard, T. C. (2018) *Why race and culture matter in schools: Closing the achievement gap in America's classrooms.* Teachers College Press.

Jones-Smith, E. (2019) *Culturally diverse counseling: Theory and practice.* SAGE Publications.

Ladson-Billings, G. (2021) *Culturally relevant pedagogy: Asking a different question.* Teachers College Press.

Ladson-Billings, G. & Tate, W. F. (2016) Toward a critical race theory of education. *Teachers College Record, 97*(1), 47-68. https://doi.org/10.1177/016146819509700104

Love, B. L. (2019) *We want to do more than survive: Abolitionist teaching and the pursuit of educational freedom.* Beacon Press.

Marx, S. (2006) *Revealing the invisible: Confronting passive racism in teacher education.* Routledge.

McIntyre, A. (1997) *Making meaning of whiteness: Exploring racial identity with white teachers.* SUNY Press.

Milner, H. R. (2020) *Start where you are, but don't stay there: Understanding diversity, opportunity gaps, and teaching in today's classrooms.* Harvard Education Press.

Nash, K. & Miller, E. (2023) Cultural competency in psychological assessment: A systematic review of current practices and future directions. *School Psychology Review, 52*(1), 89-105.

Peters, S. J. & Engerrand, K. G. (2022) Equity and excellence: Proactive efforts in the identification of underrepresented students for gifted and talented services. *Gifted Child Quarterly, 66*(2), 95-109.

Peters, S. J. & Gentry, M. (2012) Group-specific predictors of social coping among gifted subgroups. *Journal for the Education of the Gifted, 35*(1), 62-82. https://doi.org/10.1177/0162353211432047

Renzulli, J. S. (2022) *A rising tide lifts all ships: Excellence, equity, and developing the gifts and talents of all students.* Creative Learning Press.

Roberts, D. (2022) *Torn apart: How the child welfare system destroys Black families—and how abolition can build a safer world.* Basic Books.

Robinson, S. A. (2020) Transforming practice through qualitative research about twice-exceptional Black students. *Gifted Child Today, 43*(2), 120-131.

Toldson, I. A. (2019) *No BS (Bad Stats): Black people need people who believe in Black people enough not to believe every bad thing they hear about Black people.* Brill Sense.

Valencia, R. R. (2015) *Students of color and the achievement gap: Systemic challenges, systemic transformations.* Routledge.

Weinfeld, R., Barnes-Robinson, L., Jeweler, S., & Shevitz, B. R. (2013) *Smart kids with learning difficulties: Overcoming obstacles and realizing potential* (2nd ed.). Prufrock Press.

Whiting, G. W. (2006) From at risk to at promise: Developing scholar identities among Black males. *Journal of Secondary Gifted Education, 17*(4), 222-229.

Whiting, G. W. (2014) The scholar identity model: Black male success in the K-12 context. In F. A. Bonner II (ed.) *Building on resilience: Models and frameworks of Black male success across the P-20 pipeline* (pp. 88-108). Stylus Publishing.

Whiting, G. W. (2019) *Gifted Black males: Understanding and decreasing barriers to achievement and identity.* Roeper Review, 41(4), 252-264.

Woodson, C. G. (1990) *The miseducation of the Negro.* Africa World Press. (Original work published 1933.)

Worrell, F. C. & Dixson, D. D. (2018) Equity in gifted education: A universal issue. *Gifted Education International, 34*(1), 5-11. https://doi.org/10.1177/0261429418755926

Wright, B. L. & Ford, D. Y. (2017) Untapped potential: Recognition of giftedness in early childhood and what professionals should know about students of color. *Gifted Child Today, 40*(2), 111-116. https://doi.org/10.1177/1076217517690862

Wright, B. L., Ford, D. Y., & Young, J. L. (2017) Ignorance or indifference? Seeking excellence and equity for under-represented students of color in gifted education. *Global Education Review, 4*(1), 45-60.

# Chapter 5

# Brillantes y Valientes

## To Be Twice-Exceptional, Latinx/Hispanic, and Adolescent

### Alexandra Vuyk and Maureen Montanía

*What really bothers me is that I was never seen as a whole person, especially during primary school. Teachers literally told my mom when I was in first grade, "Your seven-year-old daughter has the mental age of a three-year-old." At school, they saw me as delayed, but at home I was perceived as this brilliant human being. This is unfair. I already learned how to read at age three, so of course I wasn't interested in paying attention in class in first grade when my peers were just learning the alphabet. Then in high school, I remember my ADHD was never acknowledged; I was bright, but when I had a problem, people didn't see it. At home, it was the same; they never acknowledged my ADHD, they didn't want to see it. Even now for my parents, ADHD is something I deal with in therapy and that's it; they brush it aside, they only want to see the good. I've accepted that this is something I have to live with, and I'm grateful that my family is at least more open nowadays.*

*Daniella, 2e Latina student, 18 years old*

Daniella, a female 18-year-old high school student from Asunción, Paraguay, reflects on her unique position with both giftedness and attention deficit hyperactivity disorder (ADHD). Her experience, marked by both exceptional cognitive abilities and severe attentional difficulties, typifies the twice-exceptional profile in an environment where such complexities are seldom understood. Her story is one of resilience, shaped by the family and cultural dynamics that both constrain and propel her.

"At school, they saw me as delayed, but at home I was perceived as this brilliant human being," she recalls, describing a stark dichotomy between her home and school environments. This contrast affected her educational experiences from a young age, emphasizing the misalignment between her capabilities and the expectations set by traditional educational frameworks.

Securing the necessary support was a journey of significant highs and lows. Acknowledging her socio-economic advantage while also highlighting systemic disparities that affect many others in her region, she explains:

> *Getting tested was not a problem for me, whereas many in Latin America don't have financial access to this option. I have friends, for example, who I believe are twice exceptional, but their families don't understand the importance of addressing this, so they don't get diagnosed.*

However, despite this advantage, she reveals that she was only identified as gifted with moderate attention difficulties at age nine, with no additional conditions and lacking appropriate support. Specialized assistance did not come until her teenage years, after her parents had consulted numerous mental health and educational experts, and relocated from one city to another, where they eventually found the country's sole specialist who diagnosed her as twice exceptional and provided the necessary treatment. "The last years of high school were easier," she asserts, as help finally arrived when she was 14—five years after her first diagnosis. It is apparent that even the privileged cannot be sure of receiving support in her country.

Her parents were instrumental in navigating her educational path. "My family is openminded, unlike most Latino families," she states, appreciating their progressive approach toward her diagnosis and needs. This support, however, did not always extend beyond her family circle. At school, the lack of understanding continued: "At school, they saw me as delayed, but at home I was perceived as this brilliant human being." Even within her supportive family, extended members were less understanding and her parents struggled to integrate the ADHD diagnosis with her identity, placing a main focus on the giftedness. "I remember my ADHD was never acknowledged; I was bright, but when I had a problem, people didn't see it … I deal with my ADHD privately."

High school presented both challenges and moments of subtle triumph. "Most teachers knew me and helped me," she recalls, appreciating the support from some educators who recognized her needs. However, not all responses were supportive. She describes a persistently disheartening interaction with the teacher of her favorite subject, chemistry and sciences: "This teacher would get angry and give me dirty looks every time I raised my hand, and when I asked for adaptations, she said, 'I can't give you an adaptation just because you think you're special.'"

Despite these challenges, once Daniella began therapy with a clinician who specialized in gifted and 2e individuals, she found ways to cope and excel, adapting to her learning environment in innovative ways. "In 12 years of school, I only learned the ABCs in English; everything else I achieved on my own, by reading, researching. School was a place of rebellion for me; I already knew everything they taught."

Looking forward, she embraces both aspects of her identity with a mature perspective:

*My ADHD, for me, is more a part of my personality than my high abilities because of the spontaneity, creativity, and non-linear thinking it gives me, which, even though they are characteristics also associated with high abilities, were always presented to me as something "negative"—values that the system doesn't appreciate and wants to crush, but that nevertheless are characteristics that make me say: "This is ADHD and this is who I am."*

Daniella's narrative not only underscores the educational and social hurdles she faces, but also illuminates the resilience and adaptability required to navigate life as a twice-exceptional student in a Latin American context.

## Factors Impacting 2e Latinx/Hispanic Students

Latinx/Hispanic twice-exceptional secondary students carry several intersectional identities within the educational landscape: their dual identities of both giftedness and learning difficulties, as well as the cultural richness and systemic constraints deeply entrenched in Latin American and Hispanic societies (Borland et al., 2000; Yaluma & Tyner, 2018; List & Dykeman, 2019). For these students, navigating the educational system often involves confronting compounded challenges shaped by cultural and socioeconomic factors such as limited access to resources and prevalent stigmas surrounding disability and giftedness that can obscure and complicate their identification and support (Borland et al., 2000). Additionally, familial expectations and community values play critical roles in shaping how educational experiences and personal identities are developed and perceived (Neihart, 2016).

This chapter examines the specific ways in which cultural contexts influence the educational trajectories and personal growth of these young individuals. Through a detailed narrative analysis, we present the voice of a twice-exceptional female Latina student from Paraguay whose experiences serve as an example of the complex interplay of identity, culture, and education. Her story sheds light on common challenges and provides profound insights into the intersectional experiences faced by many similar students across diverse Latin American and Hispanic settings. Our aim is to foster greater recognition of their challenges and strengths, advocating for more inclusive and effective educational support systems that can better serve the nuanced needs of twice-exceptional students within these vibrant and complex communities so that they can ultimately acknowledge and leverage their full potential.

# Social Experience

## Family Dynamics: Navigating Support and Stigma

Expanding from involving just the family unit to engaging the entire community can be a strategic approach, given that Latinx/Hispanic families place significant value on culture and community as sources of support. Correspondingly, this approach might tackle the negative impact of stigma that typically comes from Latinx/Hispanic dynamics and leaves students in conflict between their cultural identity—where typically immediate family members have not graduated or even attended school (Carrillo, 2016)—and the expectations of gifted programs, which can lead to feelings of isolation or pressure to conform to dominant cultural norms (Mun et al., 2020). Being placed in special education is a spotlight in the community, which can impact the student's self-esteem and academic motivation (Guiberson, 2009).

Furthermore, even when students do not enroll in a program or receive special education, stigma lingers as their 2e condition is apparent, requiring more social capital and a stronger mentorship group (Carrillo, 2016). Regardless, stigma is a notable aspect that arises from Latinx/Hispanic dynamics; thus, whatever the wave of support, it must not be overlooked, as clearly expressed in Daniella's narrative and personal context.

While more supportive than most, Daniella's familial situation still reflects tensions common among families dealing with twice-exceptionality, where cultural stigma influences the family's stance on ADHD:

*We went to a private school and my mom told the principal that I was intelligent, and I thought: "Sure, but I don't have good grades, so what's the point?" She never mentioned that I have ADHD. She said she didn't do it because you shouldn't talk about bad things; you have to sell yourself.*

Even when addressing the present, she explained:

*At home, they never acknowledged my ADHD; they didn't want to see it. Even now, for my parents, ADHD is something I deal with in therapy and that's it; they brush it aside—they only want to see the good.*

This reveals the complex dynamics at play between providing support and struggling to fully embrace the reality of a diagnosis that presents daily difficulties in functioning.

This conflict in perception within both Daniella's family and her culture, compounded by a late diagnosis and years of mistreatment of her complex identity, continues to complicate her journey. "What really bothers me is that I was never seen as a whole person, especially during primary school," she notes, expressing frustration at being viewed solely in terms of either her disability or her giftedness, but never both.

The stigma associated with her condition in a Latinx/Hispanic cultural context where mental health and disabilities are often misunderstood perpetuates this challenge. Emphasizing the challenges of mental health issues when concealed due to concerns over social backlash or misinterpretation, Daniella reflects:

*I deal with my ADHD privately. I don't know enough twice-exceptional Latinos, but I imagine they go through similar things if they have to deal with it privately, like keeping the negative aspects hidden; nobody can see us as a complete being, with our faults and our good qualities.*

## Friendship Dynamics: Rising to the Challenge

Daniella has demonstrated resilience and adaptability in navigating her social environment. Her unique cognitive profile has sometimes made it challenging to relate to others or engage in typical social interactions—particularly during childhood, when she was undiagnosed and faced more judgment. This is in line with the experiences of other 2e students from Chile, as many of them described themselves as reserved during their school years. The lack of likeminded peers and appropriate social settings in school contributed to feelings of isolation and stress, increasing their need to establish relationships with classmates and teachers in beneficial educational settings (Sandoval-Rodríguez & Conejeros-Solar, 2024)—similar to Daniella's experience even after childhood ("something difficult is finding friends to talk about interesting topics. I try to diversify my circles, but I have very few close friends, who are more intellectual peers").

In Fugate and Gentry's (2016) study of gifted girls with ADHD, they found that these girls often faced social challenges, including peer rejection and difficulties in maintaining friendships. Such social impairments were linked to lower self-esteem and increased risk of anxiety and depression. Supportive peer relationships and involvement in extracurricular activities helped mitigate these challenges, fostering a sense of belonging and improving their overall wellbeing. This is also evident in Daniella's narrative, as later in life she overcame her social difficulties and formed meaningful friendships and connections with peers who accepted and supported her.

For Daniella, these friendships often revolve around shared interests or mutual understanding, providing her with a sense of belonging. Her social interactions center on her capacity to engage in profound discussions and form bonds with peers who share the same appreciation for intellectual and artistic matters. This aspect of her experience is socially similar to the Chilean study, where 2e students found value in establishing relationships with other 2e peers, enriching their educational experience and supporting their twice-exceptional identity (Sandoval-Rodríguez & Conejeros-Solar, 2024). What is more, regardless of socio-demographics, this is an aspect that underscores a shared camaraderie observed among intellectually gifted individuals, irrespective of cultural backgrounds (Robinson, 2008).

In essence, Daniella's social landscape provides insight into the nuanced social dynamics of twice-exceptional individuals. Discussing her social interactions, she reveals:

> *I find it easy to connect with people because I'm very outgoing ... I'm not sure if my social life is very different from that of a neurotypical person. I talk openly about being twice-exceptional with my friends; I only have trouble talking about my high abilities because I feel like I'm boasting, but that's me.*

Daniella's present situation collides with the experiences of other 2e students (Fugate & Gentry, 2016; Sandoval-Rodríguez & Conejeros-Solar, 2024), yet gives hope that once the 2e identity is settled and they feel more at ease with who they are, they will find peers with whom to share.

Equivalently, Daniella's increasing comfort discussing and asserting her ADHD adds a distinct dynamic to her relationships. "At my age, ADHD allows me to be the spontaneous, creative friend, without a strict schedule, giving me that advantage," she explains, reflecting how the spontaneity and creativity that come with ADHD make her a vibrant and engaging companion (Fugate, 2018). Furthermore, this openness about being 2e helps foster understanding among her peers, who are generally more accepting of neurodivergence than older generations like her family. "For my generation it's easy to understand; there are no taboos compared to previous generations," she says, unveiling a distinctly healthy friendship that underscores the importance of identity integration for social adaptation and wellbeing in 2e students (Fugate & Gentry, 2016).

Understanding Daniella's unique experiences as an adolescent gifted girl with ADHD—her coping mechanisms, motivational influences, and the impact of being 2e on her academic and social lives—requires perceiving her not merely as an individual with challenges but as a student with significant potential for creativity and achievement, even relabeling her 2e from "gifted and ADHD" to "ADHG: attention divergent hyperactive giftedness" (Fugate & Gentry, 2016; Fugate, 2018).

## Friends with Many Interests

It is possible that Daniella's own experiences with expectations and misconceptions have nurtured her ability to navigate complex social dynamics and engage with friends across a broad spectrum of interests. She explains her approach to friendship, saying, "I have friends to talk about X topics and others to talk about Y topics," illustrating how the unique intellectual gifts of each of her friends aligns with different aspects of her interests and personality. Furthermore, she elaborates on how this is true regardless of whether they align with academic standards:

*With my male best friend, we usually go to the roof of his house for five hours and talk about anything in the world … [whereas with] my female best friend, I don't talk about philosophy, physics, or such topics because she's not interested; but I can talk about Taylor Swift endlessly.*

This adaptability in social settings stems from continuously navigating diverse perceptions of intelligence and ability. She critiques the narrow definitions of "intelligence" by sharing the example of her best friend:

*She is one of the smartest people I know, yet she's not seen as having high abilities because her focus is on popular culture. That always bothered me because not all highly intelligent people have academic knowledge, yet all forms of knowledge should be valued.*

This perspective allows her to appreciate a broader range of intelligences and to cultivate varied friendships—skills that might arise from managing conflicting expectations and misconceptions about her own capabilities. Consequently, she not only enriches her social life but also challenges and redefines traditional views of intelligence, showcasing her journey as a 2e individual who thrives through acceptance and meaningful connections.

## Emotional Dynamics: Coping and Growth

Daniella has experienced, and continues to experience, many challenges in her journey toward acceptance as she transitions into adulthood. The persistent dissonance between her ability to engage in advanced thinking and her difficulties with focus, organization, and motivation, whether in academic endeavors or daily tasks, fosters intermittent feelings of underachievement and inadequacy. Furthermore, the incongruity between her 2e profile and societal expectations perpetuates the struggles through myths and stigma surrounding mental health ("Even now for my parents, ADHD is something I deal with in therapy and that's it; they brush it aside—they only want to see the good").

Consequently, she developed an understanding of her own strengths and weaknesses that help her build a range of creative coping mechanisms. She has discerned positive attributes in her experience of ADHD such as spontaneity and creativity, which—combined with her extroverted nature and giftedness—are rightfully interpreted as an asset in social dynamics compared to other neurodivergent profiles (Gómez-Arízaga et al., 2016). Moreover, by discerning her needs, Daniella has engaged in proactive dialogue with teachers to advocate for adaptations and resources that improve her learning journey.

### Regular Specialized Psychotherapy

Daniella actively participates in therapy sessions and engages in self-reflection and introspection, which have been empirically demonstrated to be effective practices for the wellbeing of 2e students (Pfeiffer, 2021). They are of special relevance for gifted students with ADHD, as these individuals typically report lower self-esteem, overall happiness, and behavioral satisfaction than the general gifted population (Foley-Nicpon & Kim, 2018).

In Daniella's journey, therapy emerged as a significant bright spot after numerous hardships. Visibly moved, she recalls:

> *When I first went to therapy, I was really struggling emotionally, a result of years of untreated twice-exceptionality. From the ADHD perspective, I had a very serious emotional dysregulation; and from the high abilities perspective, I felt a deep frustration from being unseen.*

Since starting therapy four years ago, her daily life has improved markedly, empowering her with self-agency throughout her final years of high school and into early adulthood, marking a profound transformation.

Among the positive changes, she particularly emphasizes the importance of setting personal challenges as a key coping mechanism. She discovered that challenges ignite her motivation for nearly everything. "For academic and even daily life, setting challenges helps me," she explains. This strategy has transformed her approach to academic endeavors, as mentioned previously ("I set a challenge for myself last year in school: How vulgar can I make my projects without losing the best score in the class? So I did an economics class presentation about a brothel") and even her routine tasks, making them more engaging and aligning them with the unique cognitive patterns of her twice-exceptional condition.

## Wise Mind: A Favorite Strategy

This transformation is largely due to years of therapy, during which Daniella discovered a particular technique from dialectical behavior therapy that significantly improved her self-perception—Wise Mind:

*Wise Mind helped me a lot to get to know myself, to distinguish between my feelings and thoughts, and to understand the reasons behind them. As I progressed with this exercise, I began to see all the factors that brought me to where I was at that moment. I realized that being twice-exceptional was not a detriment; rather, it allowed me to express my high abilities in unconventional ways. Through Wise Mind, I developed my own system to improve.*

## Changing Boring into Fun

Daniella uses her high cognitive abilities to deal with boring tasks by setting inventive objectives. She details one of the specific techniques she uses to maintain productivity and focus: "Many times I lack motivation to tidy my room, so I set myself mental challenges that no one else knows about—for example, 'How many things can I fit into this bag in 30 seconds?'" This playful strategy not only helps her manage the symptoms of ADHD but also makes everyday activities more engaging and enjoyable.

On occasions when this approach falls short, she employs online resources to trigger hyperfixation, transforming mundane chores into engaging activities ("I look for TikTok videos on how to clean bathrooms and watch so many that I end up motivating myself to clean, because I hyperfixate on it"). By creating and meeting small challenges, she not only stays organized and productive in educational and personal settings but also maintains a sense of accomplishment and control over her environment.

## Identity Development and Personal Growth

Daniella's bold declaration, "This is ADHD and this is who I am," signifies an effort to openly embrace neurodivergence and its profound impact, not only in practical terms reflected in her social dynamics (as mentioned earlier), but also—and notably—on her self-concept. However, despite the benefits that her integration effort brought to her adaptability and social enjoyment, for her self-concept, this presents a complex ongoing challenge of assimilating ADHD while also struggling with negative feelings that might come from the burden of stigma she always carried ("I remember that when I was a child, my family treated my ADHD as something bad or negative. Now it is not like that anymore but it is still difficult"). 2e students might face considerable frustration and demoralization due to the mismatch between their potential and their actual academic achievements, leading to negative self-assessments and doubts about their abilities, as they feel their high cognitive ability is not reflected in their academic performance (Sandoval-Rodríguez & Conejeros-Solar, 2024).

Even with the advantage of openly discussing her condition with peers who understand and welcome her neurodivergence, managing ADHD privately while simultaneously trying to acknowledge it as an integral part of her personality prompts dissociation amid integration, thus making it difficult to address the issue within her family and with herself. In parallel, her struggle to feel as comfortable and open to discuss her giftedness with peers may be due to her tendency to avoid judgment or scrutiny even in safe environments, as she says, "I only have trouble talking about my high abilities because I feel like I'm boasting, but that's me." This implies that she can be publicly talented with her family and openly disabled with her friends, but not vice versa, making communicating her whole identity not feasible—which naturally impacts her general self-concept.

To overcome these obstacles, Daniella's resilience may prove instrumental. Despite the obstacles across her story, her proactive aptitude underscores a key development toward self-management and personal growth, which is indicative of her ability to leverage her twice-exceptionality as a strength. Yet her overall experience underscores a crucial need to cultivate an environment that nurtures the comprehensive growth of individuals with 2e profiles (Bal et al., 2022).

## Cultural Dynamics: Context Matters

Daniella acknowledges the challenges of living a twice-exceptional life in Latin America but does so with a sense of resilience and determination:

*The issue in Latin America is that it's very difficult to create your own system officially within the education system. Much of what it took to get where I am now was discovering a way to adapt to the official system and carve out my own space instead of searching for where or how to fit in. The world will never be built for twice-exceptional people because we are a minority, but I believe that we can still carve out our space in this neurotypical world.*

The recommendations of Olszewski-Kubilius and Clarenbach (2014) can mitigate these issues: building awareness among parents and providing supportive networks for students, which includes engaging the community in the identification process. By leveraging the communal strengths inherent in Latinx/Hispanic communities, educational systems can create a more supportive and enriching environment for 2e students. Engaging the broader community not only provides a network of support but also reinforces the cultural values and connections that are crucial to the wellbeing and success of these students.

Daniella's narrative on her cultural and familial dynamics reveals the complex challenges that 2e students face in Latin America as they navigate systems that often overlook their unique needs and face cultural stigmas that discourage open discussions about mental health. Even with family willingness to support, cultural misconceptions can lead to inconsistency, preventing a full understanding or proper addressing of their conditions. Nevertheless, Daniella's strategies to face cultural challenges within her family, friendship and emotional worlds align with existing literature on adaptive coping strategies among 2e students, emphasizing the significance of self-awareness (Dole, 2001), self-advocacy (Dole, 2001; Foley-Nicpon & Cederberg, 2021; Haase & Hancock, 2022), and social skills (Haase & Hancock, 2022). In order to demonstrate these adaptive strategies effectively, it appears essential to establish a support network tailored to address her unique needs and strengths (Wang & Neihart, 2015).

Nevertheless, while limiting cultural norms may have influenced how Daniella's family and community perceived and responded to her unique cognitive profile and needs, she challenged cultural norms and advocated for her rights, demonstrating a strong ongoing commitment to navigating the complexities of her cultural context. This determination might have its roots in the convergence of internal capacities, external opportunities, and social support —a phenomenon frequently noted in literature addressing disadvantaged 2e students who manage to bolster their self-assurance and exhibit drive despite adversity (VanTassel-Baska et al., 2009).

# Academic Experience

## 2e Students in Latin America: "Under-resourced" and Underserved

Paraguay, as a South American society, has a strong emphasis on academic performance and conformity to traditional educational norms (UNDP, 2021) which poses challenges for Daniella in navigating her 2e within the academic environment ("I never had official curriculum adaptations, because it's difficult to get them from the Ministry of Education in Paraguay"; "The Paraguayan system … drained me"; "The biggest challenge is that ADHD and high abilities are not understood in Paraguay"; "… particularly in Paraguay, … the system turns you into a little cube and everyone has to do the same thing"). These experiences align with Sandoval-Rodríguez and Conejeros-Solar's (2024) study of five 2e adolescents in Chile who were marked by late identification of their giftedness, significant challenges with executive functions, frustration with academic performance, and social isolation.

Latinx/Hispanic 2e students face significant challenges due to systemic biases and inadequate identification and support mechanisms. These students are often misidentified or overlooked due to cultural and linguistic biases, leading to either overrepresentation in special education or underrepresentation in gifted programs—if programming even exists, as in many countries they do not. Similarly, support systems for 2e students are impacted by these biases as well; when programs exist, they must deal with limited resources and culturally responsive practices hindering academic and social development.

## Delayed Diagnoses

The lack of awareness and appropriate resources for 2e students in Paraguay delayed Daniella's diagnosis until age nine and access to specialized mental health services until age 14, leaving her feeling "never seen as a whole person" until high school. This experience of late identification also occurred in Sandoval-Rodríguez and Conejeros-Solar's (2024) Chilean study, where 2e adolescents were identified primarily during their secondary education; furthermore, many of these students were only recognized for their ADHD and their giftedness was not identified until much later. This late recognition impacted their self-esteem and the support they received during their school years, similar to Daniella's experience.

Despite encountering challenges along the way, Daniella's educational journey is defined by her unwavering commitment to self-advocacy. She did not have access to accommodations and other support systems from the Ministry of Education; therefore, despite the majority of her teachers' willingness to make curriculum adaptations, she never formally received these resources and faced negative reactions from teachers who refused assistance and treated her as inferior. Fortunately, the family's readiness to assist served as a source of support, shaping her self-perception in a predominantly positive light, which provided the groundwork for her continuous path to self-awareness and acceptance. This experience aligns with the existing literature on common challenges that 2e ethnically diverse students face (Park et al., 2018; Mayes & Moore, 2016) and the significance of family support (Besnoy et al., 2015; Wang & Neihart, 2015; Neihart, 2016; Soares & de Souza 2021; Trail, 2022).

Initially, Daniella's parents played a key role in creating a supportive environment by actively seeking the right school and therapist. Subsequently, her advocacy efforts led to understanding and support from the majority of her teachers, aided by regular meetings between her therapist and teaching staff. However, the absence of ministry support meant that formal assessments remained consistently challenging, with curriculum adaptations often falling short of universality. Moreover, her performance on standardized tests and exams fluctuated due to symptoms of ADHD and unrealistic social expectations. Nonetheless, akin to her 2e nature, Daniella balanced these aspects and achieved academic success "without studying," which now presents a new dilemma as she aspires to pursue university education and fears she lacks the necessary study skills—a common struggle among 2e individuals from minority communities (Young, 2020; Sandoval-Rodríguez & Conejeros-Solar, 2024).

As Daniella reflects on her school years, she focuses on her last period, when her diagnosis encouraged her to advocate for necessary curriculum adjustments. This revolutionary phase presented new difficulties and significant insights, leaving an enduring influence on her subsequent educational experiences. Navigating academic and personal growth with varying levels of support and acknowledgment set the stage for her journey forward.

## Formal Educational Support: Insufficient, or even Inexistent

Daniella's struggles with ADHD were exacerbated by the Ministry of Education's reluctance to formally address her needs ("I never had official curriculum adaptations because it's difficult to get them from the Ministry of Education in Paraguay") and the attitudes of some teachers who outright refused to understand or accommodate her. "One specific teacher comes to mind," she remarked when asked about uncooperative teachers, adding, "Sadly, it was my chemistry and sciences teacher, and I want to be a theoretical physicist, which means it was a subject I deeply cared about." These encounters negatively impacted not only her grades but also her enthusiasm for a subject she was passionate about.

## Self-Advocacy

Despite these challenges, high school was also a time of significant growth and increased self-awareness for Daniella. She learned to advocate for herself, supported by her therapist, who regularly met with the teaching staff. She recalls the initial difficulties:

> *I found it interesting that when I mentioned that I have high abilities, the first thing teachers would say is, "If you want, I can give you more homework." I would prefer ten times less homework, but a hundred times more complex. I think that mindset of "If you're smart, you'll have to do more" is very Latin American.*

However, as time progressed, most of her educators began to recognize her unique needs and strengths, as well as how to address them.

Fostering strong relationships with teachers who understand the dual exceptionalities of these students can create a supportive learning atmosphere that nurtures both their giftedness and their need for structure and attention management (Behrens et al., 2022). Daniella reflects positively on these later years, noting, "In the last years of high school, most teachers knew me and helped me." This understanding among her teachers allowed her to conclude high school on an uplifting note, with her individual needs increasingly met and supported.

## Creativity as a Pathway

Even when faced with boredom or a lack of motivation for certain mandatory school subjects that could not be adjusted through adaptations, Daniella's coping mechanisms were notably creative and effective. She recounts an instance where she infused creativity and humor into a school project:

> *I set a challenge for myself last year in school: How vulgar can I make my projects without losing the best score in the class? So I did an economics class presentation about a brothel. The teacher told me, "I didn't like the topic, but you had the best presentation."*

This experience highlights her ability to harness her creativity and intellectual flexibility to excel academically, even when traditional learning and evaluation methods do not cater to her strengths, as she states: "For me, it's like my ADHD requires it—and my high abilities allow me to do it." This is indeed a recommended strategy for 2e students, as intellectually stimulating and creative activities can help maintain their interest and motivation (Behrens et al., 2022).

However, as mentioned previously, Daniella also recognizes that as school became easier, another challenge arose:

*I remember last year I didn't turn in a single assignment all year, but I got 100% on all exams. I did not have to learn to study, but now that I'm going to start studying abroad at university, I'm afraid of failing because I never had to learn to study.*

This underlying apprehension toward university appears to be the first potential source of genuine academic challenge.

## Burnout

Daniella's journey showcases remarkable resilience, yet it came at a considerable cost. Navigating educational challenges, confronting stigma, and embracing her identity as a 2e individual proved to be an exhausting tribulation. "The Paraguayan system drained me," she reveals. Her struggles highlight the urgent need for Latinx/Hispanic educational systems to swiftly and effectively address the diverse needs of students. "I wouldn't wish for anyone to go through so many years without treatment," she expresses, underscoring the critical importance of timely support and recognition in education. "School was a place of rebellion for me; I already knew everything they taught, but I got bad grades because I didn't want to go through the process points and stages."

As evidently exposed, college might be Daniella's first real experience with significant academic difficulty, causing a sense of unease. While she persists in navigating these challenges, her resilience may prove instrumental in overcoming these obstacles. Yet her overall experience underscores a crucial need to cultivate an environment that nurtures the comprehensive growth of individuals with 2e profiles (Bal et al., 2022).

Overall, Daniella's experience underscores the complex nature of 2e in Latin American contexts, where inclusive practices are not completely assured and traditional educational approaches prevail (Gómez-Arízaga & Conejeros-Solar, 2021). Concurrently, it emphasizes the protective influence of self-advocacy and parental engagement in education (Trail, 2022). Daniella's narrative underscores the pressing need for improved inclusive education practices for Latinx/Hispanic 2e individuals in secondary education. This is an especially serious challenge for students like Daniella in Paraguay where, despite legislative efforts, the country continues to grapple with meeting the diverse needs of gifted students due to factors such as insufficient funding, cultural misconceptions, inadequate educator training, and deficient educational infrastructure (Lobo & Vuyk, 2023; Vuyk et al., 2024).

# 2e Students in the United States: Identification and Representation Challenges

The identification of 2e students, particularly among Latinx/Hispanic populations, presents significant challenges. Due to systemic biases and inadequate assessment practices, many Latinx/Hispanic students are disproportionately identified for special education programs primarily for their learning disabilities (Guiberson, 2009). Simultaneously, there is a stark underrepresentation of these students in gifted education programs (Mun et al., 2020). This discrepancy suggests that the dual exceptionalities of these students—both their learning disabilities and their giftedness—are often not concurrently recognized. Consequently, they might first be noticed for their learning difficulties, while their exceptional cognitive or creative abilities are overlooked.

## Expectations and Biases

Teacher expectations and cultural biases can negatively impact the identification of Latinx/Hispanic students as gifted. Teachers might have lower expectations for these students, leading to fewer nominations for gifted programs. Kitano and Pedersen (2002) observed that teachers' definitions of "giftedness" often incorporated ethnic and social class assumptions, influencing who was selected. Brice and Brice (2004) found that a checklist used as a giftedness screening tool had items that were culturally biased against Latinx/Hispanic students. Similarly, Harradine et al. (2013) found that teachers often overlooked the academic potential of children of color, including Latinx/Hispanic students, due to low expectations and biases. In special education, these biases manifest as higher referral rates for Latinx/Hispanic students. Teachers and school staff, often unprepared to work with culturally diverse populations, may misidentify cultural and linguistic differences as disabilities (Guiberson, 2009).

## Language Issues

The majority of English language learners (ELLs) in the US are Latinx/Hispanic and their language proficiency affects their likelihood of being referred to gifted and special education. Furthermore, ELL students are often overrepresented in special education at higher grade levels (6-12) due to fewer supports and increased academic demands (Guiberson, 2009). Teachers' perceptions of the language barrier, along with an emphasis on standardized testing, prevent culturally, linguistically, and economically diverse students from being identified by teachers as gifted (Allen, 2017).

Moreover, Latinx/Hispanic students are referred to special education more frequently than their Caucasian counterparts. This higher referral rate does not always translate into qualification for special education services (Guiberson, 2009). However, Latinx/Hispanic students are disproportionately represented in certain disability categories within special education, particularly as learning disability and speech-language impairment, while being underrepresented in categories such as intellectual disability and severe emotional disturbance (Guiberson, 2009).

## Socioeconomic Status

Socioeconomic factors play a role in access to services and support. In Daniella's situation, she recognizes two advantages. The first is being raised in an upper-middle-class household with caring parents, thus having access to resources and support networks. Furthermore, it highlights an important nuance, particularly for Latin American students, suggesting that the level of support they receive may be correlated with their social class, as the educational and health systems typically fail to address giftedness and additional resources are scarce and expensive (Borland et al., 2000; Yaluma & Tyner, 2018; List & Dykeman, 2019). Allen (2017) noted that socioeconomic status and other factors such as levels of parental education and reduced opportunities to learn significantly impacted test scores and nominations. Lakin and Lohman (2011) highlighted that differences in test scores were highly correlated with socioeconomic status. Even overrepresentation in special education can be influenced by school and district characteristics, including diversity in student population, school district size, and spending per student (Guiberson, 2009).

## Universal Screening with Culturally Appropriate Measures

The benefits of universal screening methods to ensure more equitable identification are well documented. For instance, Lakin and Lohman (2011) highlight the advantages of these methods and Card and Giuliano (2016) support their use to identify underrepresented gifted students. In Paraguay, Vuyk et al. (2023) demonstrated the success of universal screening, showcasing its potential to improve equity in educational settings. Nonverbal ability tests like Raven's Progressive Matrices and the Naglieri Nonverbal Ability Test minimize language barriers and cultural biases, making them effective tools for assessing the cognitive abilities of students from diverse backgrounds (Lohman et al., 2008; Giessman et al., 2013; Vuyk et al., 2023).

Incorporating strengths-based approaches into the identification process is also critical. The Teacher's Observation of Potential in Students, as demonstrated by Harradine et al. (2013), helps teachers recognize potential in students of color, including Latinx students. This method focuses on identifying students' strengths and capabilities rather than their deficits, leading to a more accurate and positive identification process.

Utilizing alternative assessments, such as nonverbal ability tests and dynamic assessments, can help identify gifted Latinx/Hispanic students more accurately. These methods consider students' cultural and linguistic backgrounds, providing a clearer picture of their abilities and disabilities. Specifically, dynamic assessment methods that consider a student's ability to learn with support can help differentiate between a disability and a language/cultural difference (Guiberson, 2009). This approach helps ensure that students are not wrongly placed in special education programs due to cultural misunderstandings.

## Family and Community Involvement in School

Involving Latinx/Hispanic families in the gifted/special education referral and evaluation process is crucial. Schools should ensure that families are informed and included in discussions about their child's educational needs (Guiberson, 2009). This is not new; even back in the 1980s, Valencia (1985) emphasized the need for strategies to increase parental involvement and cooperation in identifying their children as gifted. However, the absence of parental involvement is still pervasive; Harradine et al. (2013) reported that a lack of parental advocacy was a barrier that prevented teachers from recognizing the potential in Latinx students. In special education, Latinx/Hispanic parents often report moderate levels of satisfaction with services, but also significant levels of dissatisfaction due to perceived bias, discrimination, and lack of communication from school staff (Guiberson, 2009).

### Cultural Competency

Latinx/Hispanic identity, with its unique cultural and linguistic characteristics, significantly impacts the educational experiences of twice-exceptional students. To know how to properly address this issue, ask the people who are involved in it. Qualitative data from educators, family members, and students provides deeper insights into the phenomenon of disproportionality that quantitative data alone cannot capture; their voices highlight the lived experiences of Latinx/Hispanic students and the challenges they face in being accurately identified and supported in special education (Barrio et al., 2022).

Improved cultural competency among educators, through both pre-service and in-service training, is essential to addressing the disproportionate representation of Latinx/Hispanic students in gifted/special education. Educators should receive training to develop cultural competency, which includes understanding students' cultural and linguistic backgrounds and how these factors might affect learning and behavior (Guiberson, 2009; Mun et al., 2020). Training can alter biases and improve the accuracy of nominations for gifted programs (Mun et al., 2020). Similar training is crucial in special education to reduce misidentification and inappropriate placements. Educators must learn culturally responsive practices to distinguish between cultural and linguistic differences and actual disabilities, and to accommodate the unique backgrounds of Latinx/Hispanic students (Barrio et al., 2022; Guiberson, 2009).

## Conclusion: Moving Forward

What stands out from Daniella's story is her resilience, optimism, and proactive approach—qualities not always evident among gifted adolescents, whether they receive support or not (Tan & Tan, 2014). She fits perfectly into the bold statement of Fugate and Gentry (2016), in which they call for a change of name for gifted and ADHD 2e girls:

> These girls who are gifted with ADHD have a unique ability to view the world through multiple lenses, rejecting the predetermined paths often associated with girls who are gifted and girls with ADHD. As such, we propose that researchers, educators, and parents stop seeing these girls as gifted with ADHD but rather as girls who are ADHG (Attention Divergent Hyperactive Gifted). Such a paradigm shift would then alter the focus from their challenges as girls who are gifted and as girls with ADHD and instead, highlight their motivation, strengths, perseverance, and resilience; those innate qualities that make them so very special.
>
> *(Fugate & Gentry, 2016, p. 104)*

Despite encountering numerous obstacles, Daniella maintains a steadfast belief in her own abilities, as well as in the potential of gifted adolescents in general to carve out their own place in a world that often operates under neurotypical norms: "I believe that we can still create our space in this neurotypical world."

## Things to Consider

- In Latin American contexts, ADHD and other learning differences are often minimized or ignored, affecting the willingness of families and schools to seek appropriate interventions.
- The lack of formal recognition and accommodations for 2e students in Paraguay, combined with a misunderstanding of high abilities, forces students to self-advocate and find unconventional ways to succeed.
- Encouraging self-advocacy among 2e students—like Daniella's proactive approach in later high-school years—can help them navigate these challenges, but systemic support should not rely solely on individual resilience.
- Systemic inequities mean that even within the same cultural context, identification and intervention are often limited to those with higher socioeconomic status.

## For Discussion

- How did the student's family dynamics influence her *experience* with 2e?
- How did the student's cultural background influence her *perception* of her own abilities?
- How did the cultural stigma surrounding ADHD and high abilities impact the student's *access* to resources and support systems, particularly within the educational context of Paraguay?
- How does the cultural stigma surrounding ADHD and high abilities impact *access* to resources and support systems in your educational context?
- In what ways can Latinx educators and institutions better support 2e students based on the insights provided in the vignette?
- Reflecting on the student's journey, what lessons can be drawn for other 2e individuals experiencing similar situations?

# References

Allen, J. K. (2017) Exploring the role teacher perceptions play in the underrepresentation of culturally and linguistically diverse students in gifted programming. *Gifted Child Today, 40*(2), 77-86. https://doi.org/10.1177/1076217517690188

Bal, A., Jackson, D., Mayes, R. D., & Powell, F. (2022) Unicorns and blessings: Supporting culturally diverse twice-exceptional learners through Learning Lab. *Teaching Exceptional Children.* Advance online publication. https://doi.org/10.1177/00400599221107146

Barrio, B. L., Ferguson, S. L., Hovey, K. A., Boedeker, P., & Kluttz-Drye, B. (2022) Voices beyond the numbers: A systematic review of qualitative studies of disproportionality in special education. *Preventing School Failure: Alternative Education for Children and Youth, 67*(1), 39-47. https://doi.org/10.1080/1045988X.2022.2101422

Behrens, W. A., Boswell, C., & Fugate, C. M. (2022) Supporting gifted students with anxiety, dyslexia, or attention deficit/hyperactivity disorder (ADHD) in school settings. In: F. H. R. Piske, K.H. Collins, & K. B. Arnstein (eds.) *Critical issues in servicing twice exceptional students* (pp. 65-74). Springer. https://doi.org/10.1007/978-3-031-10378-0_5

Besnoy, K. D., Swoszowski, N. C., Newman, J. L., Floyd, A., Jones, P., & Byrne, C. (2015) The advocacy experiences of parents of elementary age, twice-exceptional children. *Gifted Child Quarterly, 59*(2), 108-123. https://doi.org/10.1177/0016986215569275

Borland, J. H., Schnur, R., & Wright, L. (2000) Economically disadvantaged students in a school for the academically gifted: A postpositivist inquiry into individual and family adjustment. *Gifted Child Quarterly, 44*(1), 13-32. https://doi.org/10.1177/001698620004400103

Brice, A. E. & Brice, R. (2004) Identifying Hispanic gifted children: A screening. *Rural Special Education Quarterly, 23*(1), 8–15. https://doi.org/10.1177/875687050402300103

Card, D. & Giuliano, L. (2016) Universal screening increases the representation of low-income and minority students in gifted education. *Proceedings of the National Academy of Sciences of the United States of America, 113,* 13678–13683. https://doi.org/10.1073/pnas.1605043113

Carrillo, J. F. (2016) I grew up straight 'hood: Unpacking the intelligences of working-class Latino male college students in North Carolina. *Equity & Excellence in Education, 49*(2), 157-169. https://doi.org/10.1080/10665684.2015.1086247

Dole, S. (2001) Reconciling contradictions: Identity formation in individuals with giftedness and learning disabilities. *Journal for the Education of the Gifted, 25*(2), 103-135. https://doi.org/10.1177/016235320102500202

Foley-Nicpon, M. & Kim, J. Y. C. (2018) Identifying and providing evidence-based services for twice-exceptional students. In S. I. Pfeiffer (ed.) *Handbook of Giftedness in Children* (pp. 349-362). Springer. https://doi.org/10.1007/978-3-319-77004-8_20

Foley-Nicpon, M. & Cederberg, C. (2021). Moving beyond disabilities: Twice-exceptional students and self-advocacy. In L. Devis & D. Douglas (eds.) *Empowering underrepresented gifted students: Perspectives from the field* (pp. 116-125). Free Spirit Publishing.

Fugate, C. M. (2018) Attention Divergent Hyperactive Giftedness: Taking the deficiency and disorder out of the gifted/ADHD label. In S. B. Kaufman (ed.) *Twice Exceptional: Supporting and educating bright and creative students with learning difficulties* (pp. 191-200). Oxford Academic. https://doi.org/10.1093/oso/9780190645472.003.0012

Fugate, C. M. & Gentry, M. (2016) Understanding adolescent gifted girls with ADHD: Motivated and achieving. *High Ability Studies, 27*(1), 83-109. http://dx.doi.org/10.1080/13598139.2015.1098522

Giessman, J. A., Gambrell, J. L., & Stebbins, M. S. (2013) Minority performance on the Naglieri Nonverbal Ability Test, second edition, versus the Cognitive Abilities Test, Form 6: One gifted program's experience. *Gifted Child Quarterly, 57*(2), 101-109. https://doi.org/10.1177/0016986213477190

Gómez-Arízaga, M. P., Conejeros-Solar, M. L., Sandoval-Rodríguez, K., & Armijo Solís, S. (2016) Doble excepcionalidad: análisis exploratorio de experiencias y autoimagen en estudiantes chilenos. *Revista de Psicología (PUCP), 34*(1), 5-37. http://dx.doi.org/10.18800/psico.201601.001

Gómez-Arízaga, M. P. & Conejeros-Solar, M. L. (2021) Gifted and twice-exceptional children in the south of the world: Chilean students' experiences within regular classrooms. *Handbook of Giftedness and Talent Development in the Asia-Pacific* (pp 405-429). Springer. https://doi.org/10.1007/978-981-13-3041-4_8

Guiberson, M. (2009) Hispanic representation in special education: Patterns and implications. *Preventing School Failure: Alternative Education for Children and Youth, 53*(3), 167-176. https://doi.org/10.3200/PSFL.53.3.167-176

Harradine, C. C., Coleman, M. B., & Winn, D. C. (2013) Recognizing academic potential in students of color: Findings of U-STARS~PLUS. *Gifted Child Quarterly, 58*(1), 23-34. https://doi.org/10.1177/0016986213506040

Jung, J. Y. (2020) Career development of twice-exceptional individuals: Present and future issues. In: M. Yuen, W. Beamish & V. S. H. Solberg (eds.) *Careers for students with special educational needs: Advancing inclusive and special Education in the Asia-Pacific*. Springer. https://doi.org/10.1007/978-981-15-4443-9_5

Kitano, M. K. & Pedersen, K. S. (2002) Action research and practical inquiry teaching gifted English learners. *Journal for the Education of the Gifted, 26*(2), 132-147. https://doi.org/10.1177/016235320202600204

Lakin, J. M. & Lohman, D. F. (2011) The predictive accuracy of verbal, quantitative, and nonverbal reasoning tests: Consequences for talent identification and program diversity. *Journal for the Education of the Gifted, 34*(4), 595-623. https://doi.org/10.1177/016235321103400404

List, A. & Dykeman, C. (2019, June 25) *The Relationship of Gifted Program Enrollment to Race/Ethnicity, Gender, and SES.* https://doi.org/10.31234/osf.io/zx396

Lobo, M. & Vuyk, A. (2023) Concepciones de docentes del nivel medio de un colegio privado de Asunción-Paraguay sobre altas capacidades intelectuales en estudiantes desde una perspectiva de inclusión. *Revista Científica Estudios E Investigaciones, 12*(1), 23-37. https://doi.org/10.26885/rcei.12.1.23

Lohman, D. F., Korb, K. A., & Lakin, J. M. (2008) Identifying academically gifted English language learners using nonverbal tests. *Gifted Child Quarterly, 52*(4), 275-296. https://doi.org/10.1177/0016986208321808

Mayes, R. D. & Moore III, J. L. (2016) The intersection of race, disability, and giftedness: Understanding the education needs of twice-exceptional, African American students. *Gifted Child Today, 39*(2), 98-104. https://doi.org/10.1177/1076217516628570

Mun, R. U., Hemmler, V., Langley, S. D., Ware, S., Gubbins, E. J., Callahan, C. M., McCoach, D. B., & Siegle, D. (2020) Identifying and serving English learners in gifted education: Looking back and moving forward. *Journal for the Education of the Gifted, 43*(4), 297-335. https://doi.org/10.1177/0162353220955230

Neihart, M. (2016) The social and emotional development of gifted children: What do we know? In M. Neihart, S. M. Reis, N. M. Robinson, & S. M. Moon (eds.) *The Social and Emotional Development of Gifted Children: What Do We Know?* (2nd ed.) Routledge. https://doi.org/10.4324/9781003238928

Olszewski-Kubilius, P. & Clarenbach, J. (2014) Closing the opportunity gap: Program factors contributing to academic success in culturally different youth. *Gifted Child Today, 37*(2), 103-110. https://doi.org/10.1177/1076217514520630

Park, S., Foley-Nicpon, M., Choate, A., & Bolenbaugh, M. (2018) "Nothing fits exactly": Experiences of Asian American parents of twice-exceptional children. *Gifted Child Quarterly, 62*(3), 306-319. https://doi.org/10.1177/0016986218758442

Pfeiffer, S. I. (2021) Optimizing favorable outcomes when counseling the gifted: A best practices approach. *Gifted Education International, 37*(2), 142-157. https://doi.org/10.1177/0261429420969917

Programa de las Naciones Unidas para el Desarrollo (2021) *Segundo Informe Nacional Voluntario, Paraguay 2021*. https://www.mre.gov.py/ods/wp-content/uploads/2021/07/Segundo-Informe-Nacional-Voluntario-Paraguay-2021.pdf

Robinson, N. M. (2008) The social world of gifted children and youth. In S. I. Pfeiffer (ed.) *Handbook of Giftedness in Children: Psychoeducational Theory, Research, and Best Practices* (pp. 33-51). Springer. https://doi.org/10.1007/978-0-387-74401-8_3

Sandoval-Rodríguez, K. & Conejeros-Solar, M. L. (2024) Voices of twice exceptional students in their first year of higher education. *Gifted and Talented International*, 1-10. Advance online publication. https://doi.org/10.1080/15332276.2024.2340025

Soares, W. K. & de Souza, D. (2021) Inclusão educacional: estudo de caso de um aluno com dupla excepcionalidade. *Revista de Psicología (PUCP), 39*(1), 339-379. https://dx.doi.org/10.18800/psico.202101.014

Tan, C. & Tan, L. S. (2014) The role of optimism, self-esteem, academic self-efficacy and gender in high-ability students. *The Asia-Pacific Education Researcher, 23*, 621-633. https://doi.org/10.1007/s40299-013-0134-5

Trail, B. A. (2022) *Twice-exceptional gifted children: Understanding, teaching, and counseling gifted students*. Routledge. https://doi.org/10.4324/9781003261216

Valencia, A. A. (1985) Curricular perspectives for gifted limited English proficient students. *The Journal for the National Association for Bilingual Education, 10*(1), 65-77. https://doi.org/10.1080/08855072.1985.10668506

VanTassel-Baska, J., Feng, A. X., Swanson, J. D., Quek, C., & Chandler, K. (2009) Academic and affective profiles of low-income, minority, and twice-exceptional gifted learners: The role of gifted program membership in enhancing self. *Journal of Advanced Academics, 20*(4), 702-739. https://doi.org/10.1177/1932202X0902000406

Vuyk, A., Montanía, M., Barrios, L., & Lobo, M. (2024) Gifted education in Paraguay: Analyses from a learning-resource perspective. *Cogent Education, 11*(1). https://doi.org/10.1080/2331186X.2024.2332863

Vuyk, A., Barrios, L., Méndez, N., & Zalazar, P. (2023) Mapa de Talentos: un procedimiento piloto de detección universal del talento en estudiantes del Paraguay. *Revista Paraguaya de Educación, 12*(2), 11-32.

Wang, C. W. & Neihart, M. (2015) How do supports from parents, teachers, and peers influence academic achievement of twice-exceptional students. *Gifted Child Today, 38*(3), 148-159. https://doi.org/10.1177/1076217515583742

Yaluma, C. B. & Tyner, A. (2018) *Is there a gifted gap? Gifted education in high-poverty schools*. Retrieved from https://edexcellence.net/publications/is-there-a-gifted-gap

# Chapter 6

# From Cultural Nuances to Educational Needs

## Understanding and Supporting Asian American Twice-Exceptional Adolescents

### Tiffany Chaiko and Enyi Jen

*Kevin Lee is an eighth-grade student who attends a public school in a Midwest state. The school considers Kevin to be Asian American. However, Kevin sees himself as American, Japanese, Vietnamese, Asian, and Asian American. "I was born here like my mom and dad—so I am American; but I also am a mix, because my mom is Vietnamese and my dad is Japanese."*

*Kevin played American Youth Soccer Organization (AYSO) soccer during his elementary school years. This experience was a connector to friends and a venue to exercise natural leadership and creativity skills, as well as connect with his parents:*

> *I loved the potlucks the most, because the kids on my team brought all different kinds of foods—like fried noodles with char siu, chili and rice, and hot dogs. Before we moved, I was volunteering on my uncle's AYSO soccer team for little kids. I loved coming up with new games for the kids to play so that they could build their soccer skills while having fun. Dad and I were taking the referee training together so that I could get certified and be a line referee and a center referee to help my uncle's team on game days.*

*Kevin's native language is English. It is the language he speaks at home with his parents. Although not fluent, Kevin knows some Vietnamese and Japanese words and phrases that he has learned from participating in Vietnamese and Japanese cultural events where he and his parents live. Kevin and his parents celebrate Vietnamese and Japanese traditions with family members in home settings. Kevin also has a strong connection with his mom, which blends creativity, traditions, and cooking:*

> *I love creating fusion dishes with my mom and making up new recipes that are a riff on traditional foods that blend American, Vietnamese, and Japanese ingredients in new ways. We usually try out my new dishes at family celebrations.*

*Kevin's parents are native English speakers who understand Vietnamese and Japanese spoken at restaurants or during cultural celebrations but are not fluent speakers. Kevin's grandparents are both bilingual and were born in the United States. Kevin's parents hold professional jobs and are in leadership positions. The family moved to a Western state when Kevin was 10 years old:*

> *Moving here was a little hard. In my old neighborhood, everyone was of mixed race and diverse, from different backgrounds—born here or moved from another country or state—and we just had a lot of fun hanging out together. But here, people ask where you are from. I think that is a little weird because I was born here, so why would people ask? It gets even more strange and a little uncomfortable when someone says, "Where are you really from?" after I say I'm from here and then tell me my English is really good. Of course it is—it's my language.*

*Kevin loved math and science as a child and excelled at these subjects during elementary school:*

> *I have always loved math and science since I was a little kid. I like other subjects too, but those were the most fun. My math and science teacher knew me really well and would always find interesting projects for me to do in class after I finished the regular work. That made it fun.*

*While Kevin has done well in math and science, he struggles to focus and submit assignments in other classes. Some of the other teachers believe he is not trying hard enough:*

> *It's kind of frustrating to have success in math and science and then just forget to turn in work in my other classes even though I did it. Sometimes, it is hard for me to remember what I need to do; and other times, when it is interesting, I come up with so many ideas and doing the assignment is fast. I also get bored*

*in class sometimes if I learned the topic a long time ago; or I lose track of what the teacher is saying because I am thinking about something else.*

Kevin's fourth-grade math and science teacher recommended that he take the school's gifted identification test. However, he could not take the test because his family was moving to a new state because of a job opportunity. At his new elementary school, Kevin continued to struggle to focus and turn in work. Kevin's parents met with his fifth-grade teacher and the school counselor numerous times to facilitate the school's evaluation of his qualifications for special education services under "Other Health Impairment for Attention Deficit Hyperactive Disorder." Although Kevin's parents mentioned to the school counselor that their son had been invited to test for gifted services at his previous elementary school, Kevin was not invited to participate in the gifted program at the new school.

The learning situation became complicated when Kevin started middle school. Kevin's teachers did not recognize his strengths in middle school. Since the middle school did not provide gifted services for its students, Kevin was enrolled in high-level math classes and received special education services, which took away time from elective classes that he wanted to take in science. Because of schedule conflicts, Kevin was enrolled in basic science, technology, engineering, and math (STEM) classes:

*The math that I can do is several levels above what we are discussing in my STEM class. It is pretty boring and makes me not want to do the assignments, turn in them, or pay attention in class. It is a little strange to try to explain to the class counselor why I am getting As in pre-calc and trig and super-low grades in STEM, which uses basic math concepts. We have a little group in trig, but I do not hang out with the kids who do STEM and pre-calc because I do not feel like I fit in with them either, with my lower STEM grades and everything.*

Kevin has a different experience in his English and history classes:

*It's a mixed bag for those classes. If there is a topic that I am really interested in, I will ask complex and in-depth questions that surprise the teachers but might baffle the other students, who just look confused or make a joke out of my question. If there is a group project that I am interested in, I will usually lead it—which is fun, and we all get good grades; but the teachers sometimes congratulate the other kids in my group and seem to expect me to do well all of the time—that is really stressful. Other times, it is just hard to get motivated to do the assignments because I have so many ideas that I do not know which one to choose or how to get motivated to start.*

Kevin's parents noticed that Kevin was struggling in classes he enjoyed in elementary school. They contacted the middle school to discuss their concerns and advocate for his strengths and interests, as they had done in Kevin's elementary school. The middle-school staff member who took the call informed Kevin's mom that the school did not yet have Asian language interpreters for parent meetings, so the family would need to make arrangements because all meetings at the school were conducted in English and not in any Asian languages. Kevin's parents, both native English speakers, were surprised by the suggestion.

After a few more conversations with the school, a meeting was scheduled between Kevin's parents and his teachers. During the meeting, Kevin's parents shared information about his strengths and interests and advocated for support for his needs based on their observations and previous experiences of success and difficulties. Kevin's parents also asked detailed questions about potential opportunities for him to show his leadership and creativity skills in areas of interest that they saw developing before they moved. However, the teachers seemed to interpret them as overprotective parents. Kevin's parents felt frustrated that their advocacy, which had been accepted in previous education systems, was being misunderstood in the current situation. One teacher said to them gently, "You know, at middle-school age, we Americans encourage parents to empower the students and let them make their own decisions." Despite their best efforts to advocate for Kevin, his parents left the meeting feeling unheard. "They just don't see him for who he is," his mom said softly as they walked to the car. Kevin, overhearing, felt his stomach drop, torn between wanting to prove himself and the sinking feeling that he didn't belong.

When the family have a break in their busy schedules, they like to take walks together. Kevin has shared with his parents during these walks that he sometimes feels like he doesn't fit in with other kids who get high grades all the time, but he feels that he does fit in with kids who have similar interests. Kevin stated, "I just wish I could have more time to hang out with them" (i.e., those kids who shared similar science interests with him). He has also shared with his parents that he has already investigated several potential high schools but is worried that his inconsistent grades might prevent him from accessing higher-level high-school classes. While Kevin's parents assure him that they support his areas of interest, remind him of his strengths, and offer to help brainstorm potential compensation strategies to help him achieve his goals, they also know they need to do extra work, as success is not guaranteed.

# Introduction

Kevin's story highlights the intersecting complexities, contexts, and nuances embedded in the personal experiences of multiple Asian American twice-exceptional students. Themes of intersecting complexities and personal experiences emerge consistently in the literature on Asian Americans (Tran & Birman, 2010; Walton & Truong, 2022), twice-exceptional students (Baldwin et al., 2015; Beckmann & Minnaert, 2018; Reis et al., 2014), and twice-exceptional students as part of diverse gifted populations (NAGC, 2019). This body of work also includes research on culturally diverse gifted students (Kaplan & Mora-Flores, 2021; Plucker et al., 2021; Yeung & Mun, 2022) and Southeast Asian twice-exceptional students and their families (Park & Foley-Nicpon, 2022; Park et al., 2018). Moreover, a review of future research areas addressing all gifted students' social and emotional needs (Rinn, 2024) and our firsthand experiences working with multiple Asian American adolescents further inform our understanding. The contextual factors in Kevin's story exemplify intersecting complexities, as scholars emphasize the importance of sociocultural contexts in addressing the needs of culturally diverse gifted students (Plucker et al., 2021) and in understanding social and emotional growth (e.g., Neihart et al., 2016). Research also underscores that twice-exceptional students have unique social and emotional needs, and that addressing these needs is crucial to supporting their wellbeing and development (Baldwin et al., 2014; Peterson & Jen, 2018).

We use the term "Asian American" in this chapter to represent the diversity and complexity of cultures, ethnicities, and demographic factors that describe this heterogeneous population (Ruiz et al., 2023). Further, a national 2e community of practice defines twice-exceptional students who show high potential and creativity while simultaneously having learning difficulties and disabilities defined by state or federal criteria that produce a complex duality of paradoxical and dynamic traits, behaviors, and distinct social and emotional needs impacted by context (Baldwin et al., 2015; Beckmann & Minnaert, 2018; Peterson & Peters, 2021; Reis et al., 2014).

We developed a visual analysis to illustrate how intersecting complexities and personal experiences across multiple contexts and factors, as introduced in the vignette at the beginning of the chapter, support a more holistic and developmental understanding of Kevin as an Asian American twice-exceptional adolescent (Figure 6.1). Essentially, Figure 6.1 demonstrates that when these factors and contexts are considered together, they create a synergistic effect, resulting in a whole that is greater than the sum of its parts. A developmental and holistic perspective is particularly valuable, as it recognizes the interactive and cumulative impact of multiple factors and contexts (Peterson & Jen, 2023).

Bronfenbrenner's bioecological theory provides a framework for understanding the dynamic, interconnected components represented in Figure 6.1. This is achieved through the theory's concept of proximal processes, which influence, develop, and evolve potential over time through interactions across multiple levels of environmental contexts, ranging from macro to micro (Bronfenbrenner & Ceci, 1994; Ceci et al., 2016). Additionally, the Process-Person-Context-Time

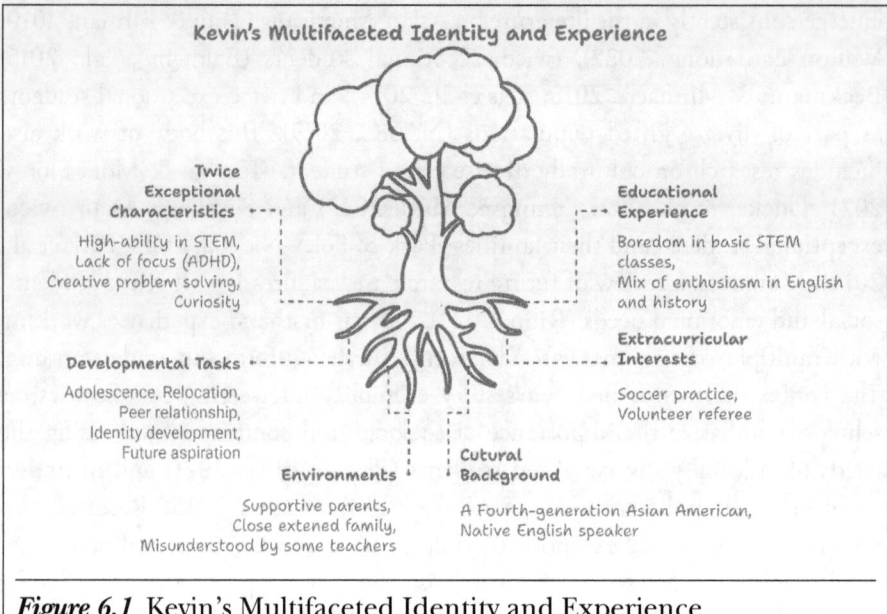

*Figure 6.1* Kevin's Multifaceted Identity and Experience

model emphasizes the complexity of these interactions over time, further enriching the framework (Tong & An, 2024).

In this chapter, we will examine how integrating a cultural focus with a holistic developmental perspective can enhance our understanding of the intersecting complexities and personal experiences of Kevin, an Asian American twice-exceptional adolescent. Kevin's lived experience unfolds within multiple bioecological, demographic, personal, cultural, social, and emotional contexts, all of which evolve in complexity over the period depicted in the vignette.

# Cultural Perspective: The Diversity of Asian Americans

The Asian American population, as defined by the US Census, consists of 41 cultural groups originating from East Asia, Southeast Asia, the Indian subcontinent, and Central Asia, as well as multiracial individuals, like Kevin in the vignette (AAPI Data, 2022). Each group has distinct histories, cultures, languages, and characteristics (Budiman & Ruiz, 2021). The majority of Asian Americans identify with 21 cultural groups, including Chinese, Indian, Filipino, Vietnamese, Korean, and Japanese, which together comprise 85% of the population. While the pan-ethnic term "Asian American," coined in the 1960s for political purposes (Choy, 2022), has historical significance, it obscures the rich diversity and cultural differences within the population (Budiman & Ruiz, 2021; Walton & Truong, 2022; Yeung & Mun, 2022). These differences span demographic factors such as nativity, generational status, socioeconomic status, education, family structure, and language, underscoring the complexity and heterogeneity of the Asian American community.[1]

However, scholars have argued that the level of complexity is even more significant than the sum of the individual parts when considering interactions between personal, family, cultural-ethnic, demographic, ecological, contextual, and historical factors (Choy, 2022). In the vignette, we introduce what this might look like in a case study. Kevin is a fourth-generation Asian American born in the United States to parents and grandparents who were born and grew up in the United States. He is both Japanese American and Vietnamese American, considered multiracial, and a member of one of the largest demographic groups in the adolescent census data. Presumably, Kevin's parents and grandparents grew up attending schools in the United States, and English is their native home language. However, Kevin and his parents understand and use Japanese and Vietnamese language during cultural celebrations. Kevin and his family lived in one state during elementary school and then moved to a new community during middle school. While these demographic elements are important when considering Kevin's experiences, they become more complex when considering the factors as an intersecting set. Additionally, Kevin's experiences are different from first, 1.5, and second-generation Asian Americans who either were born in an origin country or have parents born in an origin country and who may be unfamiliar with the United States education system. They may need assistance in translating written or oral English into a home language. There is little research on the lived experiences of second, third, fourth, fifth, or sixth-generation Asian Americans or specific Asian American cultural groups. The limited literature on Asian Americans and Asian American students, gifted Asian American students, twice-exceptional Asian American students, and twice-exceptional Southeast Asian Americans and parents primarily focuses on the lived experiences of first, 1.5, and second generations (Budiman & Ruiz, 2021; Kao & Hebert, 2006; Kitano, 2011; Park & Foley-Nicpon, 2022; Park et al., 2018; Yoon & Gentry, 2009).

Complexity can be missed when it is assumed that the Asian American population is monolithic (Budiman & Ruiz, 2021; Yeung & Mun, 2022; Choy, 2022). The nuances of personal and cultural experiences that intersect with context can be missed when success or mild behavior is assumed in the model minority myth and further confounded when nativity and generational status are assumed to be first-generation (Tran & Birman, 2010; Walton & Truong, 2022). Scholars have also found that larger political or historical contexts can impact concepts of belonging (AAPI Data, 2022; Choy, 2022). COVID-19, for example, escalated the forever foreigner stereotype and increased Asian hate incidents (Stop AAPI

Hate Campaign, 2020). It also resulted in many Asian Americans hiding their ethnic characteristics for fear of anti-Asian sentiments, Asian hate crimes, and embarrassment (Ruiz et al. 2023). Sometimes, stereotypical assumptions manifest subtly. Questions like, "No, where are you really from?" and remarks like, "Your English is really good" are microaggressions (Williams et al., 2021) that undermine a person's sense of belonging or abilities based on racial biases. Kevin feels emotionally uncomfortable when asked, "Where do you come from?" On the surface, this discomfort might seem to be tied to typical adolescent emotional changes. However, it also reflects his identity development as an adolescent, an Asian American, and someone new to the community.

Research shows that microaggressions and stereotypes negatively affect wellbeing, identity development, and social-emotional growth (Williams et al., 2021; Tran & Birman, 2010). Asian American "model" minority stereotypes and microaggressions often render the unique needs and strengths of this diverse population invisible (Cheng et al., 2017; Walton & Truong), particularly for adolescents. Thompson et al. (2020) conducted a longitudinal study with 175 high-school Asian American students, and the findings revealed complex interactions, with discrimination generally linked to negative relationship qualities and the model minority stereotype showing mixed effects—sometimes positive and sometimes negative—depending on the peer group. These stereotypes can perpetuate harmful assumptions, such as presumed success and upward mobility, regardless of actual circumstances or the notion that assistance is unnecessary. For Asian American adolescents, it may bring unnecessary stress.

Such influences may also lead to delayed or low identification of Asian American children needing learning support (Sullivan et al., 2020). For adolescents, the impact can be especially pronounced. Asian American students might hesitate to express their needs or seek help due to stereotypes, cultural or generational expectations, or fears of burdening their parents, particularly in the context of acculturation differences (Greenwood, 2022).

## Multifaceted Identity of Asian Americans

Scholars stress the importance of considering culture and context in understanding socio-emotional growth (e.g., Neihart et al., 2016). This includes having an impact on developmental processes and tasks—especially identity development, which for Asian Americans and Asian American adolescents can be complex. Scholars have found that cultural and racial identities can be fluid, adapting to different contexts and encompassing regional or subgroup micro-identities based on social dynamics, the group's familiarity with cultural nuances, family relationships, and evolving levels of acculturation. An Asian American identity, for instance, may be viewed as just one component of a broader, multifaceted identity (Ruiz et al., 2023).

The strength of cultural identity may differ when impacted by discrimination. For example, it was predicted that Filipino American youth have a weaker ethnic identity and Korean American youth have a stronger ethnic identity when experiencing racial discrimination (Woo et al., 2020). Differences also occur within single groups (Xie et al., 2024). Moreover, interest-based identities have been shown to dynamically support the expression of cultural identities among Hmong, Cambodian, Filipino, Laotian, and Vietnamese hip-hop dancers (Nguyen & Ferguson, 2020). Similarly, intersecting identities have been found to bolster the experiences of first-generation Southeast Asian twice-exceptional students (Park & Foley-Nicpon, 2022). Multiple simultaneous identity group memberships positively contribute to social and emotional wellbeing, such as being culturally and linguistically gifted bilingual students (Kaplan & Mora-Flores, 2021). For Asian American adolescents with diverse gender and sexual identities, the interplay of these factors adds further complexity and potentially significant impacts on their social and emotional wellbeing, as well as their developmental processes and tasks (Russell & McCurdy, 2023; Price et al., 2021).

Considering these insights, it is crucial to recognize the multifaceted nature of Asian American twice-exceptional adolescents' identities and the challenges they may face as they strive to balance and integrate different aspects of their identities.

## Parenting Styles of Asian Americans

Parent-child relationships significantly influence Asian American adolescents, including twice-exceptional ones (Chang et al., 2021; Greenwood, 2022; Kao & Hebert, 2006; Kitano, 2011; Park et al., 2018). Studies reveal that Asian American parents employ diverse parenting styles, which are sometimes misunderstood as less favorable. For example, cultural and acculturation conflicts often arise between first or 1.5-generation parents and their second-generation, US-born children, particularly regarding expectations, education, and career choices (Ruiz et al., 2023; Kao & Hebert, 2006). Despite these challenges, adaptive parenting styles have effectively supported Asian American twice-exceptional youth (Park et al., 2018). Child-centered approaches were used by Chinese American parents with their gifted children (Chang et al., 2021). A diversity of parenting approaches counter monolithic assumptions about Asian American parenting.

For example, Kevin and his parents have a supportive and adaptive relationship that accepts Kevin's strengths and interests. Kevin's parents were effective advocates for Kevin in some school contexts but not others. Kevin's US-born and native English-speaking Asian American parents were impacted by the model minority and forever foreigner stereotypes to different degrees, which made advocacy for Kevin's unique strengths and needs more difficult, even though they prevailed. We chose to feature the experiences of third and fourth-generation family to highlight the complex heterogeneous diversity of Asian American adolescents

Thus, when a cultural perspective is adopted, it can help to see how multiple factors and contexts may interact. Kevin, as a middle schooler, is concerned about doing well in the future. Is this because of the impact of cultural stereotypes or living up to cultural or parent expectations? Or is this a combination of factors that may include a mix of cultural factors and personal and developmental factors, including the nuances of also being twice exceptional or simultaneously gifted or of high potential and having learning differences like ADHD?

## Looking at Twice-Exceptional Adolescents Through a Developmental Lens: Social and Emotional Development

A developmental focus recognizes growth and needs across physical, cognitive, and psychosocial (social and emotional) domains over time, with the ultimate goal of fostering holistic wellbeing (Peterson & Jen, 2018). This approach to psychosocial needs and growth meets students where they are, understanding that social and emotional development occurs through continuous engagement with developmental processes and tasks without a fixed start or end point. Such engagement may involve struggles with normal developmental tasks and making sense of experiences, behaviors, and emotions (Jen et al., 2017; Peterson & Jen, 2023).

Key developmental tasks include forming an identity, establishing autonomy, developing a sense of direction or career path, building confidence, cultivating mature social relationships, and resolving familial conflicts, including emotional differentiation from family members. While all students encounter social and emotional growth and needs throughout their lives, adolescence often intensifies engagement with these processes and tasks. Although these developmental tasks are common across adolescents, gifted, twice-exceptional, and culturally diverse twice-exceptional students experience them differently (Peterson & Jen, 2018).

Twice-exceptional students may face more intense, asynchronous, or unique challenges in their developmental processes, which can also serve as opportunities for growth (Silverman, 2012). However, these differences can be unsettling if they are not understood, acknowledged, and supported within psychologically safe environments that foster the core needs of competence, belonging, and autonomy (Ryan & Deci, 2017). A lack of understanding and support may disrupt developmental processes, particularly identity formation (Branje et al., 2021).

Identity formation is a critical developmental task that becomes particularly salient during adolescence. It is a dynamic, lifelong process, but adolescence marks a period when individuals begin to construct a multifaceted self-concept. This includes aspects such as gender expression (Parra-Martiney & Treat, 2021), identities linked to interest groups and areas of strength (Nguyen & Ferguson, 2020), as well as commitments, personal goals, motivations, and psychosocial wellbeing (Crocetti, 2017; Pfeifer & Berkman, 2018). Daily experiences, close relationships, and personal narratives significantly influence this process (Branje et al., 2021).

For diverse twice-exceptional students, identity formation is further complicated by unique social and emotional needs and the duality of paradoxical strengths and weaknesses (Baldwin et al., 2015; Beckmann & Minnaert, 2018; Reis et al., 2014). This duality can be especially perplexing when strengths and weaknesses manifest inconsistently across different areas of life. Complex duality impacts self-concept in twice-exceptional students (Duyer et al., 2023). Many twice-exceptional students struggle to reconcile these contradictions, leading to low self-esteem (Gentry & Fugate, 2018), anxiety, and challenges with executive functioning (Reis et al., 2014). Recognizing and addressing these complexities is essential to supporting their identity development.

Beckmann and Minnaert's (2018) systematic review of the non-cognitive traits of twice-exceptional students shows that potential impacts extend beyond identity development and may impact many of the developmental tasks referenced above. They found that twice-exceptional students were highly motivated and showed high levels of frustration, used coping skills and had trouble with social relationships, had positive self-concept and confidence in abilities, and lacked confidence and low self-efficacy, which seemed to be impacted by social environments. The duality of traits adds another layer of complexity to the experience of developmental processes and tasks.

Adolescents' emotions are often described as "emotion storms." Brain development research highlights the increased sensitivity of emotional regions at the onset of puberty, which may be influenced by hormones (Guyer et al., 2018; van Duijenvoorde et al., 2016) or rapid cognitive and emotional development (Jansen & Kiefer, 2020). However, understanding adolescent emotional responses becomes more complex when needs or concerns are masked (Peterson & Peters, 2021), or when asynchronous development is not acknowledged (Baum et al., 2017).

Studies show that diverse gifted and twice-exceptional students may not express their needs, for various reasons. These can range from an assumption that they do not need support due to positive stereotypes (the gifted asset paradox) to a desire to avoid worrying adults, fear of making mistakes, or frustration with their dual strengths and weaknesses (Peterson & Peters, 2021; Reis et al., 2014). Family or parental expectations, particularly if they do not align with ongoing developmental tasks or the complexities of asynchronous development, can further impact on the social and emotional wellbeing of adolescent twice-exceptional students. As discussed, viewing the social and emotional needs of twice-exceptional adolescents from a developmental perspective helps us recognize duality, complexity, and intensity as part of their growth, though experienced in unique ways. In the next section, we discuss using strength-based support for the social and emotional needs of twice-exceptional adolescents like Kevin.

## Strength-Based Support for Asian American Twice-Exceptional Students

Recent insights into the needs of twice-exceptional students have shifted the focus from primarily addressing deficits to emphasizing their interests and strengths (Amran & Majid, 2019; Baum et al., 2014; Reis et al., 2014; Reis & Renzulli, 2021). By addressing both social and emotional needs, educators and counselors can support the overall wellbeing of 2e students (Baldwin et al., 2013; Silverman, 2013, as cited in Peterson & Jen, 2018). A holistic approach centered on strengths is essential for developing these students, and the Peterson Proactive Developmental Attention model provides a valuable framework for this approach. It incorporates a developmental perspective that considers personal strengths, challenges, and developmental tasks (Peterson & Jen, 2018).

However, while the strength-based approach is well recognized, a common challenge is framing actionable strength-based strategies to help develop talents. Here, we demonstrate three strength-based strategies to enhance support when working with 2e students like Kevin.

First, engaging Kevin in community-based STEM leadership opportunities could help him connect his strengths with his interests. For instance, he could start or join a community-based STEM club, such as a robotics team, or participate in maker spaces or library programs that host STEM-related activities, like coding workshops. These environments would enable Kevin to exercise his leadership and creativity skills, develop his talent for math and science, and connect with peers who share similar passions.

Second, fostering Kevin's cultural and personal interests could deepen his self-identity. Encouraging him to create a blog, YouTube channel, or social media account focused on blending Vietnamese, Japanese, and American cuisines would not only celebrate his multicultural heritage but also enhance his executive function skills through content planning and creation. This approach highlights the integration of strengths into daily experiences, reinforcing self-esteem and motivation (Baum et al., 2014).

Finally, Kevin's developmental task of identity formation, including building connections in his new community, can be supported by offering opportunities for collaboration and exploration. His leadership and creative problem-solving skills could be applied to community service projects, further contributing to his personal development and fostering a sense of belonging. As Kevin navigates significant transitions—such as moving from elementary to middle school and adapting to a new environment—these strategies can provide psychological safety, normalize his anxieties, and promote his overall wellbeing. Supporting Kevin in this way aligns with a strengths-based developmental perspective, which recognizes the interplay between personal characteristics, life events, and environmental factors in shaping his growth and success (Peterson & Jen, 2018).

# Conclusion

We recommend using a strength-based developmental focus when addressing the social and emotional needs of Asian American twice-exceptional students. This focus incorporates the impact of multiple intersecting factors and contexts on ongoing developmental processes and tasks with an end goal of wellbeing. This includes supporting strengths and interests and the duality of paradoxical traits, as well as diverse and heterogeneous cultural and demographic factors and family contexts. It also includes acceptance of asynchronous development and intersecting social, cultural, personal, and interest-based identities. Additionally, Asian American twice-exceptional students may need support expressing their needs due to a mix of complex factors and expectations.

## Things to Consider

- The model minority stereotype obscures struggles, as educators may assume students do not need support or overlook their learning challenges.
- The rigid school structure often fails to accommodate asynchronous development, placing students in lower-level STEM courses despite excelling in higher-level math.

- Schools' lack of language support services assumes all Asian American families need interpreters, overlooking their fluency and reinforcing stereotypes about foreignness.
- Schools should offer strength-based programs that connect students with mentors, leadership opportunities, and specialized learning pathways to nurture their talents.

## For Discussion

- In what contexts does the student show their strengths and interests and how might demographic and cultural contexts support or complicate matters for the student?
- What personal biases or generalized information about Asian Americans, twice-exceptional students, and gifted students might mask the nuanced experiences, behaviors, and insights of this particular Asian American student?
- What contexts can be created to provide psychologically safe spaces for Asian American twice-exceptional students to learn about developmental tasks and talk about their feelings and normalize and reframe their experiences to promote belonging?

## Note

1 To learn more about the diversity of Asian Americans, please visit the Pew Research Center website at https://www.pewresearch.org/regions-countries/asia-pacific/.

## References

AAPI Data (2024, May 8) 2024 National Overview of AA and NHPI Communities-WHIAANHI and AAPI Data. Asian American Research Center. https://aapidata.com/data/2024-national-factsheet-whiaanhpi-and-aapi-data/

Amran, H. & Majid, R. (2019) Learning strategies for twice-exceptional students. *International Journal of Special Education, 33*(4), 954-977.

Baum, S. M., Schader, R. M., & Hébert, T. P. (2014) Through a different lens: Reflecting on a strengths-based, talent-focused approach for twice-exceptional learners. *Gifted Child Quarterly, 58*(4), 311-327.

Baum, S. M., Schader, R. M., & Owen, S. V. (2017) *To be gifted and learning disabled: Strength-based strategies for helping twice-exceptional students with LD, ADHD, ASD, and More* (3rd ed). Prufrock Press.

Baldwin, L., Baum, S., Pereles, D., & Hughes, C. (2015) Twice-exceptional learners: The journey toward a shared vision. *Gifted Child Today, 38*(4), 206-214. https://doi.org/10.1177/1076217515597277

Beckmann, E. & Minnaert, A. (2018) Non-cognitive characteristics of gifted students with learning disabilities: An in-depth systematic review. *Frontiers in Psychology, 9*(504), 1-20. https://doi.org/10.3389/fpsyg.2018.00504

Branje, S., de Moor, E. L., Spitzer, J., Becht, A. I. (2021) Dynamics of identity development in adolescence: A decade in review. *Journal of Research on Adolescence, 31*(4), 908-927. https://doi.org/10.1111/jora.12678

Bronfenbrenner, U. & Ceci, S. J. (1994) Nature-nurture reconceptualized in developmental perspective: A bioecological model. *Psychological Review, 101*(4), 568-586. https://doi.org/10.1037/0033-295X.101.4.568

Budiman, A. & Ruiz, N. G. (2021) *Asian Americans are the fastest-growing racial or ethnic group in the U.S.* Pew Research Center.

Burke, P. J. & Stets, J. E. (2022) *Identity theory: Revised and expanded.* Oxford University Press.

Ceci, S. J., Ceci, S. W., & Williams, W. M. (2016) How to actualize potential: A bioecological approach to talent development. *Annals of the New York Academy of Sciences, 1377*(1), 10-21. https://doi.org/10.1037/0033-295X.101.4.568

Chang, T. F., Qin, D. B., & Wu, I. H. (2021) Parenting–acculturation match and psychosocial adjustment for academically gifted Chinese American adolescents. *Family Relations, 70*(2), 619-636.

Cheng, A. W., Chang, J., O'Brien, J., Budgazad, M. S., & Tsai, J. (2017) Model minority stereotype: Influence on perceived mental health needs of Asian Americans. *Journal of Immigrant and Minority Health, 19*, 572-581.

Choy, C. C. (2022) *Asian American histories of the United States.* Beacon Press

Crocetti, E. (2017) Identity formation in adolescence: The dynamic of forming and consolidating identity commitments. *Child Development Perspectives, 11*(2), 145-150.

Czopp, A. M., Kay, A. C., & Cheryan, S. (2015) Positive stereotypes are pervasive and powerful. *Perspectives on Psychological Science, 10*(4), 451-463.

Dixson, D. D., Jansen, L., Gentzis, E. A., & Worrell, F. C. (2024). Gifted profiles of hope: Being hopeful is associated with a talent development psychosocial profile in gifted students. *High Ability Studies, 35*(1), 21-43. https://doi.org/10.1080/13598139.2023.2206114

Duyer, S. N., Ozkaya, C., & Akdeniz, H. (2023) A systematic review of the factors affecting twice-exceptional students' social and emotional development.

*Gifted and Talented International, 38*(2), 177-189. https://doi.org/10.1080/15332276.2023.2245861

Gentry, M. & Fugate, C. M. (2018). Attention-Deficit/Hyperactivity Disorder in gifted students. In S. I. Pfeiffer (ed.) *Handbook of giftedness in children* (pp. 575-584). Springer. https://doi.org/10.037/0000038-037.

Greenwood, S. (2022, August) Being Asian in America. [Video]. YouTube. https://www.youtube.com/watch?v=LIIvqJDv6_4

Guyer, A. E., Pérez-Edgar, K., & Crone, E. A. (2018) Opportunities for neurodevelopmental plasticity from infancy through early adulthood. *Child Development, 89*(3), 687-697. doi:10.1111/cdev.13073

Jansen, K. & Kiefer, S. M. (2020) Understanding brain development: Investing in young adolescents' cognitive and social-emotional development. *Middle School Journal, 51*(4), 18-25.

Jen, E., Wu, J., & Gentry, M. (2016) Social and affective concerns high-ability adolescents indicate they would like to discuss with a caring adult: Implications for educators. *Journal of Advanced Academics, 27*(1), 39-59.

Kao, C. & Hebert, T. P. (2006) Gifted Asian American adolescent males: Portraits of cultural dilemmas. *Journal for the Education of the Gifted, 30*(1), 88-117. https://doi.org/10.1177/016235320603000105

Kaplan, S. N. & Mora-Flores, E. (2021) Urban bilingual students. In R. J. Sternberg & D. Ambrose (eds.) *Conceptions of Giftedness and Talent* (pp. 181-194). Palgrave Macmillan.

Kim, J. Y., Block, C. J., & Yu, H. (2021) Debunking the "model minority" myth: How positive attitudes toward Asian Americans influence perceptions of racial microaggressions. *Journal of Vocational Behavior, 131*, 103648.

Kitano, M. K. (2011) Issues in research on Asian American gifted students. In J. A. Castellano & A. D. Frazier (eds.) *Special populations in gifted education: Understanding our most able students from diverse backgrounds* (pp. 3-25). Prufrock Press.

Mahoney, A. S., Martin, D., & Martin, M. (2007) Gifted identity formation: A therapeutic model for counseling gifted children and adolescents. In S. Mendaglio & J. S. Peterson (eds.) *Models of counseling gifted children, adolescents, and young adults* (pp. 199–230). Prufrock Press.

National Association for Gifted Children. (2019) *A definition of giftedness that guides best practice.* https://nagc.org/page/what-is-giftedness

Neihart, M., Pfeiffer, S., & Cross, T. (eds.) (2016) *The social and emotional development of gifted children: What do we know?* (2nd ed.) Prufrock Press.

Nguyen, J. & Ferguson, G. M. (2020). "I kind of have a goal when I do it": The phenomenology of cultural variability in Southeast Asian American tricultural emerging adults. *Emerging Adulthood 8*(5), 382-396. https://doi.org/10.1177/2167696819860392

Park, S. & Foley-Nicpon, M. (2022). Excellence expected, needs overlooked: Implications for working with Asian American twice-exceptional students. *Teaching Exceptional Children, 0*(0). https://doi.org/10.1177/00400599221097020

Park, S., Foley-Nicpon, M., Choate, A., & Bolenbaugh, M. (2018) "Nothing fits exactly": Experiences of Asian American parents of twice-exceptional children. *Gifted Child Quarterly, 62*(3), 306-319. https://doi.org/10.1177/0016986218758442

Parra-Martinez, A. & Treat, A. R. (2022) The rainbow revolution: Empowering gifted LGBTQ+ learners for transformative action. In R. J. Sternberg, D. Ambrose, & S. Karami (eds.) *The Palgrave Handbook of Transformational Giftedness for Education* (pp. 287-312). Palgrave Macmillan.

Pew Research Center. (2021, April 29) Key facts about Asian Americans. https://www.pewresearch.org/short-reads/2021/04/29/key-facts-about-asian-americans/

Peterson, J. S. & Jen, E. (2018) The Peterson Proactive Developmental Attention (PPDA) model: Nurturing the rest of the whole gifted child. *Journal for the Education of the Gifted, 41*(2), 1–25. https://doi.org/10.1177/0162353218763874

Peterson, J. & Jen, E. (2023) The "d" in the Peterson Proactive Developmental Attention (PPDA) model: A lens for understanding and supporting underachievers. *Gifted and Talented International, 38*(1), 62-76.

Peterson, J. S & Peters, D. B., (2021) *Bright, complex kids: Supporting their social and emotional development.* Free Spirit Publishing.

Pfeifer, J. H. & Berkman, E. T. (2018) The development of self and identity in adolescence: Neural evidence and implications for a value-based choice perspective on motivated behavior. *Child Development Perspectives, 12*(3), 158-164.

Plucker, J. A., McWilliams, J., Guo, J. (2021) Smart contexts for 21st century talent development. In R. J. Sternberg & D. Ambrose (eds.) *Conceptions of Giftedness and Talent* (pp. 295-316). Palgrave Macmillan

Price, M. N., Green, A. E., DeChants, J. P., & Davis, C. K. (2021) *The mental health and well-being of Asian American and Pacific Islander (AAPI) LGBTQ youth.* The Trevor Project. https://www.thetrevorproject.org/research-briefs/the-mental-health-and-well-being-of-asian-american-and-pacific-islander-aapi-lgbtq-youth/

Reis, S. M., Baum, S. M, & Burke, E. (2014) An operational definition of twice-exceptional learners: Implications and applications. *Gifted Child Quarterly, 58*(3), 217-230. https://doi.org/10.1177/0016986214534976

Reis, S. M. & Renzulli, S. J. (2021). Parenting for strengths: Embracing the challenges of raising children identified as twice exceptional. *Gifted Education International, 37*(1), 41-53.

Rinn, A. N. (2024). A critique on the current state of research on the social and emotional experiences of gifted individuals and a framework for moving the field forward. *Gifted Child Quarterly, 68*(1), 34-48. https://doi.org/10.1177/00169862231197780

Ryan, R. M. & Deci, E. L. (2017). *Self-determination theory: Basic psychological needs in motivation, development, and wellness.* The Guilford Press. https://doi.org/10.1521/978.14625/28806

Ruiz, N. G., Noe-Bustamante, L., & Shah, S. (2023, May 8) *Diverse cultures and shared experiences shape Asian American identities.* Pew Research Center. https://www.pewresearch.org/race-and-ethnicity/2023/05/08/diverse-cultures-and-shared-experiences-shape-asian-american-identities/

Russell, S. T. & McCurdy, A. L. (2023) Examination of the "model minority" stereotype through ethnicity and sexual orientation heterogeneity among Asian American youth. *Journal of Adolescence, 95*(6), 1258-1273. https://doi.org/10.1002/jad.12200

Silverman, L. K. (2012) Asynchronous development: A key to counseling the gifted. In T. L. Cross & J. R. Cross (eds.) *Handbook for counselors serving students with gifts and talents* (pp. 261-279). Prufrock Press.

Stop AAPI Hate Campaign. (2020) *They blamed me because I am Asian: Findings from reported anti-AAPI youth incidents.* https://stopaapihate.org/wp-content/uploads/2021/04/Stop-AAPI-Hate-Report-Youth-Campaign-200917.pdf

Sullivan, A. L., Kulkarni, T., & Chhuon, V. (2020) Making visible the invisible: Multistudy investigation of disproportionate special education identification of U.S. Asian American and Pacific Islander students. *Exceptional Children, 86*(4), 449-467. https://doi.org/10.1177/0014402920905548

Thompson, T. L., Kiang, L., & Witkow, M. R. (2020) Discrimination, the model minority stereotype, and peer relationships across the high school years. *Journal of Youth and Adolescence, 49*(0), 1884-1896. https://: doi.org/10.1007/s10964-020-01268-0

Tong, P. & An, I. S. (2024) Review of studies applying Bronfenbrenner's bioecological theory in international and intercultural education research. *Frontiers in Psychology, 14.*1233925. https://doi.org/10.3389/fpsyg.2023.1233925

Townsen, G. & Brown, R. (2016) Exploring a sociocultural approach to understanding academic self-concept in twice-exceptional students. *International Journal of Educational Research, 80* (0), 15-24. https://doi.org/10.1016/j.ijer.2016.07.006

Tran, M. & Birman, D. (2010) Questioning the model minority: Studies of Asian American Academic Performance. *Asian American Journal of Psychology, 1*(2), 106-118. https://doi.org/10.1037/a0019965

van Duijenvoorde, A. C. K., Peters, S., Braams, B. R., & Crone, E. A. (2016) What motivates adolescents? Neural responses to rewards and their influence on adolescents' risk taking, learning, and cognitive control. *Neuroscience and Biobehavioral Reviews, 70,* 135-147. doi:10.1016/j.dcn.2015.12.010

Walton, J. & Truong, M. (2022) A review of the model minority myth: Understanding the social, educational and health impacts. *Ethnic and Racial Studies, 46*(3), 391-419. https://doi.org/10.1080/01419870.2022.2121170

Woo, B., Maglalang, D. D., Ko, S., Park M., Choi, Y., & Takeuchi, D. T. (2020) Racial discrimination, ethnic-racial socialization, and cultural identities among Asian American youths. *Cultural Diversity & Ethnic Minority Psychology, 26*(4), 447-459. https://doi.org/10.1037/cdp0000327

Yeung, G. & Mun, R. U. (2022) A renewed call for disaggregation of racial and ethnic data: Advancing scientific rigor and equity in gifted and talented education research. *Journal for the Education of the Gifted, 45*(4), 319-351. https://doi.org/10.1177/01623532221123795

Yoon, Y.S. & Gentry, M. (2009) Racial and ethnic representation in gifted programs: Current status of and implications for gifted Asian American students. *Gifted Child Quarterly, 53*(2), 121-136. https://doi.org/10.1177/0016986208330564

Williams, M. T., Skinta, M. D., & Martin-Willett, R. (2021) After Pierce and Sue: A revised racial microaggressions taxonomy. *Perspectives on Psychological Science, 16*(5), 991-1007. https://doi.org/10.1177/1745691621994247

Xie, M., Jowle, J., Pak, Ip, P. S., Haskin, M., & Yip, T. (2021) Profiles of ethnic-racial identity, socialization, and model minority experiences: associations with well-being among Asian American adolescents. *Journal of Youth Adolescence, 50*(6), 1173-1188. https://doi.org/10.1007/s10964-021-01436-w

# Chapter 7

# The Intersectionality of Native American and Twice-Exceptional Identities

Shana Lusk and Anne Gray

## Positionality Statements

**Shana:** I am a white and Indigenous woman from the Catawba Nation. My educational journey has been influenced by my racialized experiences as well as my intersectional identity. I acknowledge the privilege I hold due to my white-passing appearance, which has given me certain affordances and advantages over others. This privilege necessitates a conscious effort to silence my own voice when appropriate and to confidently share my Indigenous identity without hiding behind my white-passing appearance. Prior to my doctoral studies at the University of Connecticut, I worked as a teacher in Arizona in three schools with primarily non-white students in grades 3-8, all subjects: reading, math, English second language, and gifted. I have had the privilege of working with multiple gifted and talented Indigenous students. My commitment to writing and researching about Indigenous students is driven by my desire to stay connected to my tribe and to contribute my knowledge and experiences toward the betterment of Native American education. This has led me to work on my dissertation examining the school experiences of my fellow tribal members as well as their access to talent development from the period of school integration to present. I want to help future educators of Indigenous students see their talent and recognize their unique backgrounds within the classroom.

**Anne:** I am Biligáana, white, and I have spent my adult life as what could be called "tribal adjacent." My husband and our four children are Diné, Navajo. I have participated with them in traditional ceremonies. The majority of people within our community are Native American. We have a home and have lived on the Navajo Nation Reservation, and the times we don't live there full time we travel back regularly to be "home." I worked for six years at the local Bureau of Indian Education Community School teaching K-8 gifted, creative and talented Diné students. I strive to be a good relation to Native American educational practitioners, researchers, and academics, and to work for changes to the education system identified by this community, for this community.

We begin this chapter on the intersectionality of Native American and twice-exceptional identities with Patricia's story of resilience and resistance.

# Patricia

*Patricia Leach is a member of the Catawba tribe in the United States. She grew up on the reservation and had numerous cultural opportunities. Her grandfather was known as the tribal greeter and both her mother and father had refined skill in many tribal arts, particularly pottery. She grew up going to PowWows every year to sell their art as the family's main source of income. Despite these beautiful experiences, she lived in poverty. She recalls not having running water until she was older. Prior to entering the public school system, she was tested for academic placement. Patricia's mother has told her she tested as high IQ. She remembers teaching herself how to read before she started school. Even though she was identified as a promising future student, many of her worst experiences growing up came from the school system.*

*When she started school, Patricia was unchallenged and remembers always being bored. She remembers easily passing tests without studying. These strengths were overlooked entirely. She was treated poorly at school by adults and feels it was because she was Native American and living in poverty. Patricia stated, "They treated most of the kids from the reservation like we were dumb." In the second grade, a teacher stabbed her in the back multiple times with a pencil. She felt like she couldn't say anything, or she would get in trouble. By the third grade, Patricia was convinced that school was not the place for her. When she started middle school, her older brother had a reputation for getting in trouble and she felt like his reputation clouded the way she was perceived: "I felt like I was being judged for no reason, and I guess I just gave them a reason."* Patricia started to get in fights and skip school. She started to act out and got in trouble often and eventually she was expelled from school for her behavior. She later would go on to test out of high school at 16 with little effort.

Patricia realized that a lot of her struggles and behavioral challenges in schooling were due to attention issues. As an adult, she diagnosed herself with ADHD but didn't follow up with a doctor for a decade. She remarked, "I had been just dealing with it for so long and was used to it" and "I just thought I was different or weird." The doctor confirmed that she had ADHD as well as anxiety and prescribed medication. She was receiving medication through the tribal clinic, but due to access issues she has had to struggle with self-regulation.

Patricia has always felt proud to be Native American. She worked in many capacities after her time in school from the senior center to workforce development. Though Patricia spent many years recovering from the trauma of schooling, she decided to try again at a collegiate level. Despite a break from school, she scored high in all her college entrance exams, except math. She jokes that she thinks she that is because she always skipped school during math. She ended up getting bachelor's and master's degrees in business. Some tribal members saw her potential and recognized her talent. She was encouraged to run for tribal leadership and was elected. In 2023, she was elected as the tribe's first female assistant-chief. She hopes to serve as an example, helping other tribal members reach their full potential.

Although she has struggled with being ADHD and gifted, Patricia has experienced joy: "I enjoy the way my brain works sometimes. I don't have to put much effort into things and ideas or solutions come easily to me. Often, I don't even know how I know things but just do." The main challenge she faces is procrastination. She always knew she would do something at the very last moment and used to stress about it. "I finally learned to trust myself and my process, which has made it less stressful. I keep trying to stay organized but still struggle with 'doom piles.'"

Patricia's experiences in the K-12 educational system in the US were not good—but, more importantly, they are not unique. Little would you know …

# [In]Visibility

"Native Americans are, perversely, the most visible invisible minority" (Treuer, 2020). Native Americans[1] are misrepresented in the media, depicted as "frozen in time" (Leavitt, 2015, p. 43) from stories set in the eighteenth or nineteenth centuries, as mascots for sports teams, as negative stereotypes of drunks, living in poverty and living on government assistance; and are considered to be separate from American culture (Fryberg & Townsend, 2008; Leavitt, 2015).

Studies about Indigenous schooling often focus less on opportunities for success and more on poverty, substance abuse, and dropout rates (Brandt, 1992; Faircloth & Tippeconnic, 2010; Friese et al., 2015). Additionally, this research often homogenizes Native Americans into one grouping rather than acknowledging the over 600 culturally and linguistically distinct nations, tribes, bands, and villages within the US today. Native American students are not accounted for in educational reform. They may be mentioned in accordance with a politically correct listing of all races, as part of Title VI: Indian, Native Hawaiian, and Alaska Native Education initiatives in and around Indian Country; or, most commonly, represented by an asterisk which notes their population size, rendering insignificant or problematic results for analysis (the asterisk is used when the number of students in a subgroup do not meet the federal threshold for reporting). Native Americans have been one of the most neglected groups in educational research (Foley & Skenandore, 2003). The issue of Native American boarding schools has received the most attention in research and news coverage (Bowker 2017; Estabrook, 2023; Feir, 2016; Johnston & Zhang, 2023; Przystupa, 2020), once again relegating Native peoples to the historic past and not representing them as contemporary peoples.

Native American students suffer chronically from underrepresentation in gifted education (Gentry & Gray, 2021), are overrepresented in special education (Collier, 2012), and often feel invisible (Green, 2018) and unsupported by schools (Masta, 2018). While special reports on the state of Indian education may be published, even regularly, transformative change for the educational success of Native Americans has not happened. The American educational system continues to center Anglo and Western norms of learning behavior for academic success. For Native students to be academically successful, they are expected to assimilate to these norms (Feir, 2016) and to be resilient, daily, against the direct and indirect messaging of the wrongness of their culture.

## A Place in Gifted and Special Education Services

Patricia's mother was told Patricia was gifted during an in-home screening visit prior to her starting school. Patricia had already taught herself to read and scored highly in the tests that were administered. Unfortunately, her advanced academic abilities and intelligence were never mentioned by an educator again. In school, Patricia was unchallenged and always bored and passed tests with little effort. She remembers struggling to pay attention and feeling like she was always in trouble.

While there is a growing body of educational research literature by Native education scholars with Native communities for Native students, there is little on gifted, special, or twice-exceptional education. The extant literature in these areas often homogenizes Native Americans and makes sweeping assumptions about these youth and their experiences. (Gentry & Fugate, 2012; Gentry et al., 2014; Gentry & Gray, 2021). Native American, Black/African American, and Hispanic/Latino students historically lack proportional representation in gifted education (Gentry et al., 2019; Gentry & Gray, 2021; Peters et al., 2019). For Native American students, this perpetuates the assumption that Native students lack talent (Payne, 2011).

In special education, these same groups of students experience over-identification for services; while "American Indian/Alaska Native students are 96 percent more likely to be identified as having a disability" (Western Educational Equity Assistant Center, 2023, p. 15). Collier (2012) identified three major concerns for Native students regarding special education services: disproportionality in identification and placement, limited access to appropriate curriculum, and limited staff or personnel that come from the same cultural background. American Indian/Alaska Native students are not proportionally represented in either gifted education (under-identified) or special education (over-identified).

This under-representation in gifted education and over-representation in special education of Native American students highlights the lack of cultural understanding and the continued deficit perspective of Native peoples and cultures codified by US policies of Indian education. The misrepresentation of Native American students in these programs leaves many students feeling out of place and invisible in educational spaces (Voice Yellowfish, 2022). Additionally, the lack of representation of Native American cultures past the early 1900s in 87% of US history standards (Shear et al., 2015) and of contemporary Native American professionals across the curriculum reinforces these experiences. For us, these issues raise questions regarding their correlation to the higher dropout rate for Native American students (Western Educational Equity Assistant Center, 2023); or, as Johnston-Goodstar and Reholt (2017) identified the issue, Native American students have a high *pushout* rate.

Given the lack of information about Native Americans in both gifted education and special education, it is unsurprising that twice-exceptional research is lacking. One special education teacher stated, "I experienced an education where Native Americans were not portrayed as having active, thriving tribal communities," and revealed that her teacher training did not prepare her to work with Indigenous students (Campbell, 2022, p. 2). Furthermore, much of the terminology we use regarding gifted, special, and twice-exceptional education carries meanings specific to the education profession and is used in conversations with families by the educator from a deficit perspective.

## Tribal Critical Race Theory

Tribal Critical Race Theory (TribalCrit) is a theoretical lens that provides a framework for building dialogues which touch on the relationship of Native American/Alaska Natives to the US federal government. The tenets of TribalCrit provide grounding points for us as we discuss the experiences of Native American/Alaska Natives with the US education system and how these experiences are symptomatic of the liminal space Native people occupy in this relationship—politically, legally, and as racialized bodies (Brayboy, 2005). One of the tenets of TribalCrit is that colonization and assimilation are endemic to society (Brayboy, 2005). Native American history with schooling has largely been to force children to white values, wear white clothing, and abandon their "savage" ways. Native Americans have often been rewarded for choosing to give up their traditional culture, which creates a unique lived experience for Indigenous people (Brayboy et al., 2014). This practice continues today. Consciously and subconsciously, schools play active roles in dismissing and removing the culture of Indigenous students. A few of the ways this happens is through expected behaviors in school, styles of teaching and learning, and communication expectations.

Patricia's defiance in school partly emerged due to colonization. She felt that the judgment that befell her at such a young age came from the cultural disconnection of school and their viewpoints of her having no place there. There was plenty of intergenerational trauma that Patricia already had to contend with prior to setting foot in her elementary school. Many of Patricia's older family members mentioned being called "livestock" and "dumb Indian." Her story matches theirs in many ways and brings callbacks to the essentialization of Natives as being ignorant. Systemic racism led teachers to have lower expectations of her, take extreme disciplinary action toward her, and promote a curriculum that did not represent her. She was physically attacked by a teacher in the second grade and never reported it because she did not think she would be believed. Since Patricia was being treated like she was incapable in school, she "gave them a reason" to believe that. After the second grade, Patricia only had one way to fight back against these oppressive systems: by not listening to her teachers. She went on to get expelled from school due to a system that had set her up to fail.

## Resistance and Resilience

Patricia attended the same middle school her older brother had gone to, where he had a reputation for getting into trouble. She felt like his reputation was immediately attached to her. Patricia started getting into fights and skipping school: "I felt like I was being judged for no reason, so I guess I just gave them a reason." She was in trouble often and eventually was expelled from high school for her behavior. Even so, at 16, with no preparation and little effort, Patricia passed the high-school equivalency exam.

At school, Patricia received no recognition or fostering of her advanced intellectual and academic abilities or support for her difficulties with attention. She experienced consistent microaggressions, punctuated by actual physical aggression, from a school culture that found little value in her and viewed her primarily, if not solely, from a deficit perspective.

In contrast, Patricia was a valued member of her family and community. Her parents were renowned potters in the traditional style of her tribe. She traveled with them to PowWows where her parents made the family income selling their pottery. Her grandfather held the position of tribal greeter and Patricia participated in the traditional ceremonies of her tribal community. These are the experiences that sustained her and from which her identity as a member of her family and tribal community grew, giving her a protective resilience to her school experiences. When asked what she thought of her advanced intelligence, ease with academics, and issues with attention at that time, she replied: "I just thought I was different or weird."

In a study of protective factors associated with resilience in Navajo adolescents, a connection to their tribal culture safeguarded the youth against the negative effects of their experiences of discrimination (Galliher et al., 2011). In her research, Masta (2018) identified silence as an accommodation strategy used by Native American students attending a inantly white Midwestern school. "Accommodation" is defined as "a process in which students make the decision to adopt some practices or values for the benefit it provides the student" (Masta, 2018, p 31) The students used silence to avoid calling attention to themselves in a school climate where the attention they received was invariably negative. They used silence to withdraw from interactions that would require them to behave in ways that would conflict with their identity as a member of their tribe. Silence was also used as refusal: refusal as resistance to the assimilative policies and practices of the school that reward adaptation to dominant cultural norms.

## Educator Bias and Deficit Perspectives

For Native Americans, the further mismatch between the school environment and the home environment can lead to pushing a student out and seeing learning gaps where they might not be present. Some of the ways this can emerge is through stereotyping, having lower expectations, cultural mismatches, behavior responses, and in the curriculum and pedagogical practices. If an educator holds stereotypical beliefs about Native Americans, they might automatically think that a student is less interested in or capable of academic success. There may be a perceived lack of parent involvement which garners the need for understanding the family's cultural approach to schooling. For example, the family may feel that contacting their child's teacher about academics may be overstepping their role. Every teacher has had a different relationship with each family and therefore each teacher prior to the current year has set the tone and stage differently. Native American students could end up being disciplined more frequently due to cultural misunderstandings. One example of this is not making direct eye contact being seen as defiance in one culture and respectful in another, which could lead to further disciplinary action. Furthermore, a teacher might praise basic compliance in a patronizing way more so than with other students. Students might disengage from curricular content that makes Native Americans seem like obstacles to progress and might therefore be singled out for not paying attention or calling attention to this. Table 7.1 shows some specific examples of behavior and outcomes that might occur in the classroom based on real-life examples.

In each of these scenarios, a different choice could be made—whether by discussing the issue with students and families or considering the students' cultural lens. In Scenario 1 and Scenario 2, the teacher needs to be aware that they have characterized a student as lazy, inattentive, or uncaring. Just like any student, the communication style may be different, resulting in conflicting viewpoints about expectations. In some Native American tribes, there is a collectivist orientation, meaning they emphasize the group over oneself, leading them not to want to participate in competitive activities. The only way to understand if this is the case is by discussing this with their family or the student themselves, or considering the lens of the culture. Alternatively, the teacher could offer other pathways for sharing responses. such as writing, drawing, or more wait time to gather thoughts. In Scenario 3, the coach should consider if there is systemic bias instead of just adhering to policy. This coach did not listen to the reasoning of the parent about the importance of their son keeping their hair long. This resulted in lost opportunities to learn from one another. They should either allow the student outright on the baseball team or advocate for the student to be able to be on the team despite having longer hair. For Scenario 4, the teacher may not understand that they are asking students to write from the side of an oppressor and, more specifically, to justify cruelty that befell their own families. Even attempting this assignment could be considered disrespectful to their entire tribal community. The student should be offered a different assignment, or the assignment could be removed for the entire class. For Scenario 5, the teacher should set up norms or explain what answers should look like prior to having students think about how they would respond. If answer-sharing expectations are made apparent, it is less likely that the student will misunderstand how to respond to the directive.

*Table 7.1* Specific examples of Native American cultural differences with negative reactions

| Cultural expectations | Example | Reaction |
|---|---|---|
| *Scenario 1*: Communication expectations | A student is part of a tribe that emphasizes silence when they are unsure of the answer or are not the most important person in the room, whether that be an elder or authority figure. They do not share their thoughts on the answer to a math problem in class. | The teacher prompts them to share their thinking and interprets their silence as a lack of engagement. The teacher asks them to stay in during recess to share their thoughts since they are *not trying* in class. |
| *Scenario 2*: Participation expectations | A student is part of a tribe that emphasizes cooperation and silently opts out of competitive activities. During a classroom game where students have to hit buzzers to answer questions, the student sits at the back of their group without contributing. The other students are quick to answer the questions to win and do not engage with the student. | The teacher makes some remarks to the entire class that everyone needs to share. Instead of addressing expectations or talking with the student directly, they are docked points for participation that day. |
| *Scenario 3*: Appearance expectations | A student has been excited to be a part of the baseball team at their school. They keep their hair long as a symbol of their spirit and connection to their tribe. The baseball team has an expectation of short hair. With the encouragement of their mom, they decide to try out anyway. | The coach says that their hair is out of compliance and that they will not make it on to the team. Afterwards, they tell their mother what happened. She requests a meeting with the coach to explain the traditional reasons why their son keeps their hair long. The coach says it is out of his control and that it is a rule to participate on the team. |

(*Continued*)

*Table 7.1* Specific examples of Native American cultural differences with negative reactions (*Continued*)

| Cultural expectations | Example | Reaction |
|---|---|---|
| Scenario 4: Assignment expectations | In history class, a student from the reservation is assigned to write about the Trail of Tears. Specifically, they are asked to write about both negative and positive implications of the event. The student tells the teacher that they cannot complete the assignment because there was nothing good that occurred for their family during that event in history. | The teacher tells the student that they need to have a more neutral lens when it comes to historical events. When the student doesn't comply, they give them an incomplete on the assignment. |
| Scenario 5: Knowledge-sharing expectations | In class, a teacher asks all the students to think about how they came up with the answer to a multiple-choice question in the reading. After some wait time, they call on a Native American student who tells everyone step by step the ways they explored their answer selected. They know that when they share with family members at home, they need to tell the full story, as storytelling is a large part of their culture. The student still has more to share after two minutes. | The teacher cuts them off and asks them to summarize what they did instead of taking up so much class time. The student becomes silent, since they hadn't thought about making their answer shorter. The teacher moves on and selects another student. |

*Note.* Consider the examples above and how you would react. Consider if you have had similar reactions. How could the educator adjust their reaction?

# Academic Considerations and Recommendations

Patricia's story could have been different. School could have been a place where she was propelled forward and was able to find meaning in her life at a younger age. Instead, school was something that Patricia had to overcome. The reason for Patricia's success is her resilience. Most of Patricia's educators did not intend schooling to be an obstacle. This shows that educators and administrators must make a conscious choice to employ techniques to ensure that Native American students feel as comfortable as possible in their school environments. If intentional efforts are made, there will be fewer children who must overcome and more children who are served by the school system.

## Individual Knowledge

Many Native American tribes are thought to be the same, without separate cultures, traditions, languages, and people (Gentry & Gray, 2021). This homogenization leads to misunderstandings about the wants and desires of the community. The best thing an educator working with these populations can do is get to know the tribal members within their community. This can be done prior to a student being enrolled. Many tribes have events that are open to the public. Attend a festival, visit the tribe's cultural center, and ask the family of a student you work with how you can get to know more and/or get a sense of their tribal connection. Engaging in these ways will give you a sense of the history and a foundational knowledge to proceed in getting to know students as individuals. Many Native American art forms tie to gifts and talents like artistry as nonverbal ability, storytelling as verbal ability, dancing as math ability with rhythm counts, and other unique examples. Tribes can have varying ideas about the role of elders and how to question authority figures within and outside of the tribe. This could result in a student not speaking up or a student questioning more than other students within the class. Consider how a student from this tribe's exposure might present their gifts and how a student from this tribe might show or hide their struggles within the classroom. There could be school differences as well. A student might have attended their reservation school first and therefore have deeper knowledge of their culture but might not have the same expectations as their current school. Moreover, it is essential to consider the tribe's historical and intergenerational relationship with schooling—how many generations have lived with the legacy of boarding schools and forced integration, and whether the tribe has had to fight for state recognition. These experiences deeply shape community trust, educational engagement, and the ways in which schools are perceived by tribal families.

*Table 7.2* Steps to understanding a student's Native American culture

| | |
|---|---|
| **Step 1** | **Learn about and get to know the tribes near your school or district.** |
| Step 2 | Think about the skills and experiences that a student from this tribe may have developed through their interactions with the tribe. |
| Step 3 | Learn about the specific relationship the family and student has with the tribe. |
| Step 4 | Think about the unique lens the student has in teaching and learning. |

**Note:** Not all students who are Indigenous look Native American. This is due to colonization and assimilation. It is a good idea to ask families what cultures they identify with to ensure you are considering the right things for each child.

Once this foundation knowledge has been acquired, consider the unique relationship that each family has to their tribe. Some members are highly involved in traditions and some families have suffered through many generations of colonization and feel disconnected. By getting to know students, their culture, and their specific families, an educator is less likely to consider a student through a deficit lens by focusing on perceived shortcomings. Instead, they have a better chance of recognizing strengths and potential within their Native culture. Whenever considering if a student requires modified education, think about the differences between a deficit lens and true struggle. Make accommodations to the instructional inputs and outputs in accordance with what you have learned about your specific students first. Table 7.2 shows the basal knowledge steps an educator needs to understand before addressing a Native American student's needs.

## Cultural Responsiveness in the Classroom

Funds of knowledge were first developed to describe the accumulated abilities of Mexican-American students in Tucson, Arizona (Vélez-Ibáñez & Greenberg, 1992) and have since been used more broadly to help with cultural responsiveness. Schools have often played a role in assimilating and oppressing Native Americans (Waterman, 2019), and there is no way to erase this ideology from classroom settings. Educators need to take the time to understand the positive aspects or funds of knowledge that come from growing up Native American. Notice the cultural practices and traditions. Think about what skills come from these traditions that could show up in the classroom, such as pattern recognition, teamwork, creativity, and construction. Even tribes who have lost their language due to forced assimilation often have words they use among those in their community, giving them multiple language exposures. Moreover, Indigenous families are often more connected due to traditions of elders passing on knowledge to younger generations. Incorporating cultural practices and traditions within the classroom where appropriate could be helpful in applying these skills to subject learning. Helping to preserve language within the classroom can aid in creating classroom and cultural interconnectedness. Going back to TribalCrit, an educator who is knowledgeable about the tenets of colonization and assimilation could vet materials to ensure that Native Americans are not written about as an obstacle within the texts they are reading; locate sources written by Indigenous people in reading and social studies to ensure the Native point of view is included; and consider the behavior of their students through a cultural lens before doling out punishment.

Ways of knowing (Barnhardt & Kawagley, 2005) highlights the neglect of Indigenous cultural practices in the classroom (Gay, 2002). Schools often do not consider Indigenous worldviews, knowledge, and perspective when implementing lessons and curriculum which could improve Native American outcomes (Kawagley, 1995; McCarty & Lee, 2017). More specifically, this is a way of considering curriculum through a Native American lens and often refers to emphasizing interconnectedness of the mind and spirit in learning, learning through experiences in the local area and environment, prioritizing storytelling as a traditional art, and sharing knowledge and values of history through a Native context. Through Indigenous ways of knowing, students should have a community-centered education in which knowledge is shared and used to further their fellow tribal members. Elders are often held in high esteem in Native communities and should be invited into schools to share their cultural knowledge with educators and students to increase interconnectedness and collaboration. Cultural and spiritual practices— like rituals, ceremonies, spiritual beliefs, and stories—should be considered as part of the learning process. One example of using ways of knowing is incorporating Native American stories from the community to enhance a lesson about the environment. See how you can include these methods in the telling of other stories such as "case studies, biographies, fiction, and oral history" (University of Denver, n.d.)

Another important aspect to consider is "place-based education" (PBE)—a process coined by Laurie Lane-Zucker that emphasizes humans, animals, plants, and the environment, and their relationships with one another (Larson, 2020). PBE "emphasizes learning through an understanding of where you live and who are your neighbors" (Wisconsin First Nations, 2024). Many Native American tribes place a strong emphasis on the environment when educating their children about the world. Educators should consider the specific location of the school and its place in history. Students need to consider how long humans have lived in a location, who has lived in that location over time, what tribes are around, and who is in the classroom (Wisconsin First Nations, 2024). Implementing PBE requires that educators look into the historical context of Native Americans within the tribe, as well as how they are considered at present. Examining cultural dynamics in your area is an important piece of this history. Are Native Americans ignored, othered, or talked about through a deficit lens? The answers will help you see what is already being done to *include* Native Americans and what is actively being done to *exclude* them. Often, this will be reflected in the recognition of Native American existence, contributions, and mistreatment. A lack of mention, one-sided representation, and discussion of Native Americans solely as a victimized group are disempowering and can make Native kids feel like they do not belong in school. By including PBE with Native Americans as part of the story, you can help contribute to an environment in which Indigenous students see themselves in their curriculum. Examples of PBE include considering natural features of the land in studies (e.g., aquifers and water sources), local tourism (where people visit and why), local cuisine, civics, and service.

Every subject can incorporate Native American knowledge and perspectives. Table 7.3 shows specific examples of teachers taking accountability to decolonize education. These teacher examples highlight the steps that should be taken, but also the practicality of implementing cultural responsiveness for Native American students.

Many of the above examples can be extended to other cultures, which increases their impact. In Scenario 1, we see a teacher ensuring the Indigenous perspective is represented in the classroom. All perspectives are important to consider in teaching history. Showing multiple lenses is a way to enhance the critical thinking of all students within the classroom, while extending connection and visibility. In Scenario 2, the teacher incorporates ways of knowing into the science curriculum. Many biology-based lessons can account for Indigenous knowledge of the world. In Scenario 3, the English teacher tackles representation by way of ensuring representation in reading material and encouraging connection to self. In Scenario 4, the teacher demonstrates the math concepts that already exist within nature, their tribe, and the world. They build on funds of knowledge to make math more accessible. In Scenario 5, the teacher does not show negativity toward cultural practices or discourage the student from participating. The teacher helps them create a path to meet the classroom criteria while also honoring their culture.

## Identification and Services

For students who are labeled as needing special education or gifted services, the perceptions of these labels can vary when it comes to any parent. Many Native American communities have felt left out of discussions about schooling

Table 7.3 Examples of cultural responsiveness for Native American students

| Subject area | Example | Steps taken |
|---|---|---|
| *Scenario 1*: History curriculum | The school's history curriculum includes a unit on the Lewis and Clark expedition. However, the teacher notices that it lacks information on the Native American experience. | • The teacher examines the Native American perspective, noting that the expedition led to loss of land and cultural ways.<br>• They include stories about the forced removal of Native Americans for settlers' land.<br>• They contact a Shoshone historian to discuss the expedition's impact on their community. The lesson emphasizes the importance of considering the Native American perspective. |
| *Scenario 2*: Science curriculum | A teacher is beginning a unit on ecology and aims to include Indigenous ways of knowing in their science lessons. | • The teacher researches local tribal resources and stories to include in the lessons. They invite elders from the tribe to speak on the topic if they are interested.<br>• They investigate traditional farming techniques and teach about how Native Americans managed land.<br>• During classroom discussions, students are encouraged to explore how traditional and scientific knowledge can complement each other.<br>• The teacher considers organizing a field trip to observe traditional land management and farming practices firsthand and ask questions. |

(*Continued*)

Table 7.3 Examples of cultural responsiveness for Native American students (*Continued*)

| Subject area | Example | Steps taken |
|---|---|---|
| *Scenario 3:* English curriculum | A teacher at a new school reviews the English reading list from previous years and observes the various cultures represented. Upon examination, they note the absence of Native American representation. | • The teacher adds Native American authors to the reading list based on the genre and time period being represented.<br>• Students are asked to relate each piece of literature to their own stories of resilience, community, and more through a project or journaling. They are also asked to find their own literature to share with the class when they come across it.<br>• The teacher has students compare themes from each reading to identify similarities and differences throughout the year, highlighting interconnectedness and conflict. |
| *Scenario 4:* Math curriculum | A teacher notices some Native American students struggling with math and adjusts their teaching style to be more inclusive. | • They explore the concept of anti-oppressive math education, incorporating Indigenous knowledge and its connection to the land. They include elements of nature or Native art to examine the mathematical concepts within them.<br>• They modify problems to represent issues in the community, demonstrating that math can help present issues to bring about change or honor knowledge. Math problems become connected to the place, a story from the tribe, cultural practices, and perspectives.<br>• They ask students if they know their Native language numbers and learn together from their shared knowledge. This approach is applied to all languages represented in the classroom, where they also learn numbers one to ten. |

(*Continued*)

Table 7.3 Examples of cultural responsiveness for Native American students (*Continued*)

| Subject area | Example | Steps taken |
|---|---|---|
| Scenario 5: Timeline | A Native American student informs their teacher they will miss a few weeks of class for a ceremony that requires travel. | • The teacher conveys enthusiasm and curiosity about the ceremony, asking pertinent questions. Additionally, they inquire if the student would like to share their experience with the class upon returning.<br>• The teacher strategically adjusts the assignments scheduled during that period to ensure essential knowledge is acquired without overburdening the student.<br>• The teacher advocates for the student's attendance not to be negatively impacted by discussing the matter with administration and highlighting existing policies accommodating other religious practices. |

and thus have determined that education has little or no value and have disregarded these labels entirely. Having active and participatory conversations about what it means for their child to be in gifted and special education services can help keep families and educators on the same page. Furthermore, it ensures that families have a say about what happens within their education and are welcome participants on campus. It takes time to build trust in these situations, but if each educator works toward providing authentic, open invitations, cultural and classroom learning can continue in both environments. School staff should not have an expectation about the community's reaction to the child's needs and therefore should have open invitations about interest, concerns, indifference, or confusion. Cultural perspectives on gifts and learning disabilities can diverge considerably. For example, some Native cultures do not believe in defining someone separately from the community as being more special or different. It is important to ensure a shared understanding of these terms. Holding duality in these terms is essential in describing a student's exceptionalities and needs.

Native American students were not considered in the inception of gifted services. Like other students of color, there needs to be multiple pathways for identification. This comes with implementing universal screening and use of local norms to improve equity (Peters et al., 2019). This also means screening and considering students who are identified as needing special education. It doesn't end at twice exceptional; every student should be considered for multiple exceptionalities in their academic career. It is important not to homogenize Native American students, and this further extends to students who are already identified as twice exceptional.

## Family and Community Involvement

Involve families by giving multiple invitations for participation in the academic services of the child. Let the families set the tone for involvement and what will be done for their child in school settings to ensure they feel they are a meaningful part of the academic team. Due to historical colonization and mistreatment, some Indigenous families may approach schooling with skepticism regarding labels. Ensure that you are offering multiple entry points for involvement and communication. If phone calls do not work, send a text. If texts do not work, send an email or a letter. If letters do not work, consider a home visit. Finding volunteers for the school to help reach out could be another step in facilitating relationships. If a family does not want their child involved in services, build trust by forging relationships.

## Final Thoughts

Visible and invisible minority students are present in nearly all classrooms in the United States. Various factors in their lived experiences, including biases within the school system and life experiences outside of it, may impact their educational journey. To improve educational experiences and outcomes for Native American students, educators should take time to learn about local tribes and the students in their classrooms. Educators, families, and community members must be willing and able to adjust both inside and outside the classroom. By considering the unique challenges and opportunities presented by each student's environment, educators and parents can better support their development and help them achieve their full potential.

Currently, Patricia serves as assistant chief and has a thriving family life. Her story demonstrates the importance of resilience and maintaining cultural identity. Despite the challenges she encountered, Patricia exemplifies the qualities of a role model by maintaining her heritage and applying her skills and talents effectively. Patricia persevered despite her school experiences. She deserved better educational experiences, as do the students who follow her.

### Things to Consider

- Native American students who are also twice exceptional often face compounded marginalization due to their dual identities.
- These students may experience a disconnect between their cultural identity and school expectations, leading to feelings of invisibility, misunderstanding, and misplacement in both gifted and special education programs.
- Deficit-based interpretations of behavior (e.g., silence, lack of eye contact, resistance to competition) lead to misdiagnosis or exclusion rather than support or recognition of talent.
- Traditional cultural practices (e.g., storytelling, cooperative values, long hair, ceremonial absence) are often misunderstood or penalized in schools, instead of being seen as assets.
- One-size-fits-all strategies do not work for Native students. Teachers must build authentic relationships with families, learn about specific tribal cultures, and include community voices in planning. This requires intentional trust-building, open communication, and respect for diverse cultural values and educational perspectives.

## For Discussion

- How does a 2e Native American student experience schooling in the United States?
- In what ways might the educational experiences of a 2e Native American student differ within a reservation school setting?
- Considering that the 2e designation is primarily relevant within the Western educational system, how could such identification impact Indigenous students, positively or negatively?
- What strategies should educational institutions implement to prepare educators to effectively support and nurture the gifts and talents of Native American students?

## Note

1 In this chapter, the terms "Native American," "American Indian," and "Alaska Native", "Indigenous," "Indian," and "Native" are used interchangeably to refer to the descendants of the first inhabitants of the 49 continental states of the US. "Indigenous" is a much broader term referring to descendants of the first inhabitants of any lands that were later colonized.

## References

Adams, D. W. (1995) *Education for extinction: American Indians and the boarding school experience, 1875-1928.* University Press of Kansas.

Battiste, M. (2002) *Indigenous knowledge and pedagogy in First Nations education: A literature review with recommendations.* National Work Group on Education and the Minister of Indian Affairs, Indian and Northern Affairs Canada. https://www.nipissingu.ca/sites/default/files/2018-06/Indigenous%20Knowledge%20and%20Pedagogy%20.pdf

Brandt, E. A. (1992) The Navajo area student dropout study: Findings and implications. *Journal of American Indian Education, 31*(2), 48-63.

Barnhardt, R. & Kawagley, A. O. (2005) Indigenous knowledge systems and Alaska Native ways of knowing. *Anthropology & Education Quarterly, 36*(1), 8-23. https://doi.org/10.1525/aeq.2005.36.1.008

Brayboy, B. K. J. (2005) Toward a Tribal Critical Race Theory in education. *The Urban Review, 37*(5), 425-446.

Brayboy, B. M. J., Castagno, A. E., & Solyom, J. A. (2014) Looking into the hearts of Native peoples: Nation building as an institutional orientation for graduate education. *American Journal of Education, 120*(4), 575-596.

Campbell, J. (2022) *The Indigenous perspective on disability and special education in public schools: A professional development for school staff supporting students in special education.* Northern Arizona University. https://in.nau.edu/wp-content/uploads/sites/101/2023/02/Jaclyn-Campbell-2022.pdf

Collier, C. (2012, May-June) Special education for Indigenous students. *NABE Perspectives*, 9-10.

Estabrook, R. (2023) For the first time, Colorado details dark historical chapter of attempted forced assimilation of Indigenous children in extensive report. *CPR News*, October 3. https://www.cpr.org/2023/10/03/state-investigation-report-released-indian-boarding-schools/

Faircloth, S. C. & Tippeconnic, J. W., III. (2010) *The dropout/graduation rate crisis among American Indian and Alaska Native students: Failure to respond places the future of Native peoples at risk.* The Civil Rights Project/Proyecto Derechos Civiles at UCLA. https://civilrightsproject.ucla.edu/research/k-12-education/school-dropouts/the-dropout-graduation-crisis-among-american-indian-and-alaska-native-students-failure-to-respond-places-the-future-of-native-peoples-at-risk/faircloth-tippeconnic-native-american-dropouts.pdf/view?searchterm=faircloth

Feir, D. L. (2016). The long-term effects of forcible assimilation policy: The case of Indian boarding schools. *The Canadian Journal of Economics, 49*(2), 433-480. https://doi.org/10.1111/caje.12203

Foley, K. & Skenandore, O. (2003) Gifted education for the American Indian Student. In J. Castellano (ed.) *Special populations in gifted education: Working with diverse gifted learners.* Allyn & Bacon.

Friese, B., Grube, J. W., & Seninger, S. (2015) Drinking among Native American and White Youths: The role of perceived neighborhood and school environment. *Journal of Ethnicity in Substance Abuse, 14*(3), 287-307. https://doi.org/10.1080/15332640.2014.994723

Gay, G. (2002) Preparing for culturally responsive teaching. *Journal of Teacher Education, 53*(2), 106-116.

Gentry, M. & Fugate, C. M. (2012) Gifted Native American students: Underperforming, under-identified, and overlooked. *Psychology in the Schools, 49*(7), 631-646.

Gentry, M., & Gray. A. (2021) American Indian and Alaska Native Youth identified as gifted: Access, representation, and missingness. *Journal of American Indian Education, 60*(1-2), 123-161. https://doi.org/10.5749/jamerindieduc.60.1-2.0123

Green, E. L. & Waldman, A. (2019) "I feel invisible": Native students languish in public schools. *The New York Times,* January 2. https://www.nytimes.com/2018/12/28/us/native-american-education.html?unlocked_article_code=1.ok0.bwmY.JQmtJp7Z-8dr&smid=url-share

Johnston, T. & Zhang, C. (2023) *The Native American boarding school system*. *The New York Times*, August 30. https://www.nytimes.com/interactive/2023/08/30/us/native-american-boarding-schools.html

Kawagley, A. O. (1995) *A Yupiaq worldview: A pathway to ecology and spirit*. Waveland Press, Inc.

Larson, S. (2020, July 31). *Place-based learning, outreach, and climate change education*. National Center for Science Education. https://ncse.ngo/place-based-learning-outreach-and-climate-change-education

Leavitt, P. A., Covarrubias, R., Perez, Y. A., & Fryberg, S. A. (2015) "Frozen in time": The impact of Native American media representations on identity and self-understanding. *Journal of Social Issues*, *71*(1), 39-53. https://doi.org/10.1111/josi.12095

McCarty, T. L. & Lee, T. S. (2017) Critical culturally sustaining/revitalizing pedagogy and Indigenous education sovereignty. *Harvard Educational Review*, *84*(1), 101-124.

Payne, A. (2011) *Equitable access for underrepresented students in gifted education*. The George Washington University Center for Equity and Excellence in Education. https://files.eric.ed.gov/fulltext/ED539772.pdf

Peters, S., Gentry, M., Whiting, G. W., & McBee, M. T. (2019) Who gets served in gifted education? Demographic representation and a call for action. *Gifted Child Quarterly*, *63*(4), 273-287. https://doi.org/10.1177/0016986219833738

Przystupa, P. (2020). The archaeology of Native American boarding schools in the American Southwest. *Journal of Southwestern Anthropology and History*, *86*(2). https://doi-org.ezproxy.lib.uconn.edu/10.1080/00231940.2020.1747796

Treuer (2020). *Invisibility, disappearance, and the Native American future*. Claremont McKenna College. https://www.cmc.edu/athenaeum/invisibility-disappearance-and-native-american-future

Vélez-Ibáñez, C. G. & Greenberg, J. B. (1992) Formation and transformation of funds of knowledge among U.S. Mexican households. *Anthropology & Education Quarterly*, *23*(4), 313-335.

Voice Yellowfish, J. (2022). Value us: Stop viewing Indigenous people as disposable and invisible. *Newsweek*, April 20. https://www.newsweek.com/value-us-stop-viewing-indigenous-people-disposable-invisible-opinion-1699056

Waterman, S. J. (2019). New research perspectives on Native American students in higher education. *Journal Committed to Social Change on Race and Ethnicity*, *5*(1), 61-80.

Western Educational Equity Assistant Center (2023) *Increasing American Indian and Alaska Native high school graduation rates*. https://weeac.wested.org/wp-content/uploads/2023/09/Increasing-American-Indian_Alaska-Native-High-School-and-College-Graduation-Rates-in-the-Western-States-Brief_FINAL_ADA.pdf

Wisconsin First Nations (2024). *Place based education*. https://wisconsinfirstnations.org/place-based-education/

# Chapter 8

# Building Identity, Brick by Brick

## Being Twice Exceptional and Transgender

### Orla Dunne

Recognition of twice exceptionality has greatly increased in the gifted education literature, with gifted education professionals often having significantly more knowledge and experience with twice exceptionality than professionals in other education domains (Foley-Nicpon et al., 2013). Being twice different (or more) can lead to isolation and mental health issues for gifted adolescents (Levy & Plucker, 2003). The experiences of LGBTQ adolescents with multiple oppressed identities can also be unique by virtue of how their identities intersect (Watson et al., 2020), and how each identity is received in different spaces (Sewell, 2020). For adolescents who are twice exceptional and LGBTQ, there can be challenges in terms of being that little bit further from the mainstream or so-called "normal." These adolescents must deal with intellectual deviance from the mainstream and stigmatized sexual orientation and/or gender identity (Kerr & Multon, 2015), as well as potential social challenges beyond those experienced by their typically developing peers (Foley Nicpon et al., 2010; Seltzer et al., 2003).

This chapter examines the social and academic experiences of adolescents who are twice exceptional and transgender, with a particular focus on two individuals: Steven and Dillon. The original interviews with Steven and Dillon were conducted as part of a larger study on the experiences of gifted LGBTQ adolescents in Ireland (Dunne, 2023), which is also referenced within the chapter.

This type of case study methodology can be thoroughly useful in understanding the phenomenon of twice exceptionality, as it provides a context to examine this through individual students and catches the nuances that are the most relevant (Assouline et al., 2009).

The chapter begins by introducing relevant terminology to the topic, before discussing the research context. Following this is a literature review, which is brief both due to the lack of literature on this specific topic and to avoid repetition between other chapters within this book. Steven's and Dillon's voices are at the forefront of the rest of the chapter, starting with their experiences of being twice exceptional and transgender, within each capacity individually (gifted, autistic, transgender), and then the intersections of each identity. The chapter concludes with considerations on the value of support structures and the development of positive coping mechanisms for twice-exceptional and transgender adolescents.

# Introduction

This section establishes the foundations of this chapter and research, including terminology, research context, and an introduction to the participants.

## Definitions and Terminology

The terminology used to describe gender identity has shifted greatly over the last decade. This can be attributed to several factors: growing international awareness of gender diversity (particularly through media); increased academic literature and research; and the advocacy and activism of the transgender community themselves (E. Coleman et al., 2012). Such a rapid evolution of language naturally leads to disagreement and debate, as terms and definitions shift or become outdated, and cultural viewpoints expand (American Psychological Association, 2015). The term "transgender," or "trans," is used to describe people who do not identify with their gender assigned at birth or who defy binary gender norms (McBride, 2020; Meyer & Leonardi, 2018). The term "cisgender" relates to people who feel an alignment between the gender they were assigned at birth and their personal gender identity (Enke, 2012). "Gender-nonconforming" is an umbrella term and can be used to describe many different gender identities, including non-binary, genderfluid, genderqueer and agender (Meyer et al., 2016). Many gender-nonconforming people do not identify singularly as male or female; however, it is important to recognize that their experience of gender construction will have been shaped by their gender assigned at birth. Gender-nonconforming people may use they/them pronouns, or a variety of others.

Finally, the term "transitioning" is used to describe the stages that trans and gender-nonconforming people may go through to feel more aligned with their gender identity. For educators working with gifted transgender students, social transitioning is typically the only aspect they will need to be aware of, as medical and legal transitioning is a more private experience and often occurs as an adult. Social transitioning may include changing physical gender markers such as hair and clothing (Morandini et al., 2023), adopting mannerisms in accordance with societal expectations of gender (McGlashan & Fitzpatrick, 2018), requesting a different name and gender pronouns, and/or using different gendered facilities, such as bathrooms.

## Research Context and Background

The study referenced within this chapter is Dunne (2023), the author's own research on the experiences of gifted and talented LGBTQ adolescents in Ireland. This was a mixed methods study, with a participant sample of post-primary students (ages 13-18) and recent university students (ages 18-23) who had been identified as gifted (via either psychological or above-level testing) and attended a gifted enrichment program. A total of 120 participants fit the above criteria and identified as non-heterosexual and/or non-cisgender. There were two unique aspects to this study within the overall field of gifted LGBTQ research: the mean age of the participants (18.4)—a significantly younger mean age than most other similar studies; and the national context, as the study is the first of its kind outside the United States. All participants were able to self-identify their gender and sexual orientation—an important factor of inclusion when engaging in affirmative research with transgender and gender non-conforming participants (Sevelius et al., 2017). Overall, 14 unique gender identities were recorded. By allowing complete self-identification in these categories, the full spectrum of diversity beyond traditional singular definitions of gender can be better captured (Hammack et al., 2021).

## Participants

This chapter focuses on the experiences of two participants in the main study: Steven and Dillon. Each took part in an interview for the original study and a subsequent interview which focused on twice exceptionality. The interviews took place two years apart. At the time of the original interview, Steven was 22 and a university undergraduate, studying education. Steven is transgender, gay, autistic, and uses he/him pronouns. At the time of the original interview, Dillon was 19 and a university undergraduate, studying psychology. Dillon is non-binary, queer, autistic, and uses they/them pronouns. Both Steven and Dillon qualified to attend a gifted program by sitting above-level testing and achieving scores within the 95th percentile.

## Literature Overview

While much of the early research on twice exceptionality focused on students with learning disabilities (e.g., Vaughn, 1989), over time this has broadened to include a range of disabilities, including attention deficit hyperactivity disorder (ADHD) and autism spectrum disorder (ASD) (Reis et al., 2022). Autism spectrum conditions comprise a set of neurodevelopmental characteristics, indicated by early-onset difficulties in social communication, unusually restricted and repetitive behavior, and narrow interests (Lai et al., 2014; Lai & Baron-Cohen, 2015). Adolescents with ASD face several social challenges beyond those experienced by their typically developing peers, including demonstrating behavioral and emotional maturity, intuitively understanding environmental rules and norms (which may be taken for granted), developing age-appropriate peer relationships, and generally interpreting and navigating the social world around them (Seltzer et al. 2003; Nicpon et al., 2010). For twice-exceptional adolescents, there can be a disconnect between the age of identification of advanced abilities and an additional learning need (Reis et al., 2014); while longitudinal epidemiological data shows that diagnoses of ASD in girls and women are still typically at a later age than males (Lai et al., 2015). In terms of the delay for females to be diagnosed, we can hypothesize that this will also affect transgender males and non-binary adolescents who are assigned female at birth, who spend much of their childhood and early adolescence being socialized as female. This was the case for both Steven and Dillon, who were diagnosed as autistic as young adults. Dillon struggled with societal norms around gender and meeting "girl standards," which will be discussed later in the chapter.

There remains limited empirical research on the experiences of gifted transgender adolescents and even less on the experiences of adolescents who are trans or gender-nonconforming and twice exceptional. One study in Ireland (n=195) found that there were higher prevalence rates of bullying and cyberbullying victimization among gifted adolescents compared to the national average (Laffan et al., 2024). While there was not a noted differentiation in victimization rates for the LGBTQ and twice-exceptional participants in the study, this population did score significantly lower on satisfaction with life and significantly higher on negative outcomes, compared to the other participants. One case study with a gifted and transgender man found that as an adolescent, he had limited peer support and had experienced frequent suicidal ideation from as young as 12 (Sedillo,

2018). As referenced above, the interviews in this chapter were conducted as part of a larger study by the author (Dunne, 2023), which included interviews with other gifted trans and non-binary individuals. Three participants reported significant incidents of bullying and harassment when they were in school, including cyber harassment, verbal abuse, physical threats, and exclusion. One participant, Olivia, experienced being "outed" as a trans girl by her classmates, which led to significant bullying and caused her immense distress and isolation:

> *Some guys in my school found my Instagram and I was outed as being trans … They would message me as a group, to dehumanize me and deadname me. They made a fake Facebook page of me, where the profile picture was a crude drawing and they'd share photos from my private social media and say really awful things. Being a 15-year-old girl who was already very socially isolated at school … It was awful. Going to school, I didn't know what was going to happen. For the entire year, I never went to the [cafeteria] or PE. I was worried that if anything would happen to me, it would be there, and I started having panic attacks.*

Diverging from not only intellectual norms but also gender norms can be challenging for gifted adolescents (Kerr & Multon, 2015), particularly in an unsupportive environment. One participant in Hutcheson and Tieso (2014, p. 363) described their classes and extracurricular activities as "uncomfortably heteronormative," as they (consciously and unconsciously) reinforced heterosexuality as the norm and erased the existence of identities outside of this.

## *Building Identity, Brick by Brick*

**Steven:** *To me, my personality and autism are difficult to extricate from each other. That's why I don't agree with anyone who says they want a cure for autism, because autism is like the architecture of who someone is. In school, we learned about the history of Romanesque and Gothic churches, right? You can't change it. If you wanted to make a Gothic church into a Romanesque church, maybe you could pull it apart brick by brick, and put it into the shape of the other type of church, but then you'd have a different building. It wouldn't be the same.*

**Author:** *Do you feel like if you broke yourself down, brick by brick, and removed the autism and built you up into the other church, you would just be a completely different person?*

**Steven:** *I would be unrecognizable.*

**Author:** *How would you include your gender identity in that metaphor?*

**Steven:** *I think being transgender, in that sense, for me, is not just one thing. It's the decorations from the outside of the church, but it's also the things that are in the tabernacle.*

The above quote formed the title of this chapter. I found this metaphor to be very moving, as it describes beautifully how aspects of identity come together to create a whole person. Steven also used this metaphor to speak to the notion of "cures" for autism, as he views his autism as part of the fabric of who he is, in a positive way. The following sections each focus on these identity "bricks"—namely giftedness, autism, and gender identity.

## Gifted and Talented

Both Steven and Dillon were identified as gifted while in primary school. Steven was identified when he was 12 years old by a teacher in his school, who spoke to his parents. His strongest recollection of this was the test he would take on referral, which was an entrance test for an external gifted program—specifically, that the test had negative marking. Steven found the notion of leaving an answer blank strange and against what he considered conventional for tests. He also recalled grand fantasies about what the gifted program would be like: "I remember daydreaming that I was going to turn up and it would be Hogwarts."

Dillon approximated that they were identified around the age of seven, along with their sibling. They noted that entry into the gifted program was something which elicited a great deal of pride and praise from their parents:

> *It was framed as something to be really proud of and they were excited for us. I think I was too young to understand exactly what the test was for, so it felt almost like a run of the mill—just another thing to do.*

Steven's and Dillon's experiences of being identified as gifted were reasonably similar, with each being encouraged by parents and teachers in that respect. Parent involvement and perceptions of gifted education are important factors of gifted adolescents' access to and experiences in education (Brigandi et al., 2018; Makel, 2009). However, Dillon's strong parent support was slightly a double-edged sword, as it led to them feeling like they had to remain high achieving: "I focused heavily on academics and proving myself, because that was the way I could prove my worth."

In terms of peer relationships, gifted adolescents are often given mixed messages, encouraged to highly achieve yet sometimes ostracized for standing out (Cross, 2011), which can lead to uncertainty and anxiety surrounding social norms (Reidl Cross & Cross, 2015). Dillon described feeling lonely, particularly in primary school. Their intelligence was seen by their parents, and subsequently them, as an explanation for the social awkwardness they were experiencing:

*Being smart was something I leaned into quite a bit, especially because I had this sort of isolation from my peers at primary school. Whenever I would talk to my parents about feeling left out from my peers, they would always say things like: "Oh, it's because you're smarter than they are so don't worry about it, you're just probably on a different level."*

This was in direct contrast to Dillon's current peer relationships at university, which were positive. This is likely a combination of natural maturity with age and their own increased self-understanding:

*In terms of my closest friend, we would study together, and I also consider her extremely intelligent. We might share some frustrations over how much the workload is, but then we reassure each other that we can do it. We have a joke that we're smart cookies! [Being gifted] is no longer something that I use to separate myself from other people; it's something that brings me closer.*

On the topic of peer relationship development, Steven was asked how he would react in a scenario where he had found a test straightforward, but a classmate stated it was very difficult. This question was based on one formulated within the stigma of giftedness paradigm (Cross, Coleman, & Terhaar-Yonkers, 1997; Cross et al., 1991), which proposes that in situations where their giftedness would be evident to peers, adolescents would make conscious choices about how truthful to be about the ease of an exam. They might outright lie, tell the truth, or engage in different "copout" methods, with each choice making their giftedness more or less visible to peers. Steven found this scenario amusing and gave the following answer, offering insight into how he thinks and his overall growth:

*Well, I abhor dishonesty and I've always been uncomfortable with it. I think lying is obviously a really important skill to have—it means you're capable of abstraction and of thinking of other people's perspectives—but I hate it. Consciously or unconsciously, I don't think it would have occurred to me that it would be better to not tell the truth! Now, I think I have a lot more tact and social skills so maybe it would be different.*

Both Steven and Dillon found immense value in connecting with peers at the gifted summer camp they attended. Steven described how he was now searching for some of that connection as an adult by contacting Mensa to seek out other gifted adults: "on the Mensa website, one of the benefits that members report is being in conversations with people who don't shy away when the subject gets too complicated."

Steven described one particular challenge with being gifted, which was his perception of intelligence as fixed. This would subsequently cause him significant challenges at university, when he encountered more difficult academic tasks:

> *I think one thing that's interesting about giftedness is you get praised for not putting any effort in ... The implication is that if you are smart, then it means you don't try. People in school would say things like, "Oh, it's really incredible that you got an A+ on that test, and you didn't even study." Which made me feel like if I did have to study, or have to put effort in, it would be a problem.*

This kind of "fixed mindset" can lead to gifted students avoiding competitive situations or difficult tasks, to avoid risking failure (Siegle & Langley, 2016). Steven viewed effort and intelligence as separate, with only the latter contributing to any achievement. When Steven entered university, he struggled deeply with a sense of self, as he was now required to put in work to succeed. This coincided with being diagnosed with autism, which led to a depressive episode and Steven dropping out of university. This will be discussed again later in the chapter.

## Autistic

One of the challenges of both defining and supporting adolescents who are gifted and autistic is the difficulty in differentiating aspects of ASD and advanced abilities (Assouline et al., 2012). For Steven and Dillon, each had a significant time difference between being identified as gifted versus being identified as autistic. Steven was diagnosed as autistic approximately nine years after he was identified as gifted and felt it explained his feelings of difference from peers around him:

> *I wasn't diagnosed with autism until I was 19. I think that diagnosis was very important, because I went through a lot of distress as a child and as a teenager that, in retrospect, could probably be attributed to autism. I really struggled to interact with people. I felt weird. I do remember wondering if everybody felt the same as me internally, but maybe they're just really good at pretending.*

This feeling of isolation and questioning was similar for Dillon, who was diagnosed during university. They reflected on how their academic ability was attributed as the reasoning behind their struggles to relate with peers, particularly from their parents' perspective:

## 2e and Gender Identity

*I remember a couple of really clear occasions when I was younger, bringing it up to my parents and asking about being assessed for autism, because I felt like I was struggling. But their response was to ask what a diagnosis would do, because I was doing so well in school. So, I think excelling in academia was almost the excuse not to pursue a diagnosis or even consider it.*

Academically talented children generally may find it challenging interacting with peers, which can make it difficult to differentiate whether they are showing the social deficits typically seen with ASD or if they are simply more advanced and therefore uninterested in typical peer conversation topics (Reis et al., 2022). For Dillon, quoted above, they felt that being gifted and considered the "smart kid" obscured the difficulties and delayed their diagnosis further. Long-term social pressure to fit typical social norms can lead to the development of coping or camouflaging strategies to conceal specific behaviors (Lai and Baron-Cohen, 2015)—something which Steven also related to his gender identity:

*For most of my life I've essentially been performing to people's expectations of me, in more ways than one. Gender and autism kind of both fell into [the feeling that] I have to keep up with this performance because other people have these expectations of me that I can't always meet but I feel the need to perform to them ...*

Excessive focus on special interests is a common characteristic exhibited by twice-exceptional students with ASD (Doobay et al., 2014; Reis et al., 2022). When these interests can guide academic work and talent development, twice-exceptional adolescents can be more motivated and engaged to gain advanced skills (Reis et al., 2022). For Steven and Dillon, both found great joy in engaging with their special interests, on a personal level and as part of their friendships. Interestingly, both mentioned topics of interest that related to their university degrees. Steven, who is now doing a master's degree in clinical psychology, described having a current special interest in the history of autism—specifically the work of Hans Asperger and Leo Kanner. Dillon studied music and psychology for their bachelor's degree and wants to pursue further study in music and neural pathways. Dillon also spoke about how one particular genre of music, hyper pop, was important to them as it led to positive reinforcement of their gender identity: "hyper pop is a big deal for me, because not only is it stimming music, it's also just part of queer culture, and specifically trans culture." Rather than their niche interest isolating them from peers, both interviewees found that this strengthened their friendships and became a way for their friends to show positive attention. Steven described this as bonding:

*In terms of autism and giftedness, it is very nice to get really into super obscure, highly academic subjects. Whenever I'm upset, some of my friends who know me particularly well will ask me to tell them facts about ants because it calms me down!*

## Gender Identity

In the larger research study referenced (Dunne, 2023), gifted LGBTQ participants (n=120) were able to self-identify their gender in an open texted box, which also facilitated transgender and gender-nonconforming participants in identifying their sexual orientation in relation to their gender identity. This is an important factor of inclusion when engaging in gender-affirming research (Sevelius et al., 2017). Overall, participants used a total of 14 different labels to describe their gender, with some using multiple labels or including thick description in the open text boxes. Some of the gender labels that fall under the transgender umbrella included "non-binary," "queer," "genderfluid," "neutrois," "agender," and "transfeminine." Of eight interview participants, there were two trans men, one trans woman, and two non-binary people. Each of these participants described receiving stronger levels of affirmation at a gifted program, from both peers and staff, compared to within their school.

When considering his gender identity, Steven described the impact of meeting another trans boy, although he did not identify the reasons behind his fascination until later:

*The first time I ever met a transgender man was at [the gifted program]. I couldn't get him out of my head. Afterward I would just start to think about him and think "Imagine being so brave and being able to live your life openly." I wanted to be such an ally!*

Steven described how, a while after this, he experienced a kind of "eureka" moment about his own gender, which he recalled with great specificity:

*I was in school, in the first term of fifth year, in [gym] class. We were waiting to be picked into teams. I was thinking about how I had never really considered my gender. Then it was like I was hit with a wave of knowing: "I'm not a girl." It was like a smack to the face.*

Dillon described finding their gender identity perhaps the most challenging aspect of their identity and an ongoing journey, as it exists in both an internal and external realm:

*Being gifted was placed upon me, so it feels external. Being autistic, that's something that I just had to understand and start to identify with, so that's an internal self-discovery. But gender is harder because it's somewhere in the middle between something that's given to me by other people and something that I have to come to terms with myself.*

*Coming out and realizing I was non-binary was stressful for me because it was another tier away from normal that I was going to have to contend with. Adding transness into the mix just made me feel like life was going to be more difficult. You kind of can't separate yourself from the internalized shame about being different.*

We know gifted adolescents who experience isolation may be at a greater risk of severe mental health issues (Cross et al., 2002); while several studies which focused on gifted LGBTQ adolescents have identified themes of depression (Hutcheson & Tieso, 2014; Peterson & Rischar, 2000) and suicidal ideation (Sedillo, 2018). Transgender and nonbinary youth are generally at increased risk of poor mental health outcomes (Price-Feeney et al., 2020)—including higher rates of depression, suicidality, and self-harm—compared with their cisgender peers (Connolly et al., 2016). One participant in the larger study (Dunne, 2023), Benedict, spoke about his experience of the interaction of gender dysphoria, mental health, and a disability, which significantly affected his ability to attend school regularly. Dillon spoke about experiencing anxiety as a child in school, particularly related to social isolation and feeling different from peers. Steven spoke about how his first experience at university was challenging, leading him to drop out of his course and suffer a significant bout of depression. However, overall, Steven and Dillon found that their gender identity did present as many challenges as being twice exceptional. Dillon also emphasized the danger in only presenting LGBTQ young people as requiring help or sympathy, as they found great joy in being among their other trans and queer friends.

## Intersectional Identities

As noted in the literature review, adolescents who are gifted, LGBTQ, and hold another marginalized identity (e.g., race or ethnicity) may feel the need to compromise on certain parts of their identity or internalize one aspect to externalize another, depending on the environment (Sewell, 2020). Dillon described struggling with the intersection of their identities as a twice-exceptional, nonbinary, and mixed-race adolescent. These frustrations were also compounded by their specific school environment, which was a Catholic, all-female school with very few non-white students:

> *It was a source of oppression for me, particularly growing up in an Irish all-girls school—there were a lot of expectations for conformity. Not just in the sense of being like a "proper" girl, but as being a white girl as an extension of that ... A lot of me coming out as nonbinary was recognizing that fundamentally I didn't want to hold myself to white standards and for me, binary gender is a white standard.*

Dillon identified that their coming out (in multiple ways) was influenced by significant world events—namely the COVID-19 pandemic and racial tensions which arose in the United States at the same time:

> *I came out as nonbinary and I started to understand myself as a person of color at the same time. Like that was a lot to do with everything that was happening in America and also having to focus on myself because of the pandemic and also having time to focus on knowing more about the world. I started to think a lot about my identity, not just as something contained within me or as an extension of individuality, but as placing myself with another group of people or recognizing that I'm part of another group within a community. I almost came out as Asian, in a way. I had kind of a duality with me just from being mixed race to begin with, and also the stereotypes that are associated with gender.*

In terms of the cross-section of gender identity and autism, some recent studies suggest that trans and gender-nonconforming individuals may have higher rates of autism. One study (Warrier et al., 2020) investigated whether transgender and gender-nonconforming individuals have elevated rates of autism diagnosis or traits related to autism compared to cisgender individuals by comparing cross-sectional datasets of individuals (n=641,860) who completed information on gender, neurodevelopmental, and psychiatric diagnoses, including autism. Their overall finding was that, compared to cisgender individuals, transgender and gender-nonconforming individuals do have on average higher rates of autism, as well as other neurodevelopmental and psychiatric diagnoses. In a randomized sample of transgender adolescents (age 18-30) under the care of Ireland's National Gender Service, 14% of patients either had a formal diagnosis of ASD or had clinical features consistent with ASD without a formal diagnosis (Kearns et al., 2022). Of the total sample (n=167), only half progressed to university education. The author would caution that this is a topic which necessitates further research and educators should continue to focus on how to serve any twice-exceptional and trans adolescents, regardless of whether they are working with one student or many.

## Supports for Positive Identity Development

Over the course of Steven's and Dillon's interviews, several key support structures were identified: family, peer relationships, and inclusive spaces. In a report on parent attitudes to gifted education in Ireland, two-thirds (66%) of the total participants expressed that the gifted program Steven and Dillon attended was a positive social experience. Parental support in gifted education, along with warmth, responsiveness, and cognitive stimulation, can lead to more positive attitudes for gifted children toward their identity and academic development (Brigandi et al., 2018). Both Dillon and Steven referenced their parents' influence in their identification as gifted. Dillon's parents in particular were very encouraging of their academic skills; however, they did use their giftedness as an explanation for Dillon's self-described social awkwardness and lack of strong peer relationships, which Dillon resented slightly. Sibling relationships were mentioned in both Steven's and Dillon's interviews. Steven attributed his delayed diagnosis of autism to his parents' comparison of him and his brother's attitudes to school, as his brother was less academically focused. Steven's brother was subsequently diagnosed with ADHD. Dillon described having a very close relationship with their sister, who is also gifted, autistic, and transgender, and their shared experience of identity development:

> *In a weird way, the best form of community I have is probably just with my sister. It's like we have a tiny community where it's just the two of us. Before we both came out to each other, we were not on fantastic terms and that's just the way siblings go. Now it feels like we are nearly telepathic, because we spent time just going back and forth, trying to understand each other better, being patient, and not judging the other.*

Dillon and Steven each spoke about the value of creating positive peer relationships, particularly within the gifted enrichment program they attended. In a survey on adolescents attending the same gifted program, the development of deeper friendships was noted as a significant factor in one twice-exceptional participant's experience of the program (Cross et al., 2022): "I have Asperger's, so I've always found it hard to make friends and understand people's feelings. I feel different from groups at school but in the gifted program everyone is friendly and understanding."

Gifted students' experience at summer programs, even if short, can be instrumental in affirming giftedness among peers, enhancing independence, and building stronger self-belief (Lee et al., 2015). For gifted adolescents who are also LGBTQ, social fears like rejection, prejudice, and harassment can impact self-confidence and affect the development of strong peer relationships (Tuite et al.,

2021). It is therefore vital to create spaces where gifted LGBTQ adolescents can meet and forge friendships. Dillon described how their comfort level shifts in different spaces, particularly when considering the multiple, nuanced layers of their identity:

*There are very few environments where I'm exactly me and exactly comfortable. And it's not necessarily that being in white spaces or cishet spaces, or any of that is unbearable; it's just the little bit of extra work that you have to put in to explaining things that people haven't considered yet, or haven't been bothered to consider, or having to be a little more lenient in how much your rights get violated.*

One of the strongest predictors of a supportive educational environment for LGBTQ adolescents is the number of sympathetic educators present (Kosciw et al., 2013). Positive identity affirmation from education leaders can moderate the link between experiences of interpersonal victimization and negative mental health for LGBTQ young people (Busby et al., 2020), even during short periods like a summer camp (Gillig & Bighash, 2021). Dillon described a positive relationship with staff at the gifted program, rooted in trust and follow-through for any issues of anti-LGBTQ bullying that occurred. Leadership is an important aspect of creating an inclusive space and this theme was identified within the larger study also (Dunne, 2023), as illustrated in the below quotes:

*In my second year at the gifted program, my Residential Assistant was gay and I thought it was amazing. It was really heartwarming seeing queer people not compromising on any part of their identity and doing a good job.*

*In school, I had one teacher who always discussed queer content in course material openly. It was mentioned where appropriate and he didn't shy away from talking about the lives of queer writers or queer context if it was part of a story.*

Generally, higher levels of support from family members, peers, and academic leaders are positively associated with academic motivation and engagement (Wang & Eccles, 2012), each of which were key scaffolds for Steven's and Dillon's academic journeys.

## Developing Coping Mechanisms and Skills

Gifted children and adolescents with ASD may be more prone to symptoms of atypicality, depression, and hyperactivity than would be expected for students their age (Nicpon et al., 2010). Steven faced several challenges with his mental health after moving from school to university. He described frustration with the shift from being a high-achieving student with minimal effort to failing courses at university while needing to put in significant effort:

*Being the smart one was a huge part of my identity—more specifically, being able to do things without putting any effort into them. So, when I had to start putting effort into doing things, it was really strange. I failed my first third-level degree. And I got diagnosed with autism. It was this wave of feeling like I can't try because if I try, it means I'm not smart. Everything fell around my ears ... I dropped out of university. I actually spent a couple of years just laying perfectly still in my bed.*

Steven was directed to a national learning program, which specifically focused on executive functioning, goal-setting methods, and study techniques, along with mental health check-ins, for young adults with autism. This had a positive effect and led to his return to university to study education. This type of targeted intervention (particularly goal orientation) was like the talent development model used by Foley-Nicpon et al. (2017) during a summer camp for twice-exceptional adolescents, which also had positive outcomes.

# Final Thoughts

The theme of being or feeling different is, of course, not unique to the population discussed in this chapter. In one review, gifted adolescents concurred that the essence of being gifted was just to be different (Coleman et al., 2015). In the larger study to which Dillon and Steven contributed (Dunne, 2023), another transgender participant in the study questionnaire wrote that their negative experience in school was due to "being weird (read: autistic and non-passing)". The concept of "passing" is used in gender identity terminology to describe when a transgender person appears cisgender; however, many trans and non-binary people choose to reject this as a goal of transitioning, adopting aesthetics that challenge social assumptions about gender (McGuire & Reilly, 2022). However, in this context, the participant may also be describing their autism— that is, that they did not "pass" as neurotypical. Dillon described this idea during their interview: "I do think with autism and gender, there's always this awkward dance between who you are and how people are perceiving you." Dillon and Steven both faced challenges externally from others and internally within their own self-concept. However, each described how these challenges were positively impacted by personal growth and maturity, shifting from feeling different in a negative way (e.g., loneliness, social isolation, personal struggles) to feeling different in a positive way (e.g., building stronger relationships, academic capabilities, self-confidence). Both noted the significant impact of their time on the gifted program, as it was a space to meet others like them. This supports existing research on the value of gifted enrichment programs and having space to be with likeminded, same-age peers. Similarly, this experience of friendship development is crucial for transgender young people. Both Dillon and Steven subsequently returned to work at the gifted enrichment program they attended, expressing a desire to help young people who were like them.

The chapter will conclude with details on the participants and with their final thoughts. Steven completed his bachelor's degree in education, is now finishing his master's in psychology, and hopes to begin a PhD program next. He was an integral student figure in his university's autism inclusion program, working with students, professors, and campus staff to create a positive environment for autistic students. Steven was asked if he could offer advice to parents of adolescents who might be going through a similar identity exploration or having experiences like his and relayed the following:

*I think it's important to remember that there's no right way to do anything, both for parents and for people like me. We're all just kind of muddling through! It doesn't matter how many intersectional identities that you have—you could be twice, three times or 50 million times exceptional, but you're still a human being just trying to figure it out. You're not going to get it right 100% of the time and that's fine!*

Dillon recently completed their bachelor's degree in psychology and hopes to progress to a master's program soon, with a particular focus on the interactions of psychology and music. Dillon spoke about wanting to use their degree to contribute to humanity and a more understanding society, which values people for their exceptionalities and being beyond the norm:

I'm going into psychology because I want to create something somewhere where people are going to listen, because we have so much to say. There's so much to be understood that cis people could be learning from—not just for our sake, out of pity, but for their sake, to understand themselves better. If we create a better infrastructure, or a better system, then this is the kind of push that can lead to genuine positive environments for people like me.

## Things to Consider

- Gifted transgender youth often navigate conflicting stereotypes—such as the expectation that gifted students excel effortlessly and conform to high-achieving, neurotypical norms—alongside harmful misconceptions about transgender identities being "confusing" or "inauthentic." These stereotypes can compound, leading students to question the legitimacy of their identities or feel pressure to suppress parts of themselves to be accepted. For instance, being visibly neurodivergent or gender-nonconforming may lead to being perceived as less competent or "too different," impacting self-esteem, mental health, and the ability to access support. Challenging these stereotypes is essential for affirming both the complexity and the wholeness of twice-exceptional transgender youth.
- Recognize the crucial role of family, peer, and educator support in fostering positive identity development and resilience. Inclusive gifted programs and safe spaces can counteract feelings of isolation and stigma.

## Discussion Questions

- How do giftedness, autism, and transgender identity intersect in the lives of Steven and Dillon, and what unique challenges or strengths emerge from these intersections?
- What role do educational environments (e.g., schools, gifted programs) play in either affirming or marginalizing twice-exceptional transgender students? What qualities make a space genuinely inclusive?
- Steven uses the metaphor of a church to describe his autism and gender identity. How can metaphors like this help us better understand complex identities and what are the risks or limitations of metaphor when discussing lived experience?
- In what ways do stereotypes—around giftedness, autism, and transgender identities—impact how young people see themselves and are treated by others? How can educators and peers help disrupt these narratives?

# References

American Psychological Association. (2015) Guidelines for psychological practice with transgender and gender nonconforming people. *American Psychologist, 70*(9), 832-864. https://doi.org/10.1037/a0039906

Assouline, S. G., Foley Nicpon, M., & Dockery, L. (2012) Predicting the academic achievement of gifted students with Autism Spectrum Disorder. *Journal of Autism and Developmental Disorders, 42*(9), 1781-1789. https://doi.org/10.1007/s10803-011-1403-x

Assouline, S. G., Nicpon, M. F., & Doobay, A. (2009) Profoundly gifted girls and Autism Spectrum Disorder: A psychometric case study comparison. *Gifted Child Quarterly, 53*(2), 89-105. https://doi.org/10.1177/0016986208330565

Brigandi, C. B., Weiner, J. M., Siegle, D., Gubbins, E. J., & Little, C. A. (2018) Environmental perceptions of gifted secondary school students engaged in an evidence-based enrichment practice. *Gifted Child Quarterly, 62*(3), 289-305. https://doi.org/10.1177/0016986218758441

Busby, D. R., Horwitz, A. G., Zheng, K., Eisenberg, D., Harper, G. W., Albucher, R. C., Roberts, L. W., Coryell, W., Pistorello, J., & King, C. A. (2020) Suicide risk among gender and sexual minority college students: The roles of victimization, discrimination, connectedness, and identity affirmation. *Journal of Psychiatric Research, 121*, 182-188. https://doi.org/10.1016/j.jpsychires.2019.11.013

Coleman, E., Bockting, W., Botzer, M., Cohen-Kettenis, P., DeCuypere, G., Feldman, J., Fraser, L., Green, J., Knudson, G., Meyer, W. J., Monstrey, S., Adler, R. K., Brown, G. R., Devor, A. H., Ehrbar, R., Ettner, R., Eyler, E., Garofalo, R., Karasic, D. H., ... Zucker, K. (2012) Standards of care for the health of transsexual, transgender, and gender-nonconforming people, Version 7. *International Journal of Transgenderism, 13*(4), 165-232. https://doi.org/10.1080/15532739.2011.700873

Coleman, L., Micko, K., & Cross, T. (2015) Twenty-five years of research on the lived experience of being gifted in school: Capturing the students' voices. *Journal for the Education of the Gifted, 38*. https://doi.org/10.1177/0162353215607322

Connolly, M. D., Zervos, M. J., Barone, C. J., Johnson, C. C., & Joseph, C. L. M. (2016) The mental health of transgender youth: Advances in understanding. *Journal of Adolescent Health, 59*(5), 489-495. https://doi.org/10.1016/j.jadohealth.2016.06.012

Cross, J. R. & Cross, T. L. (2015) Clinical and mental health issues in counseling the gifted individual. *Journal of Counseling & Development, 93*(2), 163-172. https://doi.org/10.1002/j.1556-6676.2015.00192.x

Cross, T. L. (1997) Psychological and social aspects of educating gifted students. *Peabody Journal of Education*, *72*, 180-200. https://doi.org/10.1207/s15327930pje7203&4_11

Cross, T. L. (2011) *On the social and emotional lives of gifted children* (4th ed.) Prufrock Press.

Cross, T. L., Coleman, L. J., & Terhaar-Yonkers, M. (1991) The social cognition of gifted adolescents in schools: Managing the stigma of giftedness. *Journal for the Education of the Gifted*, *15*(1), 44-55. https://doi.org/10.1177/016235329101500106

Cross, T. L., Gust-Brey, K., & Ball, P. B. (2002) A psychological autopsy of the suicide of an academically gifted student: Researchers' and parents' perspectives. *Gifted Child Quarterly*, *46*(4), 247-264. https://doi.org/10.1177/001698620204600402

Doobay, A. F., Foley-Nicpon, M., Ali, S. R., & Assouline, S. G. (2014) Cognitive, adaptive, and psychosocial differences between high ability youth with and without Autism Spectrum Disorder. *Journal of Autism and Developmental Disorders*, *44*(8), 2026-2040. https://doi.org/10.1007/s10803-014-2082-1

Dunne, O. (2023) *The experiences of gifted LGBTQ post-primary students in Ireland* [Doctoral, Dublin City University]. https://doras.dcu.ie/28015/

Enke, A. (2012). Introduction: Transfeminist perspectives. In A. Enke (ed.) *Transfeminist perspectives in and beyond transgender and gender studies* (pp. 1-15). Temple University Press.

Foley Nicpon, M., Doobay, A. F., & Assouline, S. G. (2010) Parent, teacher, and self perceptions of psychosocial functioning in intellectually gifted children and adolescents with Autism Spectrum Disorder. *Journal of Autism and Developmental Disorders*, *40*(8), 1028-1038. https://doi.org/10.1007/s10803-010-0952-8

Foley-Nicpon, M., Assouline, S. G., & Colangelo, N. (2013) Twice-exceptional learners: Who needs to know what? *Gifted Child Quarterly*, *57*(3), 169-180. https://doi.org/10.1177/0016986213490021

Foley-Nicpon, M., Assouline, S. G., Kivlighan, D. M., Fosenburg, S., Cederberg, C., & Nanji, M. (2017) The effects of a social and talent development intervention for high ability youth with social skill difficulties. *High Ability Studies*, *28*(1), 73-92. https://doi.org/10.1080/13598139.2017.1298997

Gillig, T. K., & Bighash, L. (2021) Network and proximity effects on LGBTQ youth's psychological outcomes during a camp intervention. *Health Communication*, *0*(0), 1-7. https://doi.org/10.1080/10410236.2021.1958983

Hammack, P., Hughes, S., Atwood, J., Cohen, E., & Clark, R. (2021) Gender and sexual identity in adolescence: A mixed-methods study of labeling in diverse community settings. *Journal of Adolescent Research*, 1-54. https://doi.org/10.1177/07435584211000315

Hutcheson, V. H., & Tieso, C. L. (2014) Social coping of gifted and LGBTQ adolescents. *Journal for the Education of the Gifted, 37*(4), 355-377. https://doi.org/10.1177/0162353214552563

Kearns, S., Houghton, C., O'Shea, D., & Neff, K. (2022) Study protocol: Navigating access to gender care in Ireland—a mixed-method study on the experiences of transgender and non-binary youth. *BMJ Open, 12*(3), e052030. https://doi.org/10.1136/bmjopen-2021-052030

Kerr, B. A. & Multon, K. D. (2015) The development of gender identity, gender roles, and gender relations in gifted students. *Journal of Counseling & Development, 93*(2), 183-191. https://doi.org/10.1002/j.1556-6676.2015.00194.x

Kosciw, J. G., Palmer, N. A., Kull, R. M., & Greytak, E. A. (2013) The effect of negative school climate on academic outcomes for LGBT Youth and the role of in-school supports. *Journal of School Violence, 12*(1), 45-63. https://doi.org/10.1080/15388220.2012.732546

Laffan, D. A., Slonje, R., Ledwith, C., O'Reilly, C., & Foody, M. (2024) Scoping bullying and cyberbullying victimisation among a sample of gifted adolescents in Ireland. *International Journal of Bullying Prevention, 6*(1), 13-27. https://doi.org/10.1007/s42380-022-00134-w

Lai, M.-C. & Baron-Cohen, S. (2015) Identifying the lost generation of adults with autism spectrum conditions. *The Lancet Psychiatry, 2*(11), 1013-1027. https://doi.org/10.1016/S2215-0366(15)00277-1

Lai, M.-C., Lombardo, M. V., & Baron-Cohen, S. (2014) Autism. *Lancet, 383*(9920), 896-910. https://doi.org/10.1016/S0140-6736(13)61539-1

Lee, S.-Y., Olszewski-Kubilius, P., Makel, M. C., & Putallaz, M. (2015) Gifted students' perceptions of an accelerated summer program and social support. *Gifted Child Quarterly, 59*(4), 265-282. https://doi.org/10.1177/0016986215599205

Levy, J. J. & Plucker, J. A. (2003) Theory and practice: Assessing the psychological presentation of gifted and talented clients: a multicultural perspective. *Counselling Psychology Quarterly, 16*(3), 229-247. https://doi.org/10.1080/09515070310001610100

Makel, M. C. (2009) Student and parent attitudes before and after the gifted identification process. *Journal for the Education of the Gifted, 33*(1), 126-143.

McBride, R.-S. (2020) A literature review of the secondary school experiences of trans youth. *Journal of LGBT Youth, 0*(0), 1-32. https://doi.org/10.1080/19361653.2020.1727815

McGlashan, H. & Fitzpatrick, K. (2018) "I use any pronouns, and I'm questioning everything else": Transgender youth and the issue of gender pronouns. *Sex Education, 18*(3), 239-252. https://doi.org/10.1080/14681811.2017.1419949

McGuire, J. K. & Reilly, A. (2022) Aesthetic identity development among trans adolescents and young adults. *Clothing and Textiles Research Journal*, *40*(3), 235-250. https://doi.org/10.1177/0887302X20975382

Meyer, E. J. & Leonardi, B. (2018) Teachers' professional learning to affirm transgender, non-binary, and gender-creative youth: Experiences and recommendations from the field. *Sex Education*, *18*(4), 449-463. https://doi.org/10.1080/14681811.2017.1411254

Meyer, E. J., Tilland-Stafford, A., & Airton, L. (2016) Transgender and gender-creative students in pk-12 schools: What we can learn from their teachers. *Teachers College Record*, *118*(8). https://eric.ed.gov/?id=EJ1115008

Morandini, J. S., Kelly, A., de Graaf, N. M., Malouf, P., Guerin, E., Dar-Nimrod, I., & Carmichael, P. (2023) Is social gender transition associated with mental health status in children and adolescents with gender dysphoria? *Archives of Sexual Behavior*, *52*(3), 1045-1060. https://doi.org/10.1007/s10508-023-02588-5

Peterson, J. S. & Rischar, H. (2000) Gifted and gay: A study of the adolescent experience. *Gifted Child Quarterly*, *44*(4), 231-246. https://doi.org/10.1177/001698620004400404

Price-Feeney, M., Green, A. E., & Dorison, S. (2020) Understanding the mental health of transgender and nonbinary youth. *Journal of Adolescent Health*, *66*(6), 684-690. https://doi.org/10.1016/j.jadohealth.2019.11.314

Reis, S. M., Baum, S. M., & Burke, E. (2014) An operational definition of twice-exceptional learners: Implications and applications. *Gifted Child Quarterly*, *58*(3), 217-230. https://doi.org/10.1177/0016986214534976

Reis, S. M., Gelbar, N. W., & Madaus, J. W. (2022) Understanding the academic success of academically talented college students with Autism Spectrum Disorders. *Journal of Autism and Developmental Disorders*, *52*(10), 4426-4439. https://doi.org/10.1007/s10803-021-05290-4

Sedillo, P. J. (2018) The "T" is missing from gifted: Gifted transgender individuals: A case study of a female to male (ftm) gifted transgender person. *Journal of Education & Social Policy*, *5*(1), 42-52.

Seltzer, M. M., Krauss, M. W., Shattuck, P. T., Orsmond, G., Swe, A., & Lord, C. (2003) The symptoms of autism spectrum disorders in adolescence and adulthood. *Journal of Autism and Developmental Disorders*, *33*(6), 565-581. https://doi.org/10.1023/b:jadd.0000005995.02453.0b

Sevelius, J., dickey, l. m., & Singh, A. A. (2017) Engaging in TGNC-affirmative research. In A.A. Singh & L.m. Dickey (eds.), *Affirmative counseling and psychological practice with transgender and gender nonconforming clients* (pp. 231-246). American Psychological Association. https://doi.org/10.1037/14957-012

Sewell, C. J. P. (2020) Negotiating multiple identities while gifted: Reflections from black queer gifted men. *Journal of LGBT Youth*, 1-21. https://doi.org/10.1080/19361653.2020.1737298

Siegle, D. & Langley, S. D. (2016) Promoting optimal mindsets among gifted children. In *The Social and Emotional Development of Gifted Children* (2nd ed.) Routledge.

Tuite, J., Rubenstein, L. D., & Salloum, S. J. (2021) The coming out experiences of gifted, LGBTQ students: When, to whom, and why not? *Journal for the Education of the Gifted*, 44(4), 366-397. https://doi.org/10.1177/01623532211044538

Wang, M.-T. & Eccles, J. S. (2012). Social support matters: Longitudinal effects of social support on three dimensions of school engagement from middle to high school. *Child Development*, 83(3), 877-895. https://doi.org/10.1111/j.1467-8624.2012.01745.x

Warrier, V., Greenberg, D. M., Weir, E., Buckingham, C., Smith, P., Lai, M.-C., Allison, C., & Baron-Cohen, S. (2020) Elevated rates of autism, other neurodevelopmental and psychiatric diagnoses, and autistic traits in transgender and gender-diverse individuals. *Nature Communications*, 11(1), 3959. https://doi.org/10.1038/s41467-020-17794-1

Watson, R. J., Wheldon, C. W., & Puhl, R. M. (2020) Evidence of diverse identities in a large national sample of sexual and gender minority adolescents. *Journal of Research on Adolescence*, 30(S2), 431-442. https://doi.org/10.1111/jora.12488

# Chapter 9

# Students on the Move

## Cecelia Boswell

All students come to school with layers that cover who they are—some positive, some negative. Layers frame the intersectionality of the person and the educational experiences provided to each. Twice-exceptional students come with more layers. When they are homeless or from a military family, yet another layer is added. This chapter addresses the layers of twice-exceptional youth experiencing home insecurity and issues surrounding those from military families. These same students from a different race, ethnicity, or culture add more cover for educators to appreciate. Layers are not necessarily a negative; they are the fabric that creates each unique person. However:

> Research by *Children's HealthWatch* found that infants and children who experience homelessness for more than six months are at a greater risk for developmental delays, poor health outcomes, hospitalization, and being overweight than children who were never homeless or homeless for less than six months.
>
> *(Burt, 2024)*

Conversely, "Military children bloom everywhere the winds carry them. They are hardy and upright. Their roots are strong, cultivated deeply in the culture of the Military, planted swiftly and surely" (Braden, 2021).

While these quotes seem mutually exclusive, these discussions concerning transient students offers a look into both the strengths and stresses of students in these two settings as it dives into the intersectionality of students who are twice exceptional and move from school to school on an ongoing basis. Upon further investigation, the reader may find that these quotes are not antithetical. The layers that cover students' realities presented in each case converge to offer the reader insight into their world.

Not presented in this chapter are examples of similar issues experienced by migrant and immigrant youth. While not specifically addressed, the anxieties and assurances that describe the lives of the homeless and military youth apply to these students also.

## Defining the Problem

Twice-exceptional students from military families experience many of the same issues as those who are homeless. While military families may not experience poverty, they are composed of different races, ethnicities, and cultures, just as are the home insecure (US Department of Defense, 2022). Inequities expressed by an education system that brings biases toward students who arrive with different academic strengths and needs create a layer that denies possibilities for these students.

Another layer covering military students is that of accessing records from previous schools and navigating the new school's systems. Even with parents who understand the school system, twice-exceptional students must wait for the process to play out and for support to be accessed.

The layer noted in the Braden (2021) quote at the beginning of this chapter is a positive one. Military families often have access to systems that facilitate support for students. If the parent(s) have rank or commissioned status, more doors are opened that help smooth the way into the school setting (Miller, 2023). In addition, that the student's home security is not lacking facilitates the resilience noted in the quote from Braden (2024).

However, homelessness continues to grow. Statistically, it follows that the number of homeless youth who are twice exceptional is also increasing. Poverty adds to the reality that a student's giftedness and learning differences are rarely recognized (Amspaugh, 2017). This knowledge is coupled with the work of Popp et al. (2003), who found that students take four to six months to acclimatize to a new setting. While identification of services that promote their academic growth has been strengthened by targeted professional learning for educators to look more deeply into students from poverty and who are twice exceptional, more work must be done in this regard. Biases and traditional views of giftedness play an integral part in hiding twice-exceptional students who are in a situation of home insecurity. In addition, there are higher incidences of illness—physical and mental—among youth who are homeless (Ives, 2018), causing them to miss days from school. The next layer comes with students who move from school to school, creating a misalignment of coursework with each new teacher (Popp et al., 2023). For some educators, the cover is too much for meaningful examination of the realities hidden in the student.

The McKinney-Vento Homeless Assistance Act alleviates some of the issues for homeless students through the support provided in every school. However, this support focuses more on physical and emotional needs, and not necessarily on the academic needs experienced by the twice exceptional. With so many layers hiding their learning strengths and desires for appropriate instruction, students with home insecurity are concealed from the scrutiny they desperately need and deserve.

The intersectionality of students in these two life situations offers multiple layers. Their academic needs, social and emotional needs, and physical needs are many. Cultural differences between student and school can create a mismatch that slows the student's progress as they adapt to a different culture. The intersection of cultural differences and isolation brings loneliness as the student navigates the new system. Their feeling of rootlessness is a layer that may be misunderstood by the school and educators who do not look beyond the surface layer. Because extracurricular choices may be unknown or unattainable to the student, their inability to belong to a social group adds to their isolation and loneliness. The layer of learning differences and giftedness only exacerbates the situation.

Educators, parents, and students alike may feel, as Robert Frost expressed, that they have "miles to go before I sleep; … miles to go before I sleep" (Frost, 1923). While all the aforesaid may lend an air of hopelessness for both students and educators, recognition by parents and support from the school, state, and local systems can alleviate much of their anxiety, assuring a positive outlook. Parents—whether homeless or in the military—who recognize their child's needs and schools that strive to recognize each student's individual strengths and differences can create students who are resilient not for just a time, but a lifetime.

## Things to Consider

- Twice-exceptional students from transient backgrounds (e.g., military or homeless) often carry intersecting identities—race, neurodivergence, socioeconomic status—that can obscure their academic strengths and emotional needs.
- Inconsistent access to school records, varying school expectations, and narrow definitions of "giftedness" often prevent appropriate identification and support for mobile 2e students.

- Frequent school moves can lead to curriculum gaps, delays in service provision, and social-emotional disruption—all of which disproportionately impact 2e students' ability to thrive.

## For Discussion

- How can educators recognize and support twice-exceptional students who are frequently mobile?
- What changes are needed in gifted identification processes to account for students whose academic records are inconsistent or incomplete?
- In what ways might resilience and trauma coexist in homeless 2e students and how should schools respond?
- How can schools create systems of belonging and continuity for students whose experiences are marked by constant transition?

## References

Amspaugh, C. M. (2017) The relationship between school mobility and gifted identification in Connecticut public schools. University of Connecticut. https://digitalcommons.lib.uconn.edu/dissertations/1528/

Braden, K. (2021) Dandelions: Flowers of the military child. *Bunnies by the Bay*, April 14. https://bunniesbythebay.com/blogs/how-to-delight/the-dandelion-flower-of-the-military-child#:~:text=Military%20children%20bloom%20everywhere%20the,new%20lands%2C%20and%20new%20friends.

Burt, L. (2024) How does homelessness impact child health and developmental outcomes? National League of Cities, January 30. https://www.nlc.org/article/2024/01/30/how-does-homelessness-impact-child-health-and-developmental-outcomes/#:~:text=Research%20by%20Children's%20HealthWatch%20found,for%20less%20than%20six%20months.

Frost, R. (1923) Stopping by woods on a snowy evening. From E. C. Lathem (ed.) *The Poetry of Robert Frost*. Copyright 1923, © 1969 by Henry Holt and Company, Inc., renewed 1951, by Robert Frost. Reprinted with the permission of Henry Holt and Company, LLC.

Ives, J. (2018) Children experiencing homelessness for more than six months have high risk of poor health outcomes. Children's Health Watch, September 3. https://childrenshealthwatch.org/children-experiencing-homelessness-for-more-than-six-months-have-high-risk-of-poor-health-outcomes/

Miller, A. (2023) Military ranks: Everything you need to know. Military.com, May 12. https://www.military.com/join-military/military-ranks-everything-you-need-know.html

Popp, P. A., Stronge, J. H., & Hindman, J. L. (2003) *Students on the move: Reaching and teaching highly mobile children and youth* (Urban Diversity Series 116, November). Project HOPE, The College of William and Mary, National Center for Homeless

US Department of Defense (2022) McKinney-Vento Homeless Assistance Act, Pub. L. No. 100-77, 101 Stat. 482, 42 U.S.C.§ 11301 et seq. https://www.govinfo.gov/content/pkg/COMPS-10570/pdf/COMPS-10570.pdf

# Chapter 10

# Exploring the Academic and Social Implications of Being a 2e Military-Connected Teen

Kathryn Davis and Georgia McKeown

## *Hudson and Heather*

*The summer before high school can be full of emotions for any student, but when it is your fifth school since kindergarten, you may feel a little more prepared for the change. Hudson is a 14-year-old who relocated with his military-connected family to Texas this summer. He is no stranger to relocations; he and his family have moved with the United States Army seven times since he was born.*

*Hudson started kindergarten at five years old at a public school near Fort Irwin in California. Shortly after starting school, he was diagnosed with autism and started to receive applied behavioral analysis (ABA) services both at school and in the community. In second grade, Hudson was identified as gifted through an assessment at his school and started receiving services in his class and with the gifted resource teacher.*

*Challenges began for Hudson and his family when they made their first military-related move after he started receiving services at school. Hudson's mother, Heather, was a classroom teacher and felt confident in navigating the education system to ensure her son had the supports he needed. Shortly after their relocation, she realized just how cumbersome it would be to reestablish services related to his autism and gifted education needs at their new duty station.*

*Heather spent hours every week contacting providers, trying to get on waitlists with ABA therapists, registering Hudson in school, and trying to be proactive about setting up his new individualized education program (IEP) and screening for gifted education services. She was met with administrative roadblocks at nearly every step, including delayed and incomplete records transfers and convoluted inclusion criteria and service availability. Even as an experienced educator, Heather felt ill equipped and overwhelmed with the time and tenacity needed to facilitate Hudson's transition to his new school. This was compounded by her husband's Army responsibilities, often taking him away from the home for weeks at a time on training exercises, meaning Heather had to lead many of the transition-related tasks that needed to happen in person.*

*After weeks of intense advocacy and coordination, Hudson started second grade with the services and supports necessary at school to meet his 2e needs. Heather took note of her experience and quickly turned to the military spouse community to share what she had learned and strategize with other spouses for future moves. Hudson and his family have since made numerous moves, navigating the vastly different special and gifted education policies and procedures from state to state and school to school.*

*Now, almost ten years later, Heather and Hudson are advocates for other 2e military-connected families, participating on numerous panels and other advocacy events to share their experiences, resources, and strategies with others. When asked recently what he would share with other military-connected teens making school transitions, Hudson stated emphatically:*

*Basically, moving to a new school means changing the way you learn. It can kind of throw you off balance, but it also can impact you positively. You gain new experiences, you learn what it feels like to change, and then you become more flexible from learning from those experiences.*

## Introduction to Military-Connected Students

Military-connected students (MCSs) can be found in nearly every zip code in the United States. They make up about 900,000 school-age children between the ages of six and 18, and more than 80% of them attend public schools (US Department of Defense, 2022; US Department of Education, 2021; American Association of School Administrators, 2019). While the official definition of a "military-connected student" varies across education, the term is commonly defined as a student who has a parent serving in the military, including those on active duty, on reserve duty, or in the National Guard. Active-duty military personnel serve full time in the armed forces, including the Army, Air Force,

Navy, Marines, Coast Guard, and Space Force (Air & Space Force Magazine, 2021). They are often stationed at bases both domestically and internationally and are expected to be ready for deployment at any time. Reservists typically serve part-time, often balancing civilian jobs (Congressional Research Service, 2020). They are called to active duty only when needed, such as during emergencies or special military operations. The National Guard is unique in that it serves both state and federal governments; its members can be activated by state governors for domestic emergencies or by the federal government for national missions (National Guard, 2021). Some definitions of "military-connected student" include those of recently retired or veteran service members, drastically increasing the population.

# Ethnoracial Composition

MCSs are a diverse group representing many different races, ethnicities, cultures, and family structures. The ethnic and racial diversity makeup of MCSs mirrors the broader demographic trends within the US military, which is increasingly composed of service members from a wide array of racial and ethnic backgrounds. Active-duty service members who self-report as White constitute approximately 68.8% of the US military, with those identifying as Black or African American making up an additional 17.3% and Asian reporting the next-highest representation at 5.2% (US Department of Defense, 2022). Native Hawaiian or other Pacific Islander, American Indian or Alaskan Native, and multiracial identifiers each make up less than 4% of the active-duty population. Children of racial and ethnically diverse military-connected families who move and transfer to schools across the US and overseas bring their cultural and diverse ties with them into the classroom.

MCSs of color face similar challenges to those who do not come from military families. These include biases and systemic inequities within the education system, both overt and subconscious. Minority students often face biases in school placement, special education and gifted education tracking, and access to resources (Fadus et al., 2021). These are compounded for students in military-connected families, as they do not get to choose where they move or how often. Behaviors indicating stress endured from moving or deployments from MCSs of color may be interpreted by educators more negatively than for White MCSs (de Pedro et al., 2014; Trautmann et al., 2015). Instead of receiving services such as therapy, IEP placement, or 504 plans, minority MCSs may find themselves being punished by school staff. Additionally, different cultural backgrounds may play a part in what is expected from MCSs at home and in school (Reed et al., 2011; Trautman et al., 2015).

However, there are many positives that can come from the diversity of ethnic and racial backgrounds in the military. Coming from diverse backgrounds can foster resilience and adaptability in MCSs (MCEC, 2020). Exposure to different cultures and environments can help to enhance cultural competence for these students as well as those they encounter. These students may also show greater depth in social skills, including demonstrating more empathy for others as well as broader cross-cultural understanding (Williamson et al., 2018; Easterbrook et al., 2013).

## Military Parent Rank and Commission

When considering the background and experiences of military-connected families, it is important to factor in the rank and commission status of the service member parent, as these can offer insights into the family's military experiences (Wang et al., 2012). Enlisted personnel hold ranks from E1 to E9, with those ranked E5 and above being classified as non-commissioned officers (NCOs) (Miller, 2023). Commissioned officers, simplified to "officers," hold ranks from O1 to O10. These individuals typically have attended a four-year public university, college, or military academy and possess at least a bachelor's degree (Millife Guides, n.d.). Some officers may have received their education through a Reserve Officer Training Corps scholarship, committing to serve in the military for four to five years depending on their branch of service. Warrant officers, holding ranks from WO1 to WO5, are specialized officers who rank above NCOs but below commissioned officers (Miller, 2023).

Officers in the military tend to move more frequently with their families but have greater access to opportunities for continued education (Classen, 2014). Enlisted personnel may not relocate as often but are more likely to be deployed for extended periods. Due to their longer stays in one place, enlisted families may build stronger community ties; however, they have less direct access to superiors and might not have the flexibility to request leave to support an exceptional child (Classen, 2014). Officers typically have more autonomy and are more likely to have the time and support from their superiors to engage with their children's educators, doctors, therapists, and other professionals (Classen, 2014). Officers serve as leaders and managers within the military, responsible for setting schedules and calendars for their subordinates, which provides them with greater flexibility in time management (Millife Guides, n.d.).

## Family Structures

Family structures among MCSs can vary widely and may often change from one transition to another. While many MCSs live in traditional two-parent households, the demands of military service can significantly affect family dynamics. Deployments, temporary duty stations, and assignments away from home mean that one or both parents might be absent for extended periods (Russo & Fallon, 2015). This often leads to temporary single-parent households, where the remaining parent assumes full responsibility for the family (Le Menestrel & Kizer, 2019).

Since the Gulf War, the US military has evolved from being predominantly male and single to a more diverse community in terms of gender representation and family structures (Demographics of the US Military, 2020). Approximately 50% of all active-duty service members are married and 39% have school-age children (Le Menestrel & Kizer, 2019). There are 234,741 female active-duty service members, accounting for 17% of the military population (U.S. Department of Defense, 2022). Female service members are more likely to be in dual-service marriages where both partners are active-duty military or divorced with full custody of their children (Military Family Research Institute, 2017).

Extended family members, such as grandparents, may also play crucial roles in providing support during these times (Lester & Flake, 2013). However, military-connected families are often not stationed near extended family and may need either to separate from their current location to move closer or to rely on a grandparent to relocate to help. In some cases, military families may live in multigenerational households to better manage the demands of military service (Kaye et al., 2022). Additionally, blended families are not uncommon, as service members may remarry, bringing together children from previous relationships into a single household.

## Military Lifestyle Demands

While no two MCS experiences are identical, there are some common lifestyle demands, including service-related separations and frequent relocations that impact their education. These experiences can exacerbate some of the challenges faced by all 2e students, like the identification process and receiving adequate services and supports.

## Service-Related Separations

Military service is a complex career with unique expectations for work. One of the primary expectations is being ready to deploy to defend the country at any given time. Military units are deployed for months to years at a time for service operations, but preparedness also requires military units to train regularly in a variety of situations and conditions, often taking them away from their assigned duty stations for shorter stints of time. Both short and long service-related separations take the service member out of the home and community. These separations force the family to adapt to the service member's absence and disrupt typical responsibilities and activity. Additionally, these separations typically leave the home caregiver (i.e., the non-service member parent—typically the mother in many military families) to manage the daily home and school operations for the family.

Research on the impacts of service-related separations on military-connected children highlights the challenges of these frequent transitions. The average MCS has moved six to nine times during their K-12 years and experienced up to five parental deployments lasting over six months (United Services Organization, 2022). These frequent transitions significantly increase the stress levels of military families with school-age children (MCEC, 2020; Russo & Fallon, 2015). Each move necessitates finding new pediatricians and specialists; replacing items lost during the move; finding community support such as churches, daycare, or babysitters; and establishing routines in a new time zone. Additionally, the non-military spouse may be searching for or starting a new job, with up to 67% of military spouses working outside the home (Le Menestrel & Kizer, 2019). These cumulative challenges often divert both parents' and children's focus from education until life stabilizes. Evidence shows that these transitions can negatively impact MCSs in the general education system (Choe, 2021; Classen, 2014; Rylander, 2020).

Academic performance often drops during and after a parent's deployment (Classen, 2014; Rylander, 2020). MCSs frequently take on additional responsibilities at home, such as caring for siblings, doing household chores, or supporting the non-deploying parent emotionally (Choe, 2021; Russo & Fallon, 2015), which in turn reduces their capacity for studying (Rylander, 2020). Anxiety and depression can increase as children anticipate and endure a parent's deployment (Garner & Nunnery, 2018). Discipline issues at home often escalate during deployments due to the increased stress and reduced emotional bandwidth of the non-deployed parent (Jackson-Lynch, 2020; Rylander, 2020). High-school students often engage in riskier behaviors such as underage alcohol consumption and unprotected sex (Rylander, 2020). Transitions can also disrupt educational continuity, as MCSs miss school during moves and while settling into new areas, including establishing care with new healthcare providers. They may also miss school during redeployments to spend time with their returning parent (Lester et al., 2016).

While there is very little direct research regarding the intersection of MCSs and 2e teens, it can be extrapolated through what is known regarding each group's needs that there are commonalities that impact this niche group. Both involve navigating a unique set of social and emotional challenges that require consistent and thoughtful approaches to support. The interplay between the 2e student's exceptional abilities and disabilities can impact their self-esteem, peer relationships, and emotional regulation (Reis et al., 2014). Similarly, the constant transitions and pressure to show flexibility in the face of consistent change can play on a military-connected teen's self-development (Easterbrooks et al., 2013). However, with the right support systems and coping strategies, 2e and military-connected adolescents can develop resilience and thrive both academically and socially. Acknowledging and addressing their multifaceted needs is essential for fostering their overall wellbeing and helping them reach their full potential.

## Frequent Relocations

Being a military-connected family also comes with the expectation of frequent relocations. The military moves families around for a variety of reasons, including continuing education, training, and mission readiness. How often a family moves varies based on service branch and specialty, with the average MCS moving six to nine times in their K-12 years (Clever & Segal, 2013). With each relocation, families must find new housing, enroll in new schools, and navigate the complex educational policies that vary from state to state and sometimes even from school to school. These relocations often come with little notice and require families to act quickly as they prepare to move to a place they typically know little about.

Families do sometimes have the support of the Department of Defense School Liaison Program. School liaisons work as a point of contact between military-connected families, military commanders, and local school systems when it comes to barriers to academic success that are exacerbated by the military lifestyle. However, their availability and support vary across service branches and installations (Department of Defense Education Activity, 2022). There are also inconsistencies in how school liaisons perceive their role and communicate between schools, military bases, and families. Many military-connected families are unaware of the existence of school liaisons, further complicating access when they are needed most (USGAO, 2022). Another challenge is the coordination between school liaisons and the Exceptional Family Member Program (EFMPs). Due to the lack of formal guidance on collaboration, interactions can vary widely, from school liaisons handling referrals and organizing joint events to instances of no regular coordination at all.

Military families typically relocate every two to three years—a process known as a "permanent change of station" (PCS). This frequent relocation is driven by the needs of the military, including the rotation of personnel to different bases, career development opportunities, and the requirements of specific missions or units (US Department of Defense, 2022). The destinations for these relocations vary widely, both within the United States and internationally. While the military will often PCS a family to a specific base, this is not always the case. There are school and job opportunities, both domestic and international, that can move families into largely civilian locales. MCSs in these situations may lose out on having a built-in social net of other MCSs (MCEC, 2017).

Research has demonstrated that frequent, non-routine school transitions are associated with multiple challenges for students (Lleras & McKillip, 2017; Anderson & Leventhal, 2017; Bradshaw et al., 2010). Despite the challenges, many military families develop strong adaptive skills and a sense of camaraderie through their shared experiences of frequent relocation.

## Social Considerations

One of the most prominent social impacts felt by MCSs is the difficulty of social integration due to frequent relocations. The constant mobility inherent to the military lifestyle can disrupt the formation of long-term friendships and can lead to feelings of isolation and loneliness (Williamson et al, 2018). MCSs are expected to repeatedly enter new social environments, where they are the "new kid" over and over. They must rebuild their social networks from scratch or attempt to fit into already established ones. These frequent transitions can strain their ability to form and maintain meaningful peer relationships, which are crucial for social development during childhood and adolescence (Easterbrooks et al., 2013; Esqueda et al., 2012).

MCSs often face challenges establishing trust and stability in their peer relationships and may be hesitant to form close bonds out of concern they or their friends might move away (Mmari et al., 2010; Easterbrooks et al., 2013). For these students, this can lead to a type of social detachment and reluctance to invest emotionally in relationships. They might also struggle to find peers who understand their unique experiences, increasing their feelings of being misunderstood or separate from their non-military-connected peers (Rylander, 2020).

This mirrors the experiences of many 2e teenagers. They may feel set apart from their peers, in this case due to their intellectual or creative strengths. This can lead to feelings of isolation or being misunderstood by both peers and educators (Baum et al., 2014). Simultaneously, 2e students' learning disabilities or emotional challenges can make it difficult to connect with peers. This can result in social withdrawal or difficulty in forming meaningful friendships. 2e students also often experience higher levels of peer rejection and bullying compared to their peers (Bracamonte, 2010). These social challenges can exacerbate feelings of loneliness and impact these students' emotional wellbeing.

There are, once again, strengths that can also come from the social interactions within the military. The transient nature of the military lifestyle can significantly influence the identity formation of MCSs. These students often grow up in a culture that values discipline, duty to others over self, and resilience (Alfano et al., 2016; Russo & Fallon, 2015). The military community at large can provide a strong sense of identity and belonging. As an extension, MCSs are part of a unique subculture with shared values and experiences. This collective identity can be a source of pride and can contribute to a strong sense of self (Russo & Fallon, 2015). MCSs may be viewed as leaders among peers and educators—an influence that can contribute to all-round positive social growth.

However, the process of identity formation can be complex for MCSs, especially when they frequently move between different cultural and regional contexts. For instance, a student might spend their early childhood, middle-school, and high-school years spread across different regions of the US and even internationally. Each environment presents different cultural norms, expectations, and social dynamics (Williamson et al., 2018). As a result, these students often develop a hybrid identity that incorporates elements from multiple cultures and regions.

This multicultural exposure can be enriching, fostering cultural competence and a global perspective (Williamson et al, 2018; Reed et al., 2011). MCSs often become adept at navigating different cultural contexts and may develop a broad worldview (Knoblock, 2015). However, this fluid identity can also lead to challenges, such as difficulty in feeling a strong connection to any one place or community. The lack of a stable "home" base can create a sense of rootlessness, which can be unsettling for some students. These are considerations that should be viewed with empathy and understanding by educators.

## Emotional Considerations and Mental Health

The military lifestyle demands a high degree of emotional resilience from MCSs. These students must cope not only with the stress of frequent relocations, but also with parental deployments and the possibility of their parents finding themselves in dangerous situations. Parental deployments can be a significant source of emotional stress (Chandra et al., 2010; Garner & Nunnery, 2018). Adolescents may experience feelings of anxiety, sadness, and fear regarding the safety of their deployed parent (Jackson-Lynch, 2020; Rylander, 2020). The absence of a parent during critical developmental stages can lead to feelings of abandonment, worry, and sadness.

MCSs, particularly teens, are at a higher risk of mental health issues such as anxiety, depression, and behavioral problems in general compared to their civilian peers (Garnder & Nunnery, 2018; Rylander, 2020). The stress of military life, compounded by the challenges of adolescence, can take a toll on their emotional wellbeing. In some cases, the cumulative stress of military life can lead to academic difficulties—something that will be looked at more in depth in the following section (Classen, 2014; Rylander, 2020).

## Academic Considerations

There are significant academic considerations for all 2e students, as they often need access to both special education and gifted education services. This can be especially challenging for military-connected 2e students because of their frequent transitions. Regular, clear communication is necessary to ensure smooth transitions for 2e MCSs—not only between the student and parents, but also with general education teachers, specialists, school psychologists, and gifted education teachers. Additional key players include military commanders making decisions on personnel placement and deployment schedules, school liaisons, and possibly military family life counselors. With so many collaborators, any mix-up or delay in the process of the transition can produce resounding challenges for the student.

### Accessing Services

2e military-connected students' frequent transitions often interrupt access to services because providers and services typically must be reestablished in each new location. Understanding how being a 2e MCS may impact academic opportunities is critical to helping these students thrive both in and outside of school. Collaboration between old and new schools is key to creating a truly differentiated curriculum for each 2e MCS (Crepeau-Hobson & Bianco, 2010). This includes the timely transition of paperwork such as IEPs, 504s, and portfolios containing examples of student work. Streamlined transition processes are critical to helping 2e MCSs access services.

## Services in School

School-based services for 2e students can include special education services and accommodations like occupational therapy, speech therapy, and academic support related to a learning disability, in addition to gifted education services (Baum et al, 2014). Receiving these services after a military-related relocation can be difficult for 2e MCSs because of the complex system of how education service determinations are made. For example, while there are federal mandates in the Individuals with Education Disabilities Act (US Department of Education, 2004) for requiring that students have access to a free and appropriate public education, how schools meet this requirement is typically determined by a series of state and local statutes.

In many cases, this means that the assessment measures, qualifying criteria, and available services for a student may be vastly different from one school to another. Additionally, this typically means that the IEP that a 2e MCS may have had at one school will not transfer seamlessly to another. In a 2020 survey study, Partners in Promise—a nonprofit organization focused on supporting the needs of MCSs with special education needs—found that 82% of respondents reported their child was without their special education services for a month or more following a military-related relocation. Additionally, their survey found that even MCSs with previously established special education needs waited an average of 5.75 months to reestablish services after a relocation. This data suggests that the transfer of academic services for MCSs with special education needs has significant lag time, leaving the student without their support services during already challenging periods of transition.

Accessing gifted education support for 2e MCSs is similarly complex to accessing special education services. Gifted education services vary widely at the state, district, and even school level. This can be especially complicated for 2e MCSs because it means they often miss the assessment and placement windows at a new location. While initiatives like the Interstate Compact on Educational Opportunity for Military Children (Department of Defense Instruction 1342.29) strive to streamline academic placements for MCSs, access to gifted or magnet programs can be difficult because of the waitlists or lottery structures in many schools and districts. This means that the responsibility of advocating for access to these types of services and programs often falls on the family of the student, relying heavily on the knowledge and availability of the home caregiver to take on the advocacy role.

Hulsey (2011) further emphasizes the critical role of home caregiver parents as advocates for their children in special education. These parents must identify key individuals in their support system, navigate the opinions and recommendations of each new provider, gain knowledge of the rules and local processes for special education, actively engage with each service provider involved in their child's care, and maintain detailed records to facilitate a smooth transition for both the child and the new providers. However, many military-connected families have experienced advocacy that is most effective when the male service member parent participates in the IEP process (Aleman-Tover et al., 2022). Since this parent may not always be regularly available or may be unavailable altogether for some families, this can add to the stress and frustration experienced by the home caregiver parent.

### Auxiliary Services

Accessing auxiliary services can also be a challenge for 2e MCSs. Therapies accessed outside of schools have many of the same challenges as those within schools. There are shortages of providers and long wait times across many of the therapies that 2e MCSs rely on, including ABA and occupational therapies, in addition to regular scheduling delays with medical providers and specialists (Farley et al., 2021; Cramm et al., 2019). These common challenges can be compounded in military communities because often both the providers and the patients are frequently in transition. This typically leaves the home caregiver responsible for identifying providers, establishing care, transferring records, and managing billing for their child's services at each new duty station (Health Promotion and Wellness Public Health Assessment Division, 2019; Aronson et al., 2016). While auxiliary services are a significant asset to many 2e MCSs, accessing them can require a great deal of coordination and planning in times of transition.

### Transfer Delays and Academics

While policies have been implemented to address the challenges of transferring paperwork such as IEPs, 504 plans, and EFMP documents between schools, significant issues persist. Many military-connected families continue to struggle with accessing necessary services, transferring timely supports, and managing transitions to new schools (Aleman-Tover et al., 2022). These issues are compounded for students with IEPs or 504 plans, where additional frustrations include gaps in service continuity and a lack of educator familiarity with specific accommodations (MCEC, 2020). Such delays in the transfer of paperwork contribute to a noticeable lag in the initiation of services at new schools, affecting the overall support provided to students (MCEC, 2020).

The problem of delayed paperwork extends beyond special education services. For gifted students, delays in receiving and reviewing assessment records often necessitate reassessment to ensure appropriate placement, which imposes an extra layer of complexity and burden on the family (Meyer, 2022). This process can further disrupt the continuity of educational support and exacerbate the challenges faced by MCSs who frequently relocate.

The impact of these delays on students is multifaceted. Not only do they experience interruptions in their educational services, but the uncertainty and inconsistency in support can also affect their academic performance and emotional wellbeing (MCEC, 2020; Meyer, 2022). For military families, these disruptions can contribute to additional stress and frustration, as parents must navigate both the logistical challenges of relocating and the bureaucratic hurdles associated with transferring educational records.

The gaps in knowledge among educators about specific accommodations required by students with disabilities or gifted students can hinder effective support. Teachers at new schools may need time to become familiar with the unique needs of these students, which can further delay the implementation of necessary services and supports.

To mitigate these issues, it is crucial to streamline the process for transferring educational records and ensure that schools are well informed about the needs of incoming students. Enhanced communication between schools, military families, and education agencies can help reduce delays and improve the overall transition experience for MCSs. Additionally, providing professional development for educators on the specific needs of students with disabilities and those who are gifted can enhance their ability to support these students effectively from the outset.

Addressing these challenges requires a concerted effort from all stakeholders involved in the education and support of MCSs. By improving the efficiency of paperwork transfers and increasing awareness and training among educators, it is possible to create a more streamlined transition process that better supports the academic and emotional needs of these students.

## Educator Awareness and Preparedness

Despite being a large student subgroup, MCSs can be difficult for districts, schools, and teachers to identify and support. Teachers and school leaders typically know very little about the specific lifestyle demands that MCSs face; and what they do know, they often do not know how to accommodate (Ruff & Keim, 2014). Schools are taking steps to address the needs of their MCSs with student transition programming and initiatives like the Purple Star designation in many states, but research is limited on the extent to which these programs impact the MCS experience.

Recommendations from the Military Child Education Coalition (MCEC) primarily emphasize the importance of easing transitions for military families by ensuring that school staff are proactive in their communication. This includes monitoring students who are preparing for PCS, facilitating remote enrollment in programs at receiving schools, and obtaining parental consent before making changes to IEPs (MCEC, 2020). School staff are advised to actively anticipate the needs of families preparing for a PCS by gathering and maintaining updated evaluation schedules, and by keeping a detailed record of what strategies have been effective with the student at their current school (Meyer, 2022; Jagger, 2014). Shaw (2018) offers similar advice, recommending that parents collaborate with schools to keep records current and seek additional education about their child's disability to advocate effectively across different educational settings.

To further support transitioning families, receiving school staff should proactively engage with families undergoing a PCS and provide clear information about anticipated changes, such as how IEP goals might be approached differently in the new school environment. One recommendation is to maintain IEPs at the receiving school for up to six months following a PCS (Shaw, 2018). This extended time can allow MCS to better settle in and play catchup in areas they may have missed during the move.

In addition to supporting families directly, establishing key partnerships is crucial. It has been suggested that improving communication channels between military base commands and school superintendents could be beneficial (Classen et al., 2019). Such partnerships may reduce the stress associated with relocations, diminish the stigma surrounding special education, and facilitate easier access to resources, ultimately supporting a smoother transition for military families.

# Additional Considerations

The impacts of having a 2e military-connected teen often extend beyond the educational needs of that teen. Having a 2e military-connected teen in a family can impact siblings, access to extracurricular activities, and the service member's career. Understanding how the needs of a 2e MCS can ripple across the family unit is critical to establishing necessary support structures.

## Sibling Considerations

There is little research regarding the relationship between 2e students and their siblings and research on the relationships between military-connected siblings is similarly lacking. However, what is known is that both situations play a part in the dynamics between siblings, their parents, and educators.

One of the most significant considerations for military-connected families with a 2e child is the potential for sibling rivalry or unequal treatment. The stress of adapting to new schools and making new friends following a PCS or dealing with a parent's deployment can lead to increased irritability and conflict between siblings (Chandra et al., 2020; Rylander, 2020). The pressures of military life can also sometimes result in uneven attention from the parents, particularly if one child is struggling more with the various changes or if there is a deployed parent (Choe, 2021). This often exacerbates feelings of jealousy or rivalry, as siblings compete for limited home caregiver time and resources. Additionally, much of the parents' attention and resources may be focused on meeting the specific needs of the 2e child (Baum et al., 2017). This can lead siblings to feel overlooked or resentful, particularly if they perceive that their achievements or struggles are not receiving the same level of attention. Siblings in both cases might feel pressure either to excel to gain attention or to downplay their needs to avoid burdening their parents further.

The deployment of a parent is another critical factor that influences sibling relationships in military families (Chandra et al., 2010). As previously discussed, during a deployment the home caregiver takes on additional responsibilities, which can be overwhelming. In such cases, older siblings may feel compelled to step up their involvement by helping to care for younger siblings, contributing to behavior management, and assisting with more household chores (Choe, 2021; Russo, 2015). This can foster a sense of maturity and responsibility in older siblings; however, it can also create stress if they feel burdened by these additional duties (Chandra et al., 2010; Huebner & Mancini, 2005). Meanwhile, younger siblings may look to their older siblings for guidance and reassurance and thus strengthen their bond while simultaneously internalizing the imbalance in their sibling dynamic.

Despite the challenges, the military lifestyle offers unique opportunities for sibling relationships to deepen. The shared experiences of military life can create a strong sense of family identity and solidarity (Huebner & Mancini, 2005). When possible, military families may live in close-knit communities where children can find support and friendship among other military kids who understand their lifestyle. This sense of community can reinforce sibling bonds, as they share not only a familial connection but also a shared identity as military children. Much like any sibling dynamic, communication within the family is another crucial factor. Open, age-appropriate conversations about the nature of being a military family as well as what needs the 2e sibling has can help demystify the situation and foster empathy on all sides (Baum et al., 2017; Trail, 2010).

## Extracurricular Activities

Extracurricular activities play a pivotal role in the lives of MCSs and may be even more vital for those who are 2e. These activities are key in promoting social, emotional, and academic development. For MCSs, who often face unique challenges due to the transient nature of military life, participation in extracurricular activities can be a stabilizing force that significantly enhances their overall wellbeing and academic success (MCEC, 2020).

One of the most significant benefits of extracurricular activities for MCSs is the opportunity they provide for finding and fitting into established social groups (Fredericks & Eccles, 2006). As mentioned, frequent moves can disrupt friendships and make it difficult for MCSs to form lasting relationships. Extracurricular activities can be a way for 2e MCSs to quickly meet peers with similar interests. These meetings occur within familiar frameworks and help build new social connections in an unfamiliar environment. Extracurriculars such as sports teams, bands, or academic clubs create a sense of belonging and community, which is crucial for students who might otherwise feel isolated after relocating to a new school (Meyer, 2022).

Extracurricular activities offer MCSs a sense of continuity amid the constant changes in their lives. While the differences in academic curriculum have been discussed in depth, often extracurricular activities are universally recognized and available across various schools (MCEC, 2020). This continuity helps ease the transition by providing students with a familiar environment where they can pursue their interests and excel at something they already know and enjoy. Additionally, the discipline required to balance schoolwork with extracurricular commitments can instill a strong work ethic and time management skills, which are often lacking in 2e students (Reis et al., 2014).

In addition to fostering social connections and providing continuity, extracurricular activities play a crucial role in the emotional and mental health of MCSs. Participation in these activities can boost self-esteem and provide an outlet for stress and anxiety, which are common issues for students who experience frequent relocations (MCEC, 2020; Rylander, 2020). Engaging in activities they are passionate about allows MCSs to develop self-expression and self-confidence (Meyer, 2022).

Academically, extracurricular activities can enhance educational experience by promoting deeper engagement with the school. Students who participate in extracurricular activities are more likely to have higher grades, better attendance, and a stronger commitment to their education (Frederick & Eccles, 2006). For 2e MCSs, who face academic disruptions due to their numerous school transfers, these activities can serve as an anchor, keeping them engaged and motivated to succeed despite the challenges they face (MCEC, 2020; Meyer, 2022).

Extracurricular activities may also provide MCSs with opportunities for leadership and personal growth (Fredricks & Eccles, 2006). These activities often require teamwork, problem-solving, and leadership skills—valuable life skills that students can carry with them beyond their school years. These skills are also valuable for 2e students, who often want to take a more hands-on approach to their education (Kaendler et al., 2016). By assuming leadership roles in clubs or teams, 2e MCSs can gain confidence in their abilities and develop a stronger sense of responsibility.

### Impact on Service Members' Career

An issue that may not be openly discussed by military personnel is that having a child with additional needs in the military can change the trajectory of one's career. In the military, all service members are advised to enroll their spouse, children, or other dependents in the EFMP whenever a medical diagnosis occurs, especially when the service member is preparing for a new assignment (Military.com, 2023). The EFMP helps assess whether a new assignment can accommodate the medical, behavioral, or educational needs of the service member's dependents and aids in seeking a reassignment if necessary.

However, not all service members will follow through on seeking EFMP enrollment. One reason cited for inadequate screening by the EFMP before a move is the responsibility placed on the service member (USGAO, 2012). The service member is the only parent who can enroll their child and is solely responsible for updating paperwork through their child's enrollment. This issue reflects a broader concern about how enrolling in EFMP or seeking special education services for a child might negatively impact a service member's career (MCEC, 2020). According to Classen et al. (2019), junior service members may be particularly hesitant to seek services for their child due to concerns about career repercussions or a lack of familiarity with accessing resources.

The perceived stigma associated with having a child in special education can also affect access to support. The absence of appropriate supports for these families can have significant repercussions on military readiness. Specifically, it can lead to reduced individual retention of service members and hinder the economic feasibility of relocating to installations or states that lack adequate services (MCEC, 2020).

## Support for MCS and Families

There are programs designed to support military families across their various needs, reflecting the importance that military organizations and policymakers

Table 10.1 Support Services and Organizations for Military-Connected Families

| Organization or Initiative | Mission |
|---|---|
| Military Interstate Children's Compact Commission http://mic3.net | "The collaborative's mission: ease the educational transitions of school-aged, military and uniform-connected students attending public schools, to include Department of Defense Education Activity schools worldwide, and also promulgate and enforce the compact rules." |
| MCEC http://militarychild.org | "MCEC supports all military-connected children by educating, advocating, and collaborating to resolve education challenges associated with the military lifestyle." |
| School Liaison Program https://www.dodea.edu/education/partnership-and-resources/department-defense-school-liaison-program | "School Liaisons serve as the primary point of contact for PK-12th grade school-related matters. The School Liaison Program offers an array of services and resources to support students, parents, installation leadership, schools and the surrounding community." |
| Families OverComing Under Stress https://focusproject.org | "FOCUS (Families OverComing Under Stress) provides resilience training to military children, families, and couples. It teaches practical skills to help families and couples overcome common challenges related to a military life. It helps build on current strengths and teach new strategies to enhance communication and problem solving, goal setting and creating a shared family story." |
| The Protect the Rights of Military children in Special Education (PROMISE) Act http://thepromiseact.org | "Our mission is to Protect the Rights Of Military children in Special Education and disability communities to ensure they receive equal access to an education. We develop data-informed solutions that equip parents, inform leaders and enable military students to thrive. We promote the principles of diversity, equity and inclusion by advocating for the futures of our military children with unique and diverse backgrounds and needs." |

(Continued)

*Table 10.1* Support Services and Organizations for Military-Connected Families (*Continued*)

| Organization or Initiative | Mission |
|---|---|
| EFMP<br>https://efmpandme<br>.militaryonesource.mil/ | "EFMP is more than just one program or connection point, it's the work of three components: Family Support, Identification and Enrollment, and Assignment Coordination. The program assists by identifying and enrolling family members with special medical or educational needs; finding out what services are available at current or new duty stations; and supporting families with information, referrals when appropriate, and non-clinical case management to access services." |

place on serving these families. However, many military families may be unaware of or unfamiliar with these resources (Barmeier, 2014). This lack of awareness may stem from the relative newness of these programs—many of which have only been established since the 2010s—or from the self-reliant nature of military families (Janeth et al., 2022). At this time, there is no single organization dedicated to helping military families with 2e students find suitable educational settings and accommodations. Table 10.1 presents the missions of these programs.

Being a 2e MCS is rife with challenges, often related to frequent relocation and parental separation. Understanding the experiences of 2e MCSs is critical to being able to develop and employ services and supports that are designed to meet their needs. While there are numerous social, academic, and other considerations unique to 2e MCSs, there are also multiple organizations and interventions available to help educators, families, lawmakers, and other stakeholders cooperate to ensure their success. Exploring these and other ongoing initiatives targeted at 2e MCSs is critical to supporting them within and beyond the classroom.

## Things to Consider

- MCSs often move six to nine times during their K-12 years, impacting educational stability.
- Disruptions in special education and gifted services for twice-exceptional students are common, as IEPs and 504 plans do not always transfer seamlessly.
- MCSs may develop resilience and adaptability but also face difficulties with identity formation due to constant environmental changes.
- Military-connected families often experience long delays (averaging 5.75 months) in reestablishing special education services after relocation.
- Gifted programs often have rigid enrollment periods or lottery-based admissions, making access difficult for students moving mid-year.
- The Interstate Compact on Educational Opportunity for Military Children exists but is not uniformly implemented, creating barriers for 2e students.
- The stigma around special education in military culture can deter service members from enrolling their children in support programs.

## For Discussion

- What assets and constraints can you identify for 2e MCSs after reading this chapter that you may not have previously been aware of?
- In what ways is being a military-connected 2e student the same as and different from being a non-military-connected 2e student?
- How can teachers and other school support personnel obtain more information about MCSs, including 2e students?
- What initiatives or organizations shared in this chapter were new to you? What other organizations or resources might be helpful to you as someone who supports 2e MCSs?
- What unique challenges can you identify that Hudson faced as an MCS?
- What unique assets can you identify that Hudson may have had to help him succeed despite barriers?
- What might be different about school transitions for 2e MCSs compared to students who do not require special services?
- What supports can you think of that Hudson's schools could have implemented to be more supportive of 2e MCSs?

## References

Air & Space Forces Magazine. (2021, June 30). *2021 USAF & USSF almanac: DOD personnel*. Air & Space Forces Association. https://www.airandspaceforces.com/article/2021-usaf-ussf-almanac-dod-personnel/

Aleman-Tovar, J., Schraml-Block, K., DiPietro-Wells, R., & Burke, M. (2022) Exploring the advocacy experiences of military families with children who have disabilities. *Journal of Child and Family Studies, 31*, 843-853. https://doi.org/10.1007/s10826-021-02161-5

Alfano C.A., Lau, S., Balderas, J., Bunnell, B.E., & Beidel, D.C. (2016) The impact of military deployment on children: Placing developmental risk in context. *Clinical Psychology Review, 43*, 17-29, https://doi.org/10.1016/j.cpr.2015.11.003.

Anderson, S. & Leventhal, T. (2017) Residential mobility and adolescent achievement and behavior: Understanding timing and extent of mobility. *Journal of Research on Adolescence, 27*(2), 328-343. https://doi.org/10.1111/jora.12288

American Association of School Administrators. (2019). Fact sheet on the military child. AASA the School Superintendents Association. https://www.aasa.org/content.aspx?id=8998

Barmeier, M. (Moderator) (2014). Health care utilization by military-connected children and their families. In Eunice Kennedy Shriver National Institute of Child Health and Human Development and the HSC Foundation, *Military children with special health care needs: What is known? What are the gaps in research and practice?* [Working Group] Military-connected children with special health care needs and their families, April 14-15, Bethesda, MD, United States. https://www.nichd.nih.gov/sites/default/files/about/meetings/2014/Documents/military_families_summary.pdf

Barnhill J., Schaffer A.P., Consedine M., Mahoney C.D., Shuman A. (2022) *Military children in special education: The real, perceived, and unknown barriers to accessing a free and appropriate public education (FAPE).* https://thepromiseact.org/wp-content/uploads/Partners-in-PROMISE-2022-Survey-Findings-FINAL.pdf

Baum, S. M., Schader, R. M., & Hébert, T. P. (2014) Through a different lens: Reflecting on a strengths-based, talent-focused approach for twice-exceptional learners. *Gifted Child Quarterly*, 58(4), 311-327. https://doi.org/10.1177/0016986214547632

Baum, S.M., Schader, R.M., & Owen, S.V. (2017) *To be gifted and learning disabled: Strength-based strategies for helping twice-exceptional students with LD, ADHD, ASD, and More* (3rd ed.). Routledge. https://doi.org/10.4324/9781003239147

Bracamonte, M. (2010) *Twice exceptional students: Who they are and what they need.* Davidson Institute. https://www.davidsongifted.org/gifted-blog/2e-students-who-they-are-and-what-they-need/

Bradshaw, C. P., Sudhinaraset, M., Mmari, K., & Blum, R. W. (2010) School transitions among military adolescents: A qualitative study of stress and coping. *School Psychology Review*, 39(1), 84-105. https://doi.org/10.1080/02796015.2010.12087792

Chandra, A., Lara-Cinisomo, S., Jaycox, L. H., Tanielian, T., Burns, R. M., Ruder, T., & Han, B. (2010) Children on the homefront: The experience of children/military families. *Pediatrics*, 125(1), 16. https://doi.org/10.1542/peds.2009-1180

Choe, Y. J. (2021) *A multiple case study: Military-dependent children's social and emotional well-being and its impact on classroom behavior* (Publication No. 28647650) [Doctoral Dissertation, Baylor University]. ProQuest Dissertations and Theses.

Classen, A. I. (2014). *Needs of military families: Family and educator perspectives* (Publication No. 3632937) [Doctoral Dissertation, University of Kansas]. ProQuest Dissertations and Theses.

Clever, M. & Segal, D. R. (2013) The demographics of military children and families. *Future of Children*, 23(2), 13-39. https://doi.org/10.1542/peds.2009-1180

Congressional Research Service (2020) Defense primer: Reserve forces. https://crsreports.congress.gov/product/pdf/IF/IF10540

Cramm, H., McColl, M. A., Aiken, A. B., & Williams, A. (2019) The mental health of military-connected children: A scoping review. *Journal of Child and Family Studies, 28*(7), 1725-1735. https://doi.org/10.1007/s10826-019-01402-y

Crepeau-Hobson, F. and Bianco, M. (2010) Identification of gifted students with learning disabilities in a response-to-intervention era. *Psychology in the Schools, 48*(2), 102-109. https://doi.org/10.1002/pits.20528

Department of Defense Education Activity (2022) Department of Defense school liaison program. https://www.dodea.edu/partnership/schoolliaisonofficers.cfm

DePedro, K.T., Atuel, H., Malchi, K., Esqueda, M.C., Benbenishty, R., & Astor, R.A. (2014) Responding to the needs of military students and military-connected schools: Perceptions and actions of school administrators. *Children & Schools, 36*(1), 18-25. https://doi.org/10.1093/cs/cdt047

Easterbrooks M. A., Ginsburg K., & Lerner R. M. (2013) Resilience among military youth. *Future Child, 23*(2), 99-120. https://doi: 10.1353/foc.2013.0014

Esqueda, M. C., Astor, R. A., & De Pedro, K. M. T. (2012) A call to duty: Educational policy and school reform addressing the needs of children from military families. *Educational Researcher, 41*(2), 65-70. https://doi.org/10.3102/0013189X11432139

Fadus, M. C., Valadez, E. A., Bryant, B. E., Garcia, A. M., Neelon, B., Tomko, R. L., & Squeglia, L. M. (2021) Racial disparities in elementary school disciplinary actions: Findings from the ABCD study. *Journal of the American Academy of Child and Adolescent Psychiatry, 60*(8), 998-1009. https://doi.org/10.1016/j.jaac.2020.11.017

Families OverComing Under Stress. (2017). Focus: Resilience training for military families. https://focusproject.org/

Farley, B. E., Griffith, A., Mahoney, A., Zhang, D., & Kruse, L. (2022) Brief report: Identifying concerns of military caregivers with children diagnosed with ASD following a military directed relocation. *Journal of Autism and Developmental Disorders, 52*(1), 447-453. https://doi.org/10.1007/s10803-021-04936-7

Forbes, D. L. (2022). A guide to the exceptional family member program. America's Navy, December 22. https://www.navy.mil/Press-Office/News-Stories/Article/3254358/a-guide-to-the-exceptional-family-member-program

Fredricks, J. A. & Eccles, J. S. (2006) Is extracurricular participation associated with beneficial outcomes? Concurrent and longitudinal relations. *Developmental Psychology, 42*(4), 698.

Garner, J. K. & Nunnery, J. A. (2018) The children come and go: How educating military-connected students impacts the work of school teachers, counselors, and administrators. In L. D. Hill & F. J. Levine (eds.) *Global Perspectives on Education Research* (pp. 125-156). Routledge.

Huebner, A. & Mancini, J. (2005) *Adjustments among adolescents in military families when a parent is deployed: Final report to the Military Family Research Institute & Department of Defense.* Department of Human Development, Virginia Polytechnic Institute and State University. https://www.researchgate.net/publication/238513588

Hulsey, A. (2011) Military child education coalition: Building partnerships and support networks for military children with special needs. *Exceptional Parent*, 41(9), 18-20. https://www.proquest.com/education/docview/1371422033/abstract/1A6C5F8C99D341F9PQ/3

Jackson-Lynch, L. M. (2020) *Influence of one or more domestic relocations on adolescent social skills perceived by former military parents* (Publication No. 28398834) [Doctoral Dissertation, Texas Woman's University]. ProQuest Dissertations and Theses.

Jagger, J. C. & Lederer, S. (2014) Impact of geographic mobility on military children's access to special education services. *Children & Schools*, 36(1), 15-22. https://doi.org/10.1093/cs/cdt046

Janeth, A.-T., Schraml-Block, K., DiPietro-Wells, R., & Burke, M. (2022) Exploring the advocacy experiences of military families with children who have disabilities. *Journal of Child and Family Studies*, 31(3), 843-853. https://doi.org/10.1007/s10826-021-02161-5

Kaendler, C., Wiedmann, M., Leuders, T., Rummel, N., & Spada, H. (2016) Monitoring student interaction during collaborative learning: Design and evaluation of a training program for pre-service teachers. *Psychology Learning & Teaching*, 15(1), 44-64. https://doi.org/10.1177/1475725716638010

Kaye, M. P., Aronson, K. R., & Perkins, D. F. (2022) Factors predicting family violence revictimization among army families with child maltreatment. *Child Maltreatment*, 27(3), 423-433. https://doi.org/10.1177/10775595211008997

Knobloch, L., Pusateri, K., Ebata, A., & McGlaughlin, P. (2015) Experiences of military youth during a family member's employment: Changes, challenges, and opportunities. *Youth & Society*, 47(3), 319-342. https://doi.org/10.1177/0044118X12462040

Le Menestrel, S. & Kizer, K. W. (2019) Demographic and military service characteristics of military families. In S. Le Menestrel & K.W. Kizer (eds.) *Strengthening the military family readiness system for a changing American society* [online edition]. National Academies Press (U.S.). https://www.ncbi.nlm.nih.gov/books/NBK547615/#:~:text=Family%20Status&text=Overall%2C%20about%2050%20percent%20of,(DoD%2C%202017%

Lleras, C. & McKillip, M. (2017) When children move: Behavior and achievement outcomes during elementary school. *Journal of Educational Research, 110*(2), 177-187. https://doi.org/10.1080/00220671.2015.1060930

Lester, P., Aralis, H., Sinclair, M., Kiff, C., Lee, K.-H., Mustillo, S., & Wadsworth, S. M. (2016) The impact of deployment on parental, family and child adjustment in military families. *Child Psychiatry and Human Development, 47*(6), 938-949.

Lester, P. & Flake, E. (2013) How wartime military service affects children and families. *Future of Children, 23*, 121-141. https://doi.org/10.1353/foc.2013.0015

MCEC (2020) Social justice. https://www.militarychild.org/upload/images/MGS%202022/WellbeingToolkit/AL_4_1_Social_Justice_interactiv.pdf

Meyer, M. S. (2022) On the move: Helping military-connected gifted students navigate non-promotional school transitions. In J. A. Castellano & K. L. Chandler (eds.) *Identifying and serving diverse gifted learners: Meeting the needs of special populations in gifted education* (pp. 23-34). Routledge. https://doi.org/10.4324/9781003265412-6

Military.com (2023) The Exceptional Family Member Program: EFMP. https://www.military.com/benefits/tricare/the-exceptional-family-member-program.html

Military Child Education Coalition (2017). The challenges of supporting highly-mobile, military-connected children in school transitions. https://militarychild.org/upload/images/CPRL/Military_Student_Transitions_Stu.pdf

Military Child Education Coalition (2020). Military kids now 2020 survey: Summary report. https://militarychild.org/wp-content/uploads/2024/05/MCEC_2020EdSurvey_digital.pdfhttps://www.militarychild.org/news/press-releases/2020/mcec-survey-reveals-significant-concerns-for-militaryconnected-students

Military Child Education Coalition (2023) Mission and vision. https://www.militarychild.org/about/mission-vision

Military Family Research Institute (2017) Military women and marriage: A fact sheet. www.healthymarriageinfo.org/wp-content/uploads/2017/12/militarywomenmarriage.pdf

Military Interstate Children's Compact Commission (n.d.) Background. https://mic3.net/background/

Military OneSource (n.d.) Advancing in the Military. Millife Guides. https://www.militaryonesource.mil/resources/millife-guides/military-career/#learn-about-re-enlisting-and-rising-through-the-ranks

Military OneSource (n.d.) Military and family life counselling. https://www.militaryonesource.mil/non-medical-counseling/military-and-family-life-counseling/

Miller, A. (2023, May 12) Military ranks: Everything you need to know. Military.com. https://www.military.com/join-military/military-ranks-everything-you-need-know.html

Mmari, K., Bradshaw, C., Sudhinaraset, M. & Blum, R. (2010) Exploring the role of social connectedness among military youth: Perceptions from youth, parents, and school personnel. *Child & Youth Care Forum, 39*, 351-366. https://doi.org/10.1007/s10566-010-9109-3

National Guard (2021) About the Guard: Army National Guard. https://www.nationalguard.mil/About-the-Guard/Army-National-Guard/

Operation Autism (2024) What does the Exceptional Family Member Program (EFMP) do for my family? https://operationautism.org/healthcare/efmp/

Partners in Promise (2020) Military special education evaluation. https://thepromiseact.org/wp-content/uploads/Partners-in-PROMISE-2021-Military-Special-Education-Survey-Resource-Partner-Report.pdf

Reed S. C., Bell J. F., & Edwards, T. C. (2011). Adolescent well-being in Washington state military families. *American Journal of Public Health, 101*(9), 1676-1682.

Reis, S. M., Baum, S. M., & Burke, E. (2014) An operational definition of twice-exceptional learners: Implications and applications. *Gifted Child Quarterly, 58*(3), 217-230. https://doi.org/10.1177/0016986214534976

Russo, T. J. & Fallon, M. A. (2015) Coping with stress: Supporting the needs of military families and their children. *Early Childhood Education Journal, 43*(5), 407-416. https://doi.org/10.1007/s10643-014-0665-2

Rylander, N. J. (2020). *A qualitative narrative exploration of the social, emotional, and academic needs of military-connected students* (Publication No. 28093293) [Doctoral Dissertation, Northcentral University]. ProQuest Dissertations and Theses.

Shaw, A. (2018). Educational resources for military-based families. *The Exceptional Parent (Online), 48*, 72-82. https://www.proquest.com/magazines/educational-resources-military-based-families/docview/2002001226/se-2

Trail, B. ((2010). Parenting twice-exceptional children through frustration to success. In J. L. Jolly, D. J. Treffinger, & T. F. Inman (eds.) *Parenting Gifted Children* (pp. 387-398). Routledge. https://doi.org/10.4324/9781003237020

Trautmann, J., Alhusen, J., & Gross, D. (2015) Impact of deployment on military families with young children: A systematic review. *Nursing Outlook, 63*(6), 656-679. https://doi.org/10.1016/j.outlook.2015.06.002

US Department of Defense (2022) 2022 demographics: Profile of the military community. https://download.militaryonesource.mil/12038/MOS/Reports/2022-demographics-report.pdf

US Department of Education (2004) Individuals with Disabilities Education Act. Public Law 108-446. https://www.congress.gov/bill/108th-congress/house-bill/1350/text

US Department of Education (2022) Veterans and military families. https://www.ed.gov/veterans-and-military-families

United States Government Accountability Office (2012a) Military dependent students: Better oversight needed to improve services for children with special needs. https://apps.dtic.mil/sti/pdfs/AD1170040.pdf

United Services Organization (2022) How long is a military deployment? https://www.uso.org/stories/2871-how-long-is-a-military-deployment#:~:text=Some%20service%20members%20are%20deployed,pre%2Ddeployment%20training%20as%20well.

Wang, L., Elder, G. H., & Spence, N. J. (2012) Status configurations, military service and higher education. *Social Forces*, *91*(2), 397-422. https://doi.org/10.1093/sf/sos174

Williamson, V., Stevelink, S. A. M., Da Silva, E., & Fear, N. T. (2018) A systematic review of wellbeing in children: a comparison of military and civilian families. *Child and Adolescent Psychiatry and Mental Health*, *12*(46). https://doi.org/10.1186/s13034-018-0252-1

# Chapter 11

# Considerations for Serving Twice-Exceptional Homeless and High-Mobility Students

Yvette R. Robinson

## Macartney and his Shark Tooth Collection

*The backseat of the car always feels safe to me because the yellow streetlight overhead shines like a nightlight. No matter where my mom and I are, every night, I stare at my collection of shark teeth until I'm too sleepy to keep my eyes open. The box of teeth goes with me no matter where we go and no matter how many times we move. It is always the first thing that I pack up each time my mom and I have to go live somewhere new. It is my most prized possession. Most sharks must keep moving to stay alive and they adapt to whatever new ocean they migrate to. This makes me feel like I have a lot in common with them. My name is Macartney. I have lived in lots of new places, but most of them have been close to the beach and that is great for me. Sometimes we stay in motels; sometimes with people my mom knows. When I was little, we lived with some of my mom's different relatives. But big fights would always happen and we had to leave to live elsewhere. We have stayed in homeless shelters a couple of times, but those made mom the crankiest because the people there were always telling her what to do. Now that I am 13, we don't try going to shelters at all because some of them don't allow boys over 12 to stay there. We usually only stay in the same place for a couple of months before we have to pack up and move again so mom can find a new job. I don't mind nights like this when we sleep in the car because, on these nights,* mom and I talk until really late about all kinds of things. My mom is so smart and knows a lot about all sorts of stuff like history, poetry, and space. She pushes me to ask questions and think really deeply about everything, even sharks.

Changing schools is the worst part. I never know what to expect at the next school or how the new teacher will treat me. Most of them don't like how my brain is always running all around the room and they don't believe that I really am trying to stay focused on what they are saying. Most of my teachers think I am just a bad kid and that I don't take school seriously. They get upset at me for my messy work and because my assignments are not finished. Some kids tease me because of my junky clothes. However, many kids at PE ask me to be on their team because I am good at many different sports.

A few years ago, when I was ten, I started a new school, and the class was learning about sharks on the day I got there. Ms. Thurston, my teacher, was impressed by how much I already knew about sharks. I told her about my shark tooth collection, the sharks I liked the best, and why I thought sharks and I had a lot in common. It was the first time that I noticed how some people's eyes "smile" when they understand how my brain works and how, for certain things, it works really efficiently. Ms. Thurston usually gave the class the option of completing our assignments in different ways. This helped my brain absorb more of what we were learning. She would give me extra time to complete assignments when I needed to. Other times, when I finished my work fast, she gave me hard little projects to work on that usually had something to do with sharks but were kind of still connected to what we were learning about. Leaving Ms. Thurston's class was more difficult than some of the other moves, but I was happy that I got to learn better about how my brain works. On my last day, I hugged her goodbye. She told me, "Macartney, tell your mom that she is raising an impressive young man, and I hope I get to read about you one day when you become a famous ichthyologist."

Ms. Thurston helped me understand that it wasn't that my brain couldn't focus but that it focused differently and on lots of things all at once. This helped me understand why I enjoy searching for sharks' teeth and why I can do it for a long time whenever mom and I go to the beach. While mom sleeps on her towel, I walk back and forth on the shore, pushing the shells around with my foot. My eyes skim over the sand and shells, and my mind fills up with a chorus of shell names. That's a lettered olive, an auger, a coquina, a jewel box, some cockles, a Florida cone, Florida buttons, sunray venus, slipper shell. After a little bit, I can see patterns in the types of shells, and I know if I have a good chance of finding a new tooth to add to my collection. When I keep my eyes steady, it is just a matter of time before I see the familiar black corner sticking out. Finding another tooth for my collection is my reward for controlling the steering of my brain. When I find a new one, I sort through my brain files, trying to figure out what type of shark it belonged to. Long and thin, it probably was a sand shark; short and thin, it probably was a lemon shark or maybe a reef shark. Every once *in a while, Mom looks with me and one time, we found a great white shark tooth and we both jumped up and down. On the ride back to the motel that day, I remembered thinking that I wished everything felt like looking for and finding shark teeth.*

Homelessness is a challenge facing an ever-growing number of American families with school-age children. The condition has reached levels unprecedented in the United States since the Great Depression (Tobin, 2016). School-age children have been continually identified as the fastest-growing segment of the homeless population for nearly 25 years (Becker & Boxill, 1990). During the 2021-2022 school year, public schools identified 1,205,292 students who experienced homelessness—that is, 2.4% of students enrolled in public schools, a 10% increase on the previous year. From the 2004-2005 to 2021-2022 school years, the number of students who experienced homelessness increased by 79% (National Center for Homeless Education, 2023). In New York City alone, the number of families with children living in Department of Homeless Services shelters had risen to 19,400 by the end of 2023 (Institute for Children, Poverty & Homelessness, 2019).

The mobility of children experiencing the foster care system is similar to that of children experiencing homelessness. There are approximately 400,000 children in the American foster care system. Although efforts are made when the child first enters foster care to ensure the stability of their placement in a home, many of these placements do not last. Factors undermining placement stability range from the caregiver's inability to cope with the child's trauma-induced behaviors to the caregiver's inability to cope with the impossible demands of the foster care system. Any number of factors can lead to the foster child's caregiver calling the case worker to request that the child be moved to a new home. Children in foster care may find themselves being moved from home to home dozens of times throughout their childhood until they turn 18 and are discharged from the system to face adulthood. According to Casey Family Programs (2023), of the children who have been in foster care for more than 24 months, 59% have been in and out of three or more homes. It is not uncommon for older children to experience ten to 15 different homes and school placement changes during their time in foster care. With each move comes a loss of friends and meaningful connections. With each change in school, records, grades, evaluations, and progress that the child has made may be lost. Among the children caught up in the growing number of homeless and high mobility (HHM) students are students navigating their education with gifts and challenges. This presents an intricate labyrinth of needs for educators to work through, as they must understand, support, and cultivate the learning experience for all students.

# The Hows and Whys of Homelessness and High Mobility for Students

Housing is essential for developing a sense of stability, certainty, and belonging. It is a vital component of child-rearing as it provides space for routines and predictability. Housing gives us space to store our belongings, maintain food supplies, and support the health and safety of our families. The place we call home helps us feel settled, established, and rooted. However, for 1.5 million people, conditions often outside of their control disrupt the options available to them for where they will call "home."

US housing prices have risen significantly for 11 consecutive years. In 2021, the housing market saw the highest jump in over 20 years (Bahney, 2022). The meteoric rise of housing prices, flanked by stagnating wages and the lack of a living minimum wage, has created unmanageable conditions for many families. American society has also seen a widening divide between the skills and credentials required to move from a low-paying job to one offering better wages; for those who did not have the opportunity to complete a high-school diploma or degree or obtain specialized work skills, the proliferation of low-paying jobs keeps them trapped in a cycle of working long hours in multiple jobs to barely scrape by. These conditions, combined with difficulties in accessing affordable childcare, underemployment, and the rising cost of goods, mean the inevitability of homelessness for families living on the margins of society increases. As we saw with Macartney and his mom, permanent housing was out of reach despite his mom having work.

Risk factors that increase the likelihood of homelessness among parents of young children include estrangement from extended family, parents who themselves have a childhood history of instability, growing up in foster care, and abandonment by their parent or parents. Incarceration of an income-earning household member can cause the remaining caregiver to lack sufficient funds to cover household expenses. Growing up in poverty, lacking a high-school diploma, having a child at a young age, and working in low-wage jobs are also common themes of homeless families with young children. A large percentage of homeless mothers have histories of severe physical or sexual abuse (Gültekin et al., 2014). Finally, substance abuse and a recent history of mental health hospitalization indicate an increased likelihood of homelessness (Bassuk et al., 1997).

While concentrations of homelessness are more likely to be seen in urban areas, substantial rates of homelessness can be found in suburban and rural areas as well. The lack of funding available for support services in many rural communities means families must navigate the challenge of homelessness on their own. The dearth of affordable housing units for individuals working minimum or low-wage jobs adds to the already pressurized state. Currently, 5.8 million housing units are needed to house America's low-income families (National Center on Family Homelessness, 2014). The vulnerability of people in poverty in landlord/tenant relationships increases the likelihood of being taken advantage of by the landlord, such as when a building becomes uninhabitable and the family does not have the resources to make a legal challenge. Once a family becomes homeless, they often must spend a higher-than-normal amount of money on basics such as food, transportation, and laundry as they lack their own amenities. This impedes efforts to escape homelessness because it uses up available financial resources that would otherwise go toward saving up for housing deposits and downpayments.

When a family loses access to their primary residence and lacks sufficient resources to relocate to a new permanent residence, their options of where to live next can vary significantly. "Couch surfing" or "doubling up" can occur when a homeless family moves into a single-family home that is already occupied by others. Families may couch surf or double up to avoid the stigma associated with going to a homeless shelter or when there are no shelters or shelter spaces available. This is a standard solution for many homeless families. Doubling up can provide access to much-needed support for homeless parents. Homeless mothers in doubled-up living arrangements can benefit from having more people available to help with childcare. However, crowding can negatively impact children in doubled-up arrangements where a lack of quiet space can interfere with concentration on schoolwork. Children in crowded households may be viewed as a burden or nuisance, leading to strain in family environments (Bush, 2017). If the dynamics in the home become unsafe, strained, or contentious, the family can find themselves discharged and homeless all over again. Macartney and his mom experienced the volatility of doubling up, even with family.

Motels and hotels may be an option when minimal funds are available. A homeless family may move into a motel for an extended period. Although this option is costly, it offers a certain level of autonomy that doubling up or a shelter does not provide. Hotels and motels do not require credit checks, income verification, large amounts of money upfront, or separate utility payments. This is also true for trailer parks and campgrounds. These conditions may be cramped and offer little in the way of a comfortable space for students to focus on school. When families lack the funds and resources to stay in a motel or campground, they may seek shelter in automobiles or other spaces not intended for habitation, such as in abandoned buildings, under bridges, in wooded areas, down alleyways, or on sidewalks.

Larger cities and communities with denser populations may have emergency shelters or transitional housing facilities for homeless families. Shelters generally provide supportive services but often offer little autonomy and typically have firmly set schedules. Shelters can often be densely populated with other individuals with varying degrees of healthy functioning. The schedule in a shelter can hinder parents' routines, and threats of being referred to child protective services may be suggested or overtly made by shelter staff. Adults and children staying in a shelter may be stigmatized by others in their community, and their plight can be blamed on some ill-perceived moral failing. Children who live in shelters may get teased or be bullied by their peers at school because of where they live. To avoid all these issues, parents may opt to have their child taken care of by others when they become homeless. This separation of the child from their parent can cause a negative experience, such as feelings of abandonment or loss.

## Adverse Experiences and Their Impact on HHM Students

Homelessness predictably brings a host of harmful exposures and experiences. Being a victim of violence and witnessing violence are not uncommon for children experiencing homelessness. Families experiencing homelessness suffer disproportionately from chronic health conditions that may contribute to poorer health outcomes. HHM children have higher rates of emergency room visits and hospitalizations (Ives, 2018). Homeless children also suffer disproportionately from asthma, anemia, malnutrition, lice, scabies, depression, anxiety, dental problems, ear infections, and respiratory infections. They are at increased risk of trauma-related injuries and skin infections (Gültekin et al., 2014). Depression and anxiety were also identified as elevated mental health risks associated with school-age children staying in shelters (Karr, 2012). HHM students often see a breakup of their family due to cramped conditions or shelters that do not allow unmarried parents to be housed together.

The anguish that comes with not knowing where you are going to go to sleep that night or if you will have food to eat can profoundly impact a child's emotional state. Youth experiencing homelessness sleep less than their housed peers, with 33% indicating that they slept fewer than four hours each night on average. Children experiencing homelessness are also twice as likely not to eat breakfast before attending school (Institute for Children, Poverty & Homelessness, 2019).

Upon receiving a new HHM student, office personnel at the school may be left to make their best determination of grade placement and educational needs based on the limited data that they receive. This can result in the child losing valuable learning time. The child may arrive at a class with the same title as the one they left, but the new teacher may approach instruction differently or the class may be on an entirely different section of the course. This misalignment of coursework can result in gaps in the child's learning. This can be particularly detrimental in math, as it requires a structured progression of knowledge and skills. Educational time can also be lost when a student joins a class and repeats previously learned content. Popp et al. (2003) noted that it can take four to six months to recover academically from each school transfer. Because Macartney and his mom moved so often, it is likely that an individual education plan (IEP) was never even completed. Had an IEP been part of his records and had those records been received in a timely manner, he may have received more consistency in the accommodations that he was given.

Their difficulties may be the only patterns observed for struggling unidentified twice-exceptional students, while their giftedness remains unseen. This could result in the child being placed in special education and remedial programs where the proper pedagogy needed to meet their needs may be lacking. The unchallenged child can become bored and begin exhibiting further behavior problems, resulting in disciplinary actions and ultimately becoming even further detached from school. Children who live in shelters may also experience mistreatment from peers. They may be teased about the condition of their hair, the quality of their clothes, or where they live (e.g., a shelter; a car). This can be made worse by the implicit bias of teachers, who may only see an uninterested, disorganized student who sleeps in class and is poorly groomed. Getting to school and attending consistently can also be a challenge. Opportunities for school-provided transportation often mean long early morning and afterschool commutes. HHM students may be kept out of school to care for younger siblings when other childcare options are absent. Increased rates of illness and mental health for the child can mean more healthcare appointments and missed school days.

Findings related to the neuropsychology of HHM students consistently indicate a high degree of challenges. The impact of homelessness on children and youth includes "changes in brain architecture that can interfere with learning, emotional self-regulation, cognitive skills, and social relationships" (Luby, 2015, p7). Students experiencing homelessness are at increased risk of developmental issues pertaining to physical development, mental health, and school success. They experience a significantly higher prevalence of developmental delays in communication and social and emotional development. Homelessness in youth may also affect neurocognitive functioning (e.g., poor decision-making; reckless behaviors; risk-taking; emotional outbursts). It may also lead to an increased likelihood of adverse childhood experiences such as trauma and abuse (American School Counselor Association, 2018). Additionally, Obradovic et al. (2009) found that the gap in achievement between HHM students and their low-income and advantaged peers was present as early as second grade and persisted through elementary school. Researchers have also found that students experiencing homelessness are more likely to be retained and perform below their peers in grades earned and test scores (Masten et al., 2015).

While economically disadvantaged students graduate at rates below their more affluent peers, graduation rates for students experiencing homelessness are markedly lower still. Close to 75% of homeless students drop out before graduating from high school. Only 69% of California high-school students during the 2017-2018 academic year who experienced homelessness completed high school in four years, compared to the statewide average of 83% (California Department of Education, n.d.) The graduation rates of children from foster care are some of the lowest of all students nationwide (National Center for Homeless Education, 2023). Colorado foster care students graduated high school at the rate of 23%.

## McKinney Vento Homeless Assistance Act

The formal definition of "homelessness" used by the public school system comes from legislation implementing solutions to HHM students' struggles to receive a quality education. The McKinney-Vento Homeless Assistance Act (initially adopted by Congress in 1987 as the Stewart B. McKinney Act) was the first federal response to homelessness and brought much-needed attention to the issue of children who are homeless. It serves as the primary piece of federal legislation for educating children and youth experiencing homelessness in US public schools. It creates a framework of offices and services to improve HHM students' educational outcomes. The act was reauthorized as Title X, Part C of the No Child Left Behind Act in January 2002. The legislation's definitions offer guidelines that help school personnel clarify which children are considered homeless, what resources will be provided, and what safeguards they will be afforded. These guidelines are essential considerations when school resources for all students are often stretched thin and decisions must be made on how best to utilize them.

District and school administrators in local education agencies (LEAs) responsible for complying with McKinney-Vento must determine whether the law applies in each situation. They must ask, "Is this particular child or youth homeless?" If so, the administrator must answer a second question: "What does McKinney-Vento require the LEA to do?" The nationally applicable definition says the term "homeless" refers to "individuals who lack a fixed, regular, and adequate nighttime residence" (within the meaning of Section 103(a)(1)). The act gives examples for clarification, including:

> (i) children and youths who are sharing the housing of other persons due to loss of housing, economic hardship, or a similar reason; are living in motels, hotels, trailer parks, or camping grounds due to the lack of alternative adequate accommodations; are living in emergency or

transitional shelters; are abandoned in hospitals; or are awaiting foster care placement
(ii) children and youths who have a primary nighttime residence that is a public or private place not designed for or ordinarily used as a regular sleeping accommodation for human beings (within the meaning of section 103(a)(2)(C))
(iii) children and youths who are living in cars, parks, public spaces, abandoned buildings, substandard housing, bus or train stations, or similar settings; and
(iv) migratory children (as such term is defined in section 1309 of the Elementary and Secondary Education Act of 1965) who qualify as homeless for the purposes of this subtitle because the children are living in circumstances described in clauses (i) through (iii).

---

**Services Available to McKinney-Vento Eligible Children**

Children identified as McKinney-Vento eligible can receive various federally funded services. These include:

- tutoring, supplemental instruction, and enriched educational services that are linked to the achievement of state standards;
- expedited evaluations of homeless children and youths, including educational programs for gifted and talented students, children with disabilities, and English learners, programs in career and technical education, and school nutrition programs;
- referral services to homeless children and youths for medical, dental, mental, and other health services;
- transportation for students to enable them to remain at their home school when possible; and
- early childhood education programs for preschool-aged homeless children.

---

McKinney-Vento goes beyond just clearing the way for enrollment and supporting educational stability. It also provides directives in granting students appropriate full or partial credit when they change schools, instructions to consult with prior schools about partial coursework completion, and instructions to evaluate the student's mastery of partly completed courses and offerings of credit recovery. It also directs state and local education agencies to consider issues related to homelessness prior to taking disciplinary action and states that children cannot be disciplined for homelessness-related truancy. McKinney-Vento also mandates state and local agencies to provide training on the traumatic impacts of homelessness and how to provide trauma-informed support to their district's school staff.

Implementation of services occurs mainly at the state and local levels. At the local level, McKinney-Vento requires that every school district designate a local homeless education liaison to build awareness within the school system and the community about the needs of children and youth experiencing homelessness and the necessity for schools to address them. At the state level, the act creates the role of a state coordinator, usually a staff member within the state department of education. The state coordinator provides support to the local liaisons. At the federal level, McKinney-Vento has a federal coordinator and national technical assistance center. The Every Student Succeeds Act (ESSA) is a federal law signed by President Obama in 2015 that governs the United States' K-12 public education policy. ESSA aims to provide all children with a quality education and includes provisions related to accountability, state standards, assessment, and support for struggling schools. It replaced the No Child Left Behind Act. Although ESSA does not explicitly focus on homelessness like McKinney-Vento, its provisions are aimed at supporting the educational needs of disadvantaged and vulnerable student populations, including homeless students. ESSA does specifically describe provisions and instructions for children in foster care, outlining their rights and directing schools to ensure students are able to enroll and succeed. The law removes institutional barriers within schools—such as transportation, immunization, physical examination requirements, fees, residency and birth certificate requirements, and lack of school records—which impede homeless families' ability to enroll their children. States must have procedures in place to eliminate barriers to academic and extracurricular opportunities, such as magnet schools, summer school, career and technical education, advanced placement, online learning, and charter school programs.

## The Intersectionality of Twice-Exceptional HHM Students

HHM students frequently face bias from teachers about their aptitude and behavior. LaFavor et al. (2020) found teachers perceived HHM students as less competent and engaged, regardless of objective testing. Similarly, ensuring that gifted children from disadvantaged or minority backgrounds are identified and served is a pervasive challenge that plagues many school systems. Considerable research has examined how educators fail to equitably identify gifted children from racially, culturally, economically, and linguistically diverse backgrounds.

In an empirical analysis of teacher nominations for gifted programs in Georgia, McBee (2006) found that teachers were significantly less likely to nominate students from lower socioeconomic status backgrounds. When educators are experienced in identifying behaviors consistent with giftedness and have a lens for cultural diversity, their likelihood of identifying gifted behaviors could be increased.

The innate characteristics of gifted children endure even when navigating upheavals in their home lives. Gifted children who face the grimmest circumstances will continue to demonstrate the behaviors that evidence their intellectual capacities, although their environment may influence differences in how their abilities manifest. Homelessness can impede the identification of a gifted child as they exhibit declines in academic achievement and display undesired behaviors that are common when frequently changing schools. Changing schools disrupts the consistency of students' educational experiences and relationships. It can make it even more difficult for educators to track and identify patterns of behavior and achievement that might allow them to be recognized as gifted or twice exceptional. The achievement of HHM students may decline as their stress levels surpass their ability to cope. Gifted children experiencing homelessness or adversity may also feel pressures from their environment to mask their talents in order to "blend in" with their peers. As we saw with Macartney, his mind was still working hard at learning, noticing patterns in the behaviors of his teachers, and using what he observed to his advantage to get teachers to like him. Amspaugh (2017) noted:

> [The] lack of identification for students with gifted education needs limits the ability to advocate for or gain access to gifted education services within or beyond the school, ultimately contributing to the ongoing underrepresentation of homeless and highly mobile (HHM) students in gifted education programs.
>
> *(p. i)*

Added to this, students with learning disabilities are rarely referred for gifted services (Sansom, 2015).

McKinney-Vento can play a particularly significant role in adequate service provisions for twice-exceptional students experiencing homelessness, as the law is clear in its instruction to schools to ensure that assessments of HHM students occur quickly and services are put in place in a timely manner. Implementation of McKinney-Vento policies with HHM gifted children is dependent on the laws and procedures among individual states and school districts, as there is no nationwide policy regarding gifted identification or services. Further, the law does not give direction as to how to address the needs of a student who moves between districts with variations between their policies.

## Practical Considerations for Improving Educational Outcomes

HHM students can be "invisible" to schools and educators due to the reluctance of children and families to share information about being homeless or in foster care. This reluctance can be attributed to the stigma and misconceptions that are often associated with homelessness. Schools may not be aware that families arriving in their front offices to enroll children are homeless; that a child attending their school has become homeless; or that a new child has arrived because they were recently placed in a new foster home. Despite how hidden these children may be, based on the number of children living in homelessness and typical class sizes, there is likely at least one child in every classroom in America who is or has been homeless. If schools are going to improve in their work and outcomes with twice-exceptional HHM students, they must critique their earliest engagements with these students. We do not know how many of Macartney's teachers were aware that he was experiencing homelessness.

Schools play a crucial role in the long-term success of twice-exceptional HHM students, even if they attend for only a short time. Just as Ms. Thurston profoundly influenced Macartney's understanding of his mind, educators can help HHM students make sense of their strengths and challenges, empowering them to use their unique abilities to their advantage. Understanding the factors shaping HHM students' experiences allows educators to design a school system that leverages strengths and fosters resilience in their social-emotional development, regardless of how long they stay. To effectively support HHM students, schools should engage in proactive and strategic planning by:

- identifying and accounting for previously unreported homelessness;
- promptly obtaining and reviewing previous academic records;
- conducting timely screenings for disabilities and advanced learning needs;
- providing thorough resources and referrals for additional educational support; and
- encouraging consistent school attendance through supportive measures.

By taking these steps, schools can create a supportive and inclusive environment that meets the needs of twice-exceptional HHM students and helps them thrive. If each of Macartney's schools had included surveys with the intake paperwork, that information might have signaled to his teachers to assess his strengths and challenges differently.

> **Screening for Housing Instability**
>
> Identifying HHM students often requires building rapport and recognizing subtle indicators of homelessness. Schools should screen for housing instability in a sensitive, non-threatening manner (Karr, 2012), using enrollment questionnaires with questions such as the following:
>
> - Do you have safe and permanent housing?
> - Where do you live and how long have you been there?
> - Have there been any changes in your housing situation in the past year?

Improvements in gifted identification for students from low socio-economic families is imperative, particularly in the case of students like Macartney who exhibit exceptional abilities alongside disabilities (twice exceptional). Professionals must be sensitive and skilled in discerning how frequent moves can obscure students' strengths and how strengths can obscure learning difficulties. Amspaugh (2017) found that high-mobility students who attended school in districts that had consistent gifted identification practices in place had similar rates of gifted identification as their peers who were not high mobility. Their mobility status had no impact on their likelihood of being identified as gifted in these schools. Conversely, she found that highly mobile students in districts with minimal identification practices had virtually no chance of gifted identification. These findings can be applied to work with HHM students in that if schools place more consistent emphasis on gifted identification practices, it is likely that fewer HHM students will be missed.

# Pity is Not Helpful

All teachers receiving more foundational knowledge of how giftedness can manifest in children from adversity and how it can manifest in twice-exceptional students could augment improvements in HHM students' identification practices. The role of teachers as protective buffers, especially in the early years, can have a lasting effect on the lives of children. For teachers to be supportive, they need to be familiar with the characteristics and teaching strategies appropriate for each exceptionality and know what impact both exceptionalities have on the student. Because it is unlikely that one teacher will have enough knowledge and expertise in all needed areas, teachers can collaborate, share their knowledge, and act as mentors, coaching students with interest and talent in particular areas (Robinson, 1999).

Siegle et al. (2010) found that when teachers explicitly considered socio-economic status as a factor in reviewing a student's profile, they were more likely to identify gifted traits. By acknowledging the influence of socio-economic status, schools could purposely use this information in identification to move toward more equitable identification practices. To further support identification, schools can ensure standard practices are in place to closely monitor students' work in a wide range of skills during the first few weeks. In their monitoring efforts, schools should anticipate learning regressions when they know a child has experienced frequent changes in school placement.

Identification is only the first step toward ensuring quality education for HHM twice-exceptional students. To effectively support HHM-gifted children, educators must adopt a strength-based approach to learning rather than focusing solely on deficits. Pity is not helpful. By identifying and nurturing their abilities and interests and providing opportunities for advanced learning, educators can empower twice-exceptional HHM students to realize their full potential. Through tailored support and a strength-based approach, educators can facilitate the academic and social-emotional growth of twice-exceptional HHM children, enabling them despite their circumstances. In Macartney's case, by ensuring he is in a classroom that motivates his learning and takes stock of his innate strengths, educators are much more likely to cultivate a student who is a lifelong learner.

Once the school has developed a more in-depth understanding of the child's strengths and challenges, prompt attention must be paid to ensure that they receive the correct level of rigor and ample opportunities to learn in their zone of proximal development. Related to the assumption that children living in poverty cannot be expected to learn at high levels are teaching practices in low-income schools that emphasize basic skills instead of higher-level thinking and problem-solving. Higher-order thinking skills are presumed unattainable by students who have not mastered "the basics," leading to a reliance on drills rather than exploration and student-generated understanding (Popp et al., 2003). Enhancing instruction to incorporate advanced thinking skills does not hinder achievement but rather, in most cases improves students' academic performance. The researchers identified several vital ingredients that increased the success of such approaches, such as orderly classroom management that is flexible enough to provide varying grouping and instructional practices that promote student choice and student creation of meaning. Additionally, logical connections with students' backgrounds can be building blocks for future learning. Rigorous learning that captures the student's interest can be a healing distraction from life's harsh and unpleasant aspects. Studies on the predictors of success and resilience of HHM students have found that they include general cognitive skills, early literacy skills, self-regulation skills, and positive health outcomes (Obradovic et al., 2009). This research underscores the potential of HHM students to succeed, even in the face of challenging circumstances.

# The Role of Motivation

Self-efficacy, self-determination, intrinsic motivation, and consistent school attendance also correlate with the educational success of HHM students, further emphasizing their capacity for achievement. Bandura's (1977) theory of self-efficacy posits the following:

- Individuals tend to engage in proactive behaviors when they perceive themselves capable of effectively managing challenging situations.
- Individuals' confidence in their ability to cope with difficulties is crucial in determining their coping behaviors. The degree of individuals' belief in their own efficacy influences their willingness to confront threatening situations; they are more likely to avoid situations they perceive as beyond their capabilities and to approach those they feel competent to handle.
- Individuals' efficacy expectations influence the amount of effort they invest and the duration of their persistence when facing obstacles and adverse circumstances.
- Individuals who persist in confronting activities perceived as threatening but largely safe gradually accumulate positive experiences that reinforce their sense of efficacy, steadily reducing their fears and defensive behaviors.
- Self-efficacy is the underlying determinant of a person's persistence in engaging in behaviors even when encountering obstacles and unpleasant experiences.

Self-determination theory (Deci & Ryan, 2002) can also support the success of twice-exceptional HHM students. Self-determination factors can "facilitate self-motivation and well-being, or thwart initiative and positive experience across diverse settings, domains, and cultures" (Deci & Ryan, 2002, p. 9). Self-determination requires autonomy, relatedness, and competence—all of which can be supported in the classroom. Lastly, internal motivation can support the success of HHM students. Intrinsic motivation is the undertaking of an activity without external incentive; personal satisfaction is derived through self-initiated achievement. Understanding the concept of intrinsic motivation, how it drives academic success, and how it can be utilized and taught in the classroom is essential. "Autonomy support from a teacher enables the self-determined motivation in students" (Reeve et al., 1999, p. 537). Exposing students to career pathways and practical applications of the lesson can help children develop meaning in their lives for the lesson.

While research on giftedness and twice exceptionality among HHM children is limited, studies on intellectually gifted youth who have overcome adversity are robust and can offer valuable insights on how best to foster success. Increased self-esteem leads to increased motivation, persistence, and an internal locus of control—all protective factors noted in the literature. Regardless of the type of services provided, there is broad agreement on the importance of gearing the curriculum to the student's strengths and interests rather than their weaknesses (Baum et al., 1991). Experiences connected to the student's abilities and interests are the most valuable for learning skills and developing processes.

## Additional Considerations

Attendance was identified as a determining factor for homeless students' success or lack of achievement (Tobin, 2016). Students who are bored in school or not accurately placed in a program that matches their skill level may disengage and develop poor attendance patterns. To strengthen student connection to the learning environment, teachers, and peers, schools should facilitate innovative ways for marginalized students to get involved, such as creating a "new student" lunch group as an effortless way for new students to meet new classmates.

Educators and school administrators should ensure that parents have a comprehensive understanding of services that can be provided to support their students. However, researchers have suggested that school administrators often receive minimal professional development (e.g., Baum et al., 2017; Fugate et al., 2020). Administrators serving HHM students often do not fully understand what the law requires to meet their unique needs. Educators should examine personal beliefs about highly mobile students to recognize biases and perceptions. To enhance understanding, schools should ensure that all educators receive professional development in successfully working with HHM students and their families. For secondary students, ESSA dictates when a student experiences out-of-home placement at any point during high school, an education provider may waive course or program prerequisites or other preconditions for placement in courses or programs under the jurisdiction of the education provider. This part of the legislation can give advocates of twice-exceptional and gifted HHM students the ability to move them into more challenging classes. Schools can also consider the following:

- Have homeless and gifted liaisons track and collect data on trends.
- Broaden the diversity of families depicted in the books and materials in the classroom to include homeless, foster, and other mobile family and youth situations.
- Recognize that positive parenting by partnering with and supporting families in various ways can further improve educational outcomes for twice-exceptional homeless youth.
- Provide laptop training for the whole family.
- Consider the cost associated with homework projects. Some projects require materials students may be unable to afford, impeding their ability to do the assignment.
- Be sensitive when assigning students to write about a summer vacation, conduct a backyard science project, construct a family tree, or bring in a baby picture, as these may be impossible for a child who has moved frequently or suddenly. Instead, offer several alternatives from which all students can choose.

# Final Thoughts

The needs and considerations of homeless and highly mobile students, as their own demographic, are often overlooked and warrant closer consideration. Changing schools, poor attendance, unnecessary special education placements, poor academic performance, grade retention, and high dropout rates characterize the education experience of some homeless students. Despite the intention of legislation like McKinney-Vento to support school placement stability, many HHM students still find themselves changing schools often.

Implicit bias and deficit thinking among educators may result in efforts to try to "fix and manage" children who are homeless instead of building on their interests, gifts, and talents. It is imperative that children who are homeless or experiencing foster care are seen as multidimensional, with skills and abilities that fuel their hopes, aspirations, and passions. Increasing the awareness and competence of educators regarding the multifaceted effects of poverty and homelessness is of the utmost importance. The experiences of homelessness do not automatically bring about negative life trajectories for these children. Jozefowicz-Simbeni and Israel (2006) provided an alternative strength-based narrative to this deficit perspective: "burgeoning research has begun looking into the strengths of homeless students and has found such youths to possess numerous qualities that can lead to positive adaptation to adulthood, including being strong and resilient, as well as possessing spiritual values" (p. 37). To the extent that low-income and culturally diverse twice-exceptional HHM children and youth have more experience overcoming adversity, they may possess a greater range of flexibility in coping strategies that can be shared with others.

> ## Things to Consider
>
> - Without formal identification as gifted, students cannot access or benefit from gifted education services or supports, either within school or in external programs.
> - The lack of identification contributes to systemic underrepresentation of HHM students in gifted education, reinforcing educational disparities.
> - If HHM students are not recognized as gifted, teachers, families, and students themselves lack the necessary leverage to advocate for enrichment opportunities or accommodations.
> - Identification challenges for HHM students are often compounded by unstable living situations, disrupted schooling, and lack of consistent records, making access to testing or nomination more difficult.

## For Discussion

- What are the classroom indicators that a child and their family may be struggling with homelessness?
- What are the learning needs of a child who is twice exceptional and homeless or high mobility?
- How can educators make the curriculum and classroom more culturally sensitive to the needs of a child experiencing homelessness or foster care?

## References

American School Counselor Association (2018) The *school counselor and children experiencing homelessness.* https://www.schoolcounselor.org/Standards-Positi

ons/Position-Statements/ASCA-Position-Statements/The-School-Counselor-and-Children-Experiencing-Hom

Amspaugh, C. M (2017) *The relationship between school mobility and gifted identification in Connecticut public schools.* University of Connecticut.

Bahney, A (2022) Home prices in 2021 rose 16.9%, the highest on record. *CNN Business*, January 25.

Bandura, A (1977) Self-efficacy: Toward a unifying theory of behavioral change. *Psychological Review, 84*(2), 191-215. https://doi.org/10.1037/0033-295X.84.2.191

Bassuk, E. L., Buckner, J. C., Weinreb, L. F., Browne, A., Bassuk, S. S., Dawson, R., & Perloff, J. N. (1997) Homelessness in female-headed families: Childhood and adult risk and protective factors. *American Journal of Public Health, 87*(2). 241-248. https://doi.org/10.2105/AJPH.87.2.241

Baum, S. M., Schader, R. M., & Owen, S.V. (2017) *To be gifted & learning disabled: Strength-based strategies for helping twice-exceptional students with LD, ADHD, ASD, and more* (3rd Ed.). Routledge.

Becker, J. & Boxill, N. (1990) *Homeless children: The watchers and the waiter.* Haworth Press.

Bush, H. & Shinn, M. (2017) Families' Experiences of Doubling Up After Homelessness. *Cityscape (Washington, D.C.), 19*(3), 331-356.

California Department of Education (n.d.) DataQuest. https://dq.cde.ca.gov/dataquest/

Gültekin, L., Brush, B. L., Baiardi, J. M., Kirk, K., & VanMaldeghem, K. (2014) Voices from the street: Exploring the realities of family homelessness. *Journal of Family Nursing, 20*(4), 390-414. https://doi.org/10.1177/1074840714548943

Fugate, C.M., Behrens, W.A., & Boswell, C. (2020) *Understanding twice-exceptional learners: Connecting research to practice to practice.* Routledge.

Institute for Children, Poverty & Homelessness (2019) No longer hidden: The health and well-being of homeless high school students. https://www.icphusa.org/maps_infographics/no-longer-hidden-infographic/

Ives, J. (2018). Children experiencing homelessness for more than six months have high-risk of poor health outcomes. *News Medical Life Sciences,* September 3. https://www.news-medical.net/news/20180903/Children-experiencing-homelessness-for-more-than-six-months-have-high-risk-of-poor-health-outcomes.aspx

Jozefocz-Simbeni, D. M. & Israel, N. (2006) Services to homeless students and families: The McKinney-Vento Act and its implications for school social work practice. *Children and Schools, 28*(1), 37.

Karr, C. (2012). *Homeless children: What every health care provider should know.* Health Care for the Homeless Clinicians' Network. https://www.slideserve.com/tabib/homeless-children-what-every-health-care-provider-should-know

Lafavor, T. (2018) Predictors of academic success in 9- to 11-year-old homeless children: The role of executive function, social competence, and emotional control. *Journal of Early Adolescence, 38*(9), 1236-1264. https://doi.org/10.1177/0272431616678989

Learning Policy Institute (2021) Students experiencing homelessness. https://learningpolicyinstitute.org/sites/default/files/product-files/Students_Experiencing_Homelessness_BRIEF.pdf

Luby, J. L. (2015) Poverty's most insidious damage: The developing brain. *JAMA Pediatrics, 169*, 810-811. https://doi.org/10.1001/jamapediatrics.2015.1682

Lafavor, T., Langworthy, S.E., Persaud, S. et al. (2020) The relationship between parent and teacher perceptions and the academic success of homeless youth. *Child Youth Care Forum, 49*, 449-468. https://doi.org/10.1007/s10566-019-09538-0

McBee, M. T. (2006) Nomination and identification of traditionally underrepresented students for gifted programs: Insights from a population dataset. (Publication No. 9949332880302959) [Doctoral Dissertation, University of Georgia]. University of Georgia.

Masten, A.S., Fiat, A.E., Labella, M. H. & Strack, R. A. (2015) Educating homeless and highly mobile students: Implications of research on risk and resilience. *School Psychology Review, 44*(3), 315-330.

McKinney-Vento Homeless Assistance Act, Pub. L. No. 100-77, 101 Stat. 482, 42 U.S.C.§ 11301 et seq.

National Center for Homeless Education (2023) School year 2021-2022 EHCY data summary. https://nche.ed.gov/wp-content/uploads/2023/12/SY-21-22-EHCY-Data-Summary_FINAL.pdf

National Center on Family Homelessness. (2014). The character and needs of families experiencing homelessness. https://www.air.org/centers/national-center-family-homelessness

Obradović, J., Long, J. D., Cutuli, J. J., Chan, C.-K., Hinz, E., Heistad, D., & Masten, A. S. (2009) Academic achievement of homeless and highly mobile children in an urban school district: Longitudinal evidence on risk, growth, and resilience. *Urban Education, 51*(2), 197-220. https://doi.org/10.1177/0954579409000273

Rahman, M., Turner, J., & Elbedour, S. (2015). *The U.S. homeless student population: Homeless youth education, review of research classifications and typologies, and the U.S. federal legislative response*. National Association for the Education of Homeless Children and Youth. https://www.researchgate.net/publication/276327394_The_US_Homeless_Student_Population_Homeless_Youth_Education_Review_of_Research_Classifications_and_Typologies_and_the_US_Federal_Legislative_Response#fullTextFileContent

Ryan, R. M. & Deci, E. L. (2002) Overview of self-determination theory: An organismic dialectical perspective. In E. L. Deci & R. M. Ryan (eds.), *Handbook of self-determination research* (pp. 3–33). University of Rochester Press.

Popp, P. A., Stronge, J. H., & Hindman, J. L. (2003) Students on the move: Reaching and teaching highly mobile children and youth (Urban Diversity Series 116, November). Project HOPE, The College of William and Mary, National Center for Homeless

Reganick, K. A. (1997). Prognosis for homeless children and adolescents. *Childhood Education*, *73*(3), 133-135.

SchoolHouse Connection (2023) Data to action: How to use searchable data profiles. https://schoolhouseconnection.org/wp-content/uploads/2024/04/20230314-Data-to-Action-How-to-Use-Searchable-Data-Profiles-1.pdf

Siegle, D., Moore, M., Mann, R., & Wilson, H. (2010) Factors influencing in-service and preservice teachers' nominations of students for gifted and talented programs. *Journal for the Education of the Gifted*, *33*, 337-360. https://doi.org/10.1177/016235321003300303

Tobin, K. J. (2016) Homeless students and academic achievement: Evidence from a large urban area. *Urban Education, 51*(2), 197-220.

Wright, T. (n.d.) young, gifted, and homeless, Part 1. *Access Health News*. https://accesshealthnews.com/young-gifted-and-homeless-part-1/

Wrenick, K., Myers, K., & Mejia, T. (n.d.) Highly mobile students' presentation. Colorado Department of Education. https://www.cde.state.co.us/postsecondary/highly-mobile-students-presentation

Walsh, K. & Harvey, B. (2015, September) *Family experiences of pathways into homelessness: The families' perspective.* Housing Agency. https://www.housingagency.ie/sites/default/files/45.%20Family-Experiences-Report-PDF.pdf

Zima, B. T., Bussing, R., Forness, S. R., & Benjamin, B. (1997) Sheltered homeless children: Their eligibility and unmet need for special education evaluations. *American Journal of Public Health, 87*(2), 236-240.

# Chapter 12

# How Diverse Identities Affect the Social and Academic Experience

Debra A. Troxclair

*As an adolescent during high school, Carolyn vividly recalled being given "nerve medicine" as a preschooler; even as a four-year old, she perceived that this was indicative of an inherent fault. She also recalled her paternal grandmother exclaiming in broken French/English, "Carolyn, excité, excité!" because she got so very excited about things like family gatherings, holiday events, and outings. Her mother once described her as living from one holiday to the next. As soon as Halloween was over, she was planning and plotting to celebrate Thanksgiving; and as soon as the turkey leftovers were in the refrigerator, she was begging for a Christmas tree. As an only child, she looked forward to having others around to engage with. Carolyn was an only child born ten years after a sibling who had died when she was only six weeks old. She was an intense and sensitive, White, highly intelligent female from a family of lower socioeconomic status, who grew up in a racially mixed neighborhood of a southern US city.*

*She remembered that starting elementary school was an exciting adventure as she got to ride the school bus, and for the first time she was surrounded by other children of her own age as a first grader. She thoroughly enjoyed her brief enrollment in a suburban elementary school before moving to the city in the middle of first grade. She and her mom (her parents were separated at this time) moved from the suburbs to the city and lived next door to the parochial school she was to attend. She was all excited to return to the academic environment and was looking forward to making new friends. However, after attending a meeting with her mom and the principal of her new school, she learned that she "did not cut the mustard" for their first-grade class as she had not attended kindergarten. She would be given a two-month trial* in first grade but was told by the principal that she would have to repeat first grade instead of moving to second grade if she did not meet the required benchmarks before the end of the year.

Her mom worked with her nightly and after the trial period she not only met the benchmarks but was at the top of the first-grade class. Carolyn learned how to read before the end of first grade as she sat on her dad's lap on the bus while traveling to the public library during their weekly visits together. Her dad would read aloud and point out the words as he read. On her own, she quickly connected these read-aloud sessions with the phonics instruction she was receiving in her new first-grade class.

The only other time her mother had any further contact with any of her teachers in her K-12 education was in that first-grade classroom. Carolyn remembered being given a note to take home to her mother, who became quite upset. A subsequent phone call with her teacher resulted in her mother scolding her for being rude. The teacher reported that she "raised her hand too often," which made the other children "feel bad." Carolyn recalled being mortified at this news and learning that it was rude to be excited about school. She quickly applied this feedback and tempered her enthusiasm and excitement in the classroom. She made a real effort not to be rude anymore in class. But in doing so, she established an inner voice which shamed her and generated dissonance about being smart, excited, and enthusiastic about learning. This set in motion a lifetime of doubting her abilities and helped her to generate a distorted identity of being highly intelligent.

Carolyn suggested her love of reading originated from the bond she forged with her dad on their weekly visits to the public library. After first grade, she read just about every book in the elementary school library. However, her mother frequently chastised her for "always having her nose in a book," and this comment impacted both her confidence and her identity. In addition to school and reading, she taught herself how to sew on her grandmother's vintage, foot-pedal-powered sewing machine. She was fascinated with the colors and textures of fabric and by the time she was in eighth grade, her home-made clothes had both creative flair and a professional appearance. These activities were just the beginning of her creativity and artistic talents. On Saturdays during junior high, she took time out of social activities with friends, as she was part of a group of adolescents who visited nursing homes putting on skits and plays; she spent more time caring for the elderly than playing sports. Carolyn recalled some traits aligned with anxiety, such as nail-biting, picking at cuticles, and twisting her hair around her fingers when she was "thinking." She was a worrier during her elementary and secondary years.

Throughout the remainder of elementary school and on through her high-school years, she had a cohort of good friends and a best friend named Nancy, and she got very good grades in everything except math. Yet despite outward appearances, several confusing memories lingered. Why had she been given "nerve medicine" and why was it so wrong to be an eager participant in the classroom? Why was reading books a bad *thing? Seeds were planted for imposter syndrome to sprout and bloom in her life. Why was she so different for doing these things? The answers to these questions would not come to her until after college, when she was in graduate school.*

*Carolyn explained that her parents had separated when she was in elementary school but reunited when she began high school. While this increased the family finances, the socioeconomic status of her family barely met a middle-class ranking. Her dad was a high-school graduate and a military veteran whose occupation was in the service industry as a waiter and maître d in a local restaurant. Her mom had not finished high school. She was a "beauty-school dropout"; but after a short stint as a hair stylist, she earned high-school credentials and secured a civil services clerical position in the social services department of a huge metropolitan hospital.*

*When it was time to go to high school, Carolyn was told that she would have to attend the public high school, as the budget of this working-class family could not withstand parochial school high-school tuition. On her own, Carolyn researched scholarships and presented a proposal to her parents. There was one parochial high school with a business education curriculum which offered work-study scholarships where students could work in the school office after school for tuition reduction. Upon presenting this proposal to her parents, they realized that the tuition for this parochial school was far less than they had thought, so Carolyn's self-advocacy had a positive outcome. She was told that tuition was all the family budget could withstand and that she would need to find a part-time job to earn money for extra expenses she might accrue. She began working in a part-time job after school and on Saturdays, starting in her junior year of high school. She was active in a church-affiliated youth group all during high school and she graduated in 11th place out of a class of 120 students*

*This high school had a reputation for its high-performing business education graduates. But in Carolyn's senior year, the school added college preparatory math and science courses, and she enrolled herself on those courses instead of taking additional business education courses at the high-school guidance counselor's suggestion, without seeking parental input. Upon graduating high school, when she voiced her desire to go to college, her working-class parents once again insisted that they could not afford to send her to college. Déjà vu all over again! They suggested that it was in her best interests to get a secretarial job, and that she would have to pay them room and board for living at home after high school, as this was the expectation among their social class. This time, Carolyn was proactive in self-advocacy upon her parent's proclamation of their plans for her. She presented completed paperwork for college admissions, along with grants/work-study loans, and she made arrangements to work additional hours at her high-school job. In this instance, Carolyn was demonstrating positive behaviors of a well-integrated gifted child.*

*About this time, her parents were also concerned about a relationship between Carolyn and her "high-school sweetheart," whom she met in her senior year of high* school. But this determined young adult was not swayed by their apprehension. After all, they had ill-advised her about both high school and college. This relationship made her feel like she was part of her peer group, who had begun partnering off and even getting married right after high-school graduation. As the relationship developed further during college, Carolyn started to demonstrate progressive emotional distress from it. It was during these years that she first began experiencing more significant anxiety-related symptoms/behaviors and struggling with additional dissonance in her perception of her cognitive and academic abilities.

Carolyn attended the local university and majored in business administration, but the stress of the relationship, the lack of fit between her interests/skills and the content of the business administration degree program, and financial reasons caused her to drop out for a while. With coursework equivalent almost to an associate degree in business administration, Carolyn took time out from college and worked as a legal secretary. She saved some money, searched her soul, and realized that what she really wanted to be was a teacher. After all, she recalled that she used to line up her stuffed animals in her bedroom and teach them lessons when she was in first grade. Being a student had always provided her with a sense of accomplishment and affirmation of her ability, so being an elementary school teacher seemed to be logical career choice. This option had always been in the back of her mind, but she had pushed it aside as she wanted the financial security that came with a business administration degree, and she knew that financial prosperity would not result from a job as a teacher if she pursued a degree in elementary education. She took courses in library science as part of that degree program, which reminded her of the pleasure she had gained from reading all the books in her elementary school library.

She returned to college with a vengeance after significant boredom while working as a legal secretary. She switched majors to elementary education and minored in school library science. She made the dean's list and gained confidence in her academic and cognitive abilities as a result, but those lingering childhood messages still popped up from time to time. Upon graduating, she thrived as an elementary school teacher and solidified the relationship her parents had warned her about by marrying the man she had met in high school. Carolyn graduated with significant student loan debt but managed to repay those loans after a significant length of time. The thought of a scholarship had not entered her mind because of her misunderstanding of her true abilities.

As her marriage soured and her anxiety increased, Carolyn returned to graduate school, where she had gained confidence and an improved academic identity, and began a master's degree in early childhood education. In her last course on that degree program, she studied gifted education. After the first week's reading assignment, and reminiscent of her undergraduate shift in majors, she changed her major from a master's degree in early childhood to a master's degree in gifted education, which required her to take additional courses instead of graduating that term.

*Her advisor on that graduate gifted education course was the first person to officially notice her gifts and talents and directly confront her with her ability. Carolyn often still hears the words uttered by her mentor: "Carolyn, do you not know how smart you are?" She completed a master's degree in special education with an emphasis in gifted education, pursued identification for gifted programming for her young son, and got a divorce.*

*While her passion for gifted education was growing, she sought counseling to understand more about her role in her failed marriage. During those sessions, she learned more about why she struggled with her self-concept and why she worried constantly, and she began to formulate and value a more accurate self-concept, both as the parent of a gifted child and as gifted herself. The courses she took in gifted education provided her with some of the answers to the questions she had been asking herself since she was in elementary school. Upon graduating with a master's degree, her mother added another stanza to the song when she asked, "Well, now are you satisfied? Have you finally gotten this school thing out of your system?" This time, however, Carolyn, did not even bother to self-advocate with her parents. Instead of jarring her self-concept, she used those words as motivation for what was to come next.*

*Carolyn once again thrived as a classroom teacher for gifted students. In this role, she took a group of parents to a parent's day event at a nearby university. There she met a mentor who stalked her relentlessly until she agreed to enroll on a doctoral program in gifted education. Carolyn quickly acquiesced to the offer of the position of graduate research assistant on a doctoral program once she had other words to challenge the old tapes in her mind. When phoning to accept the offer, she heard different words this time: "Carolyn, do you not know how smart you are?"*

*During her doctoral-level studies, she delved into studying twice-exceptional gifted learners and was able to parent her twice-exceptional gifted child differently. She also was finally getting answers to those tormenting questions: why had she been given "nerve medicine" as a small child? Why was it so wrong to be an eager participant in the classroom? Why was reading books a bad thing?*

*This vignette paints a picture of the importance of teachers and how educational opportunity can make a difference in the lives of those within the intersectionality of less-than-optimal generational socioeconomic disadvantage, giftedness, and anxiety/obsessive compulsive disorder (OCD).*

## Was Carolyn Gifted or Twice Exceptional?

There is no one right answer to this question. There are several problematic incidences or recollections of life experiences noted by the subject of the vignette that impacted her life which can be attributed to the overlapping or combined traits of giftedness, twice-exceptionality, and/or lower socioeconomic status. Carolyn's life was impacted by traits related to each of these labels either individually or in a variety of combinations which could have been mitigated had her parents and teachers understood the impact of behaviors of giftedness, twice-exceptionality, and anxiety/OCD.

Carolyn demonstrated high cognitive ability and critical thinking skills in first grade, learning to read quickly by herself, without having had the prerequisite kindergarten instruction. She made connections on her own between her sessions reading aloud with her dad and the phonics instructions she received in class. Her interest in reading continued throughout elementary school, as she voraciously consumed as many of the library books in her school library as possible. She maintained high grades in elementary school and high school in all subjects except for junior high math.

Stutler (2018) explained research findings indicating that gifted girls "challenge themselves with difficult literature, critical and empathic thinking, and problem finding, and as the girls read and make meaning, they are involved in constructing their lives' purpose. They are youthful self-actualizers" (p. 18). Carolyn's passion for literature allowed her to read and make meaning in and around three interconnected areas of intelligence and intensity: intellectual, imaginational, and emotional overexcitabilities. Carolyn may have interpreted her mother's comment about her "always having her head stuck in a book" as reflecting a concern about an unhealthy obsession, instead of a gifted young girl's passion for literature which impacted her life positively in multitudes of ways.

Carolyn's self-advocacy is a positive characteristic of giftedness that she displayed early on in life. More mixed messages were provided by Carolyn's parents, who accused her of being disrespectful when she self-advocated and investigated high-school scholarships on her own, and again when they were outwitted by their strong-willed daughter who was adamant about getting a college education. Despite their misgivings, they permitted her to live at home (without charging her room and board) and attend the local university. But the message they gave her was similar to that which she received from the principal when she was in first grade: "We really don't think you can do this, but we will give you a trial period." Roeper (1982) explained that a well-integrated gifted child feels compelled to stand up for their convictions and is willing to risk isolation for doing so. The seemingly misguided advice of Carolyn's parents about her self-advocacy efforts was not driven by poor parenting skills; it was the result of social patterns rooted in the family's low socioeconomic status. Their own actions were the only ones they had observed, as they did not enjoy the same advantages growing up as they afforded their daughter by sending her to parochial schools for her K-12 education.

Carolyn's mother was astute in seeking medical advice when she questioned the behaviors of her pre-school daughter, which resulted in dosing the child with "nerve medicine." However, because of Carolyn's young age at the time of her medical diagnosis, it is uncertain if her high psychomotor activity resulted from giftedness or from traits associated with generalized anxiety. Silverman (1993) explained that gifted individuals with psychomotor overexcitabilities have significant capacity for being active and energetic and display an organic surplus of energy in the form of rapid speech, marked excitation, and intense need for physical action—which could possibly explain her grandmother's comments of "Excité!"

Twice-exceptional gifted children with generalized anxiety can experience increased irritability and emotional meltdowns and have very low levels of tolerance for distress (Kircher-Morris, 2021). Many "adults chalk up this outwardly visible irritability to a child being spoiled or picky or high maintenance, instead of seeing it as a sign of a potential emotional problem" (Kircher-Morris, 2021, p. 193). Regardless of the cause, Carolyn's grandmother's comments of "Excité!" were indicative of some aspect of giftedness/twice-exceptionality/anxiety or OCD.

As a very young child, Carolyn recalled embracing several mixed messages about her real identity. Self-definition, an adolescent crisis, may occur earlier for gifted children because of their intensely analytical approach (Roedel, 1984). Early on in life, Carolyn began suspecting that there was something inherently wrong with her after being administered "nerve medicine" for either intense-psychomotor activity or generalized anxiety. This impacted both her self-concept and her self-esteem.

## What is it Like to Be 2e and from a Lower Social Class?

Carolyn and her family were not impacted by cultural or ethnic diversity issues. However, their intergenerational low socioeconomic status shaped her parents' mindsets, leading them to question her desire to extend her education beyond high school. This was not what they were used to in their family and social circles. Lower socioeconomic status is determined in part by one's parental education level, employment status, income, and income status (US Department of Health and Human Services, 2023). Parents who did not attend college themselves because of their own family's income growing up are unlikely to be able to identify with their children's desire for a college education and may send messages to their children that they are living outside their financial means if those children express a desire to continue their education after high school. Destin et al. (2019) asserted that children from lower socioeconomic families hold deficit mindsets associated with their socioeconomic circumstances and academic achievement.

Ingram (2021) asserted that the interaction between race and social class needs to be addressed, rather than a focus on one to the exclusion of the other. The diversity issue in a lower social class remains extensive, even today. "Only a quarter of American adults today were raised by a parent with a degree, and by that measure, three-quarters of adults fall into the lower social-class origins category" (Ingram, 2021, para. 7).

Ingram (2021) explained the need to focus equally on social class disadvantage, not just on diversity issues of gender, race, and national origin, as "social class disadvantage prevails in every economy around the world" (para. 1). According to Ingram, individuals from lower social class origins are defined as "those who through the conditions of birth and upbringing have had relatively less access to money, to contacts who promote their upward mobility, and to the cultural know-how necessary to get ahead in school" (para. 3). He went on to note that social class origins are measured along the dimensions of family income during early years, parents' level of education, and parents' occupations (para. 3). Ingram explained that "a person's social class origins leave a cultural imprint even if the individual gains money or status later in life," and that "this disadvantage matters for individuals, organizations, and society as it materially reduces their career potential and general well-being" (para. 4).

According to Wilson (as cited in Ingram, 2021), "it's impossible to understand racial disadvantage without also considering social class disadvantages" (para. 26) Social class inequity is intertwined with racial inequity so closely that remediation cannot occur without attention to the impact of lower social class. To mitigate the powerful negative effects of social class disadvantages, we must expand our diversity, equity, and inclusion efforts to increase the representation of individuals from lower social class origins. According to Ingram (2021), research demonstrates that for those from higher social class origins, race is not a factor in upward mobility. However, for those from lower social class origins, race does matter—and it matters for all races. This notwithstanding, Blacks from lower social class origins are still less likely than those from other races with similar backgrounds to become upwardly mobile.

The impact of being from a lower social class family is not just about finances. According to Gorman (1998), parental attitudes toward higher education have the potential to influence their children's attitudes and their likelihood of obtaining a college degree. As a child growing up, Carolyn did not perceive her family as being financially disadvantaged, as they looked the same financially as the other working-class families in her neighborhood. She did notice that she was the only latchkey kid in the neighborhood at that time and her mother was the only mom who worked outside the home. She picked up on the pitying facial expressions of some of her friends' mothers when playing with them after school, as she was asked if her mother knew where she was. During Carolyn's childhood and adolescence, her family's income did provide for decent housing, food, and medical care; but there was no family home or car—the family rented decent but not extravagant housing and relied on public transportation to get around the city.

There were no extracurricular activities like dance lessons and recitals or art and music lessons; but in seventh grade, the teacher organized a short-lived ukulele group and Carolyn was able to participate with a rented second-hand instrument. She often accompanied a classmate who was in a local ballet academy to performances and watched from the wings, longing to relevé, plié, jeté, and pirouette alongside her friend on the stage. In her elementary school years, summer vacations involved staying with her paternal grandmother while her mother worked full time. There was no home library and the only books in the home were from the public library. However, Carolyn was given a book by her grandmother's neighbor—a biography of Jane Adams, the founder of Hull House in Chicago. She read and reread that book until she had almost memorized it. It was a treasured possession.

There were no weekend getaways or family vacations during Carolyn's elementary-school and high-school years, but the church-affiliated youth group sponsored summer beach trips and group members could earn money working on a snowball stand to pay for them. Carolyn did not experience air travel until she was an adult in graduate school but recalled a train trip with her grandmother as a young child to visit her aunt in a nearby state. Carolyn's family barely afforded her the opportunity to attend a parochial elementary school and high school; and were it not for her self-advocacy and good advice from her high-school guidance counselor, she probably would not have attended university upon graduation.

In the parochial school system at that time, there were no "gifted" classes. In fact, Carolyn did not even hear the term "gifted" until she was enrolled on a master's degree program, and she only took a deep dive into learning about twice exceptionality during courses for her doctoral degree. However, her advanced academic abilities were noted by her elementary-school teachers. One teacher would arrange the class in rows from the smartest (by the door to the hallway) to the least smart (the last person in the last row next to the windows). Carolyn and her best friend, Nancy, rotated the first position in the classroom seating arrangement in their fourth or fifth-grade classroom.

Carolyn recognized that her lower social class origins impacted her self-concept and social emotional development. The messages she received from her parents, who unknowingly mirrored misperceptions of who she was, were counterbalanced by their sacrifice of providing parochial K-12 schooling, which had a substantial positive impact on her life. The trajectory of her life as an undiscovered/unidentified gifted learner with anxiety/OCD from a lower social class would have been sizably different without that high-school guidance counselor and her master's degree program advisor. Additionally, the trajectory of her son's life would not have been impacted by her access to educational opportunities that provided relationships which promoted her to a higher social class status, resulting in a different way of life for him as well.

## Twice Exceptionality

Throughout her elementary-school and high-school years, and even into college, Carolyn's anxiety/OCD was masked by her high intelligence and stellar academic ability. While there was little money for extracurricular activities that would have nurtured her creative abilities, the traditional academic foundation provided in parochial schools established a solid foundation for successfully transitioning out of a lower social class. She demonstrated some traits such as worry, nervousness, and nail-biting (Fugate et al., 2020, p. 248).

Kircher-Morris (2022) lists the following types of OCD: fear of contamination; looking for things to be "just right"; magical thinking; and aggressive obsessions (pp. 49-50). Carolyn recalled participating in the "just right" OCD category. This type of OCD is fueled by a desire to "do something until it feels right" and can result in doing things repeatedly until they seem correct. Kircher-Morris explained that this might look like perfectionism in an academic setting (p. 49).

Carolyn did experience the obsessive thinking patterns found in those with anxiety, but as a 2e gifted learner, she masked her them with verbal and logical thinking skills. However, these thought patterns still strongly impacted her well-being and overall academic performance (Kircher-Morris, 2021). She experienced the traumatic loss of her nuclear family when her parents separated for a few years as a young child but did not experience any separation anxiety. In fact, she enjoyed spending time with her father and other family members throughout her childhood, even when her parents were separated. She considered opportunities to spend time with family other than her parents as "adventures."

However, Carolyn recalled that even in high school, it took her a long time to let go of worries and she experienced periods of restlessness. She also feared making wrong decisions and lacked confidence (Baum et al., 2017). As part of her giftedness, Carolyn was an overthinker at a very young age who managed to mask her anxiety somewhat; but she did seek reassurance by asking many questions and uttering negative self-critical thoughts, which is how many gifted learners deal with anxiety (Kircher-Morris, 2021).

In high school, procrastination resulting from unhealthy perfectionism began to be an issue, resulting in grades that were lower than expected—especially in math and senior-year science courses. The perfectionism was modeled for her by her maternal grandmother, who lived with her and her parents when she was in high school. Carolyn was expected to complete household chores and did so unwillingly, as is the case with many high-school-aged adolescents. However, if she did not make perfect hospital corners on the beds or did not scrub the sink spotlessly after doing the dishes, her grandmother would chastise her with the mantra: "If you are going to do something, do it perfectly, or don't do it at all." She would have identified her high-school self as a "meticulous or perfectionistic student," as she repeatedly checked, rechecked, and sometimes changed answers, and as she often asserted that the assignments just did not feel "good enough." She would procrastinate beginning assignments until the last minute and become frustrated after submitting assignments that did not meet her own standards.

As a senior in high school, she heard horror stories of university students who reported back to their former high-school classmates about how difficult college algebra was. Many reported failing the course entirely. She made up her mind to circumvent the stress by determining how to get a low score on the math section of the ACT test so that she would be placed in remedial algebra in college. This is an avoidance behavior which is consistent with anxiety disorders pertinent to gifted learners (Kircher-Morris, 2021). She achieved her goal, but this deliberate attempt at self-sabotage most likely resulted in a lower overall composite score on that test. This deliberate action surely impacted scholarship possibilities.

# Finding Joy

Successful academic accomplishments, creativity, and a spiritual connection were overarching aspects of Carolyn's life which brought her joy. Throughout her education, school provided her with a sense of accomplishment and much joy through affirmation of her high cognitive abilities. She was attracted to creative endeavors and there were several creative opportunities exposed by extended family members.

Carolyn reported that she was and is happiest when engaging in creative activities. In her elementary-school years, she was fortunate to have a significant circle of friends in the neighborhood and school she attended. She and her best friend, Nancy, shared similar interests and spent many hours together. One of their shared interests was to sketch "floorplans" for dream houses; they would devote hours of playtime over weekends to this activity. They also created playhouses in Nancy's garage where they imaginatively portioned out the space and decorated their apartments with found items from their backyard sheds.

As an older elementary-school-aged child, she taught herself how to sew, first following patterns for making dolls' clothes and later making her own clothes. In addition to basic construction, she learned how to alter dress patterns to her small size. During her summer vacations, when visiting her paternal grandmother, she watched as her grandmother spent hours embroidering elaborate leaf and floral patterns onto linen tablecloths and pillowcases. While financially unable to attend ballet classes, watching in the wings while her friend performed in local performances opened up her world to music and dance, to which she otherwise would not have been exposed.

During Carolyn's high-school years, the church-affiliated youth group performed plays each summer which provided social and creative experiences for cast members and stagehands. Nightly rehearsals afforded the opportunity to participate in social activities other than sports. These activities provided social-emotional connections and a sense of belonging in her teens. During her undergraduate college years, she watched her aunt paint with oils and watercolors and longed to learn how to do this herself.

As a young adult, Carolyn finally had the opportunity to enroll in formal art classes. Learning to draw and paint offered her distractions and joy during some of the hardest years of her life as she redirected herself away from a dysfunctional marriage toward the stresses of single motherhood.

The gift of a religious-affiliated elementary-school and high-school education, provided thanks to the financial sacrifice of her parents, underpinned the development of a spiritual life which would be strengthened and enhanced throughout the adult life challenges she faced as a divorced single mother.

## Acknowledging Challenges

As a young child from a lower social class family whose parents were separated and later reunited, Carolyn felt grief and loss and experienced sadness due to the differences between her own family structure and that of most of her school friends, whose families were intact and outwardly more stable than her own. As an adolescent, she reported challenges of feeling different from her peers, despite being a part of a group of age-related peers socially—especially since in US culture, "different" usually means "defective" in some way. As an adolescent, she erroneously postulated that although she was very smart—as evidenced by her high grades and overall academic achievements—she was unlike many of the smart peers around her because she was totally lost at math. Her confidence was again shattered in high-school chemistry class when she never learned the skill of balancing chemical equations.

Gaesser (2018) explained that anxiety is part of giftedness and identifies some stress factors unique to this population that can impact their self-concept:

> [They may need] greater stimulation and deeper discussion about topics of interest to them ... they may recognize the nuances and complexities of concepts and individuals which leads them to question inconsistencies/interrelationships ... they may possess a desire to explore a variety of interests which can become overwhelming ... [Consequently,] they receive mixed messages about their giftedness.
>
> *(Gaesser, p. 187)*

Gifted girls may struggle with conflicting messages pertaining to cultural or social ideas that make high intelligence less socially acceptable for their gender. Inappropriate school placements, self-concept challenges, and perfectionism can also impact the stress levels of all gifted learners.

As an adolescent, Carolyn experienced the challenge of a lack of parental financial and economic support when she sought to attend university after graduating high school. This challenge was followed by the major disappointment of a problematic marriage and the loss of family stability for her son. The stresses she experienced at this stage in her life allowed symptoms related to anxiety to flourish. Additionally, she watched her highly gifted child deal with issues of anxiety related to attention deficit hyperactivity disorder (ADHD) in his early academic years.

## Coping Mechanisms

The coping mechanisms that provided Carolyn with the greatest comfort were engaging in academic achievement and the joy she found in academic challenges and experiences, such as those afforded by undergraduate, graduate, and doctoral degree programs. Engaging in creative pursuits also provided distractions and a sense of fulfillment during hard times. While Carolyn longed to be a ballet dancer as a child, she found solace during stressful years in a required modern dance course on her undergraduate elementary education degree program. After the course was over, she enrolled in adult ballet classes and found joy from engaging in those classes. Her interest and skill in sewing clothes morphed into a passion for quilting, which helped fill the hours when her son left home and moved into his adult life. Carolyn was also able to reboot her passion for visual arts, which she had put on hold as a young adult, by taking advanced art classes in watercolors and pastels later in life.

The rituals of her spiritual life as a child and adolescent developed into a strong faith as she overcame obstacles, learning how to put losses from significant relationships behind her. Bibliotherapy along with individual counseling, membership of support groups as an adult, and learning about gifted education and twice-exceptional gifted individuals combined to enable her to develop a stronger self-concept and mitigated the impact of being a smart but different twice-exceptional individual from a lower socioeconomic status family.

## Carolyn Today

Eliminating boredom through engagement by learning something new and engaging in some type of creativity has provided Carolyn with diverse ways to manage her days. Creative projects and crafts gave her something to look forward to when struggles were intense. She still struggles with worry but has learned that in life, there are often things which are not within her ability to control or eliminate. She has learned to autocorrect when thoughts or worries won't leave her brain. Through counseling, support groups, and her own research, she learned strategies to interrupt the messages being played in her mind. The counseling technique of eye movement desensitization and reprocessing has provided tools to reduce worrying thoughts; while participation in support groups put her in contact with others who had similar behaviors and provided models for breaking the negative cycle of worry.

Learning about twice-exceptional gifted learners has also been a great source of information, which has provided her with answers to the questions she had asked herself as a child ("Why was I given 'nerve medicine'?" "Why was it so wrong to be an eager participant in the classroom?" "Why was reading books a bad thing?"). In learning about twice-exceptional gifted learners with ADHD, she became aware of the social-emotional aspect of executive functioning skills, and that anxiety is one aspect of ADHD. According to Kaufman (2010), the social-emotional strand of executive function skills consists of response inhibition (impulse control), emotional control, and adaptability (p. 4). While Carolyn was familiar with most executive skills in the metacognitive strand (goal setting; planning/strategizing; sequencing; organization of materials; time management; executive/goal-directed attention; task persistence; and working memory), she acquired knowledge of something called "set shifting." According to Goldberg (as cited in Kaufman, 2010), set shifting involves releasing a certain stiffness of mind, when there is great difficulty moving within and between tasks or thoughts (p. 7). Carolyn observed that in her earlier adult years, it took her a long time to process and let go of emotions and she would ruminate on negative feelings. She was able to draw a parallel between the way her mind would get stuck in these thought patterns and the inability of a child with ADHD to break a behavior pattern. Starting each day with a daily spiritual devotional was a practice she began in graduate school. Reading and reflecting on positive uplifting thoughts was a way of reframing negative thoughts into more positive internal self-talk.

## Carolyn's Final Thoughts

Carolyn suggested that twice-exceptional gifted learners from less-than-optimal social class families should use their cognitive abilities and problem-solving skills to self-advocate for educational opportunities despite parental objections. They should seek support from school counselors and college admission counselors to look for scholarships or options for individual counseling. They should learn about the traits of being gifted and those applicable to any impediments to embrace all such gifts, whether they relate to an additional disability or social class status. Adolescents should seek creative outlets for any arts that catch their interest.

Students should be encouraged to explore the cultural dynamics associated with lower socioeconomic status—not as a means of distancing themselves from their families, but to cultivate empathy and effectively articulate their developing identities to parents whose life experiences may not have included access to opportunities for upward mobility. Reassuring their parents that they will still be part of their family of origin is key to impacting generational ideologies.

Twice-exceptional learners should learn about how their giftedness can result in overexcitabilities, which may or may not be severe or negatively impact their wellbeing. These overexcitabilities should not be confused with the way in which anxiety or OCD impacts their giftedness. In their giftedness resides their superpowers of high intelligence, critical thinking, and problem-solving. Individuals with anxiety can possess superpowers too. According to Sinclair (2017), people with anxiety have a heightened sense of perception, which results in an ability to sense the energy of others, increased empathy, a higher IQ, the life-saving instinct that results from anxiety, and an ability to see through lies (paras. 2-5). People with these superpowers often become uncomfortable around people who are overly negative, because they have a heightened sense of empathy that can readily detect others' emotions (paras. 1-2). Anxiety is a survival skill because it makes one more aware of what is going on around one, which can sometimes even save lives (para. 3).

Hobson (2023) shared a phrase—"putting things in perspective"—that can help to reduce anxiety. He explained that the brain is wired to evaluate all possible negative events, and that the anxious brain creates egocentric stress which leads to distress and can be debilitating (paras. 4-5). There are negative emotion areas of the brain clustered in between the evaluative areas and the attention areas. When something bad happens, the brain structure itself generates emotions, evaluates them, and focuses or attends to them; and the emotions become personally relevant. Left to its own default, the brain tends to ruminate as it directs, redirects, and shifts between anxious thoughts and non-anxious thoughts (para. 7). This thought pattern can be interrupted by "putting things into perspective" (para. 12). By using future reflection, you can imagine yourself a year into the future and how you will be interacting with the thoughts that are causing you anxiety now. Hobson explained that pulling yourself out of the present is an effective strategy which allows you to see yourself more objectively and less emotionally.

Teachers of twice-exceptional gifted learners need to help these students develop an inner voice ("Carolyn, do you know how smart you are?") which reminds them of their abilities when they become frustrated by the worries and doubts of anxiety. Teachers of the gifted need professional development on the impact of disabilities and diversity in order to be able to guide and provide emotional support for these learners, who may not have had the benefits of modeling such behaviors in their home/family environments. Parents of twice-exceptional gifted learners need to learn how their family environment and social class status can "make or break" the financial, social, and emotional lives not only of their children, but of their grandchildren and beyond. Parents and teachers need to look out for advances in the field of neuroscience for strategies to help their gifted, twice-exceptional children better manage anxiety which, while perhaps not debilitating, does impact their lives. Gifted and twice-exceptional gifted children may experience anxiety resulting from stress factors unique to gifted learners—from the school experience itself; from self-concept challenges; from perfectionism (Gaesser, 2018).

Well-informed teachers play an important role in their students' lives. In addition to understanding who they are because of their gifts, and despite any negatives in their lives, these children require adult support, and teachers can enlighten parents of children like Carolyn. This vignette and the narrative that accompanies it paint a picture of the importance of, and the need for, well-trained teachers who understand the nature and needs of gifted and twice-exceptional learners. These children may not appear to be impacted by diversity on the outside but often experience inner diversity resulting from socioeconomic class. Providing appropriate educational opportunities can significantly impact students facing the combined challenges of socioeconomic disadvantage, giftedness, and anxiety or OCD. Appendix D provides more information regarding the social emotional profiles and traits of highly gifted students.

## Things to Consider

- High achievement often conceals mental health struggles in gifted learners. Carolyn's anxiety and OCD traits were misinterpreted or unacknowledged for years, highlighting the need for nuanced, trauma-informed, and culturally responsive identification practices.
- Repeated feedback discouraging her enthusiasm and intellect shaped Carolyn's internal narrative. These moments are crucial: they reveal how educators' comments—however subtle—can reinforce or erode self-belief, particularly in gifted girls.
- Carolyn's trajectory changed when key mentors recognized and named her giftedness. Supportive educators, access to gifted education courses, and counseling were all instrumental in her identity formation and healing.

## For Discussion

- In what ways can school systems more effectively identify and support twice-exceptional learners, especially those who mask their challenges with high performance?
- What are the long-term effects of mixed messages and mislabeling (e.g., being "too excitable" or "too eager") on gifted girls' self-worth and academic identity?
- How can educators and counselors support twice-exceptional students in reframing anxiety or perfectionism as part of their neurodivergence—not as flaws?

## References

Baum, S., Schader, R., & Owen, S. (2017) *To be gifted and learning disabled: Strength-based strategies for helping twice exceptional students with LD, ADHD, ASD, and more* (3rd ed.). Prufrock.

Destin, M., Hanselman, P., Nuonyrmpo, J., Tipton, E., & Yeager, D. (2019) Do students mindsets differ by socioeconomic status and explain disparities in academic achievement in the United States? *AERA Open, 5*(3) https://doi.org/10.1177/2332858419857706

Fugate, M., Behrens, W., & Boswell, C. (2020) *Understanding twice-exceptional learners: Connecting research to practice.* Routledge.

Gaesser, A. (2018) Befriending anxiety to reach potential: Strategies to empower our gifted youth. *Gifted Child Today, 41*(4), 186-195. DOI:10.1177/1076217518786983

Gorman, T. (1988) Social class and parental attitudes toward education: Resistance and conformity to schooling in the family. *Journal of Contemporary Ethnography, 27*(1), 10-44.

Hobson, N. (2023) *Emotionally intelligent people use a brilliant 4-word phrase to rewire the brain and reduce stress.* Inc. https://www.inc.com/nick-hobson/emotionally-intelligent-people-use-a-brilliant-4-word-phrase-to-rewire-brain-reduce-stress.html

Ingram, P. (2021) The forgotten dimension of diversity. Social class is as important as race or gender. *Harvard Business Review*, January-February. https://hbr.org/2021/01/the-forgotten-dimension-of-diversity

Kaufman, C. (2010) *Executive function in the classroom: Practical strategies for improving performance and enhancing skills for all students.* Paul H. Brookes Publishing.

Kircher-Morris, E. (2021) *Teaching twice-exceptional learners in today's classrooms.* Free Spirit Publishing.

Kircher-Morris, E. (2022) *Raising twice-exceptional children: A handbook for parents of neurodivergent gifted kids.* Prufrock Press.

Roedel, W. (1984) Vulnerabilities of highly gifted children, *Roeper Review, 6*(3), 127-130. https://doi.org/10.1080/02783198409552782

Roeper, A. (1982) How the gifted cope with their emotions. *Roeper Review, 5*(2). https://psycnet.apa.org/doi/10.1080/02783198209552672

Silverman, L. (1993) *Counseling the gifted and talented.* Love Publishing.

Sinclair, G. (2017) *People with anxiety disorders are hiding these 5 superpowers.* Spiritualify. https://blog.spiritualify.com/if-you-have-anxiety-disorders-you-are-hiding-these-5-superpowers/

Stutler, S. (2011) Gifted girls' passion for fiction: The quest for meaning, growth, and self-actualization. *Gifted Child Quarterly, 55*(1), 18-38. DOI:10.1177/0016986210383979

U.S. Department of Health and Human Services (2023) CDC socioeconomic factors. https://www.cdc.gov/dhdsp/health_equity/socioeconomic.htm

Wilson, A. (2018) Don't ignore class when addressing racial gaps in intergenerational mobility. Brookings. https://www.brookings.edu/articles/dont-ignore-class-when-addressing-racial-gaps-in-intergenerational-mobility/

# Chapter 13

# Depression and Suicidal Behaviors among Twice-Exceptional Secondary Students

Jennifer Riedl Cross and Tracy L. Cross

*Daniel[1] was a happy child: thoughtful, engaged and socially aware—"normal" to all who knew him. Things changed when he began school, however. His kindergarten teacher quickly became frustrated with his inattention to instructions and lack of interest in her lessons. In the first grade, he received a diagnosis of attention deficit disorder, without hyperactivity. Medication, which sometimes had negative side effects, led to improvements in school. Without special education supports, however, Daniel was performing at an average level. A chance administration of the Cognitive Abilities Test in the third grade took his teachers by surprise, when he scored in the 99$^{th}$ percentile. A move to the gifted magnet school in the fourth grade did not help the situation, with an untrained teacher in an understaffed classroom. Only in the sixth grade did Daniel finally have a good fit, when he was moved to a private school specializing in twice-exceptional students.*

*Now that he was receiving attention to both his strengths and challenges, Daniel thrived. With the help of his mother, who had learned how best to encourage his productivity, Daniel's academic performance and enjoyment in school reached new levels. Unfortunately, the school ended after the eighth grade and Daniel returned to the public high schools, where he received no services for his disability. At the same time, he decided to stop taking the medications that had helped to control his attention deficit hyperactivity disorder (ADHD). The new environment proved toxic, and Daniel's academic performance made a precipitous decline. He befriended others who had little interest in school and together they explored substances, truancy, video games, and guns. The only class that sparked his interest was in automotive customization. Despite his passion for this class, he was unable to pass his other classes in time to graduate. His depression deepened as he lost interest in what appeared to him to be a dim future. His girlfriend's announcement that she might be pregnant led him to dark thoughts about the burden his sad life would be on their child. He resisted taking required courses in community college and had made the decision to drop out days before taking his own life at age 18. At the request of his mother, in the hope that others could learn from his experience, Daniel was the subject of a psychological autopsy: a detailed case study of his life and death by his own hand (T. Cross et al., 2020).*

Everyone experiences depression at some point in their lives. It may be an acute, fleeting, hours-long episode following a negative experience or a chronic, long-term, debilitating response to one's environment (J. Cross & Cross, 2017). The American Psychological Association (2013) defines "depression" as "Sad, empty or irritable mood, accompanied by somatic and cognitive changes that significantly affect the individual's capacity to function" (p. 155). In some cases, depression may lead to suicidal behaviors, which can range from thinking about killing oneself to trying to do so. For a variety of reasons, twice-exceptional students may be at increased risk of depression and possibly even suicidal behaviors. This chapter explores the intersection of mental health and multiple exceptionalities.

## Understanding Suicidal Behavior

Suicide has been the subject of research and theorizing for centuries. Multiple theories based on research and anecdotal evidence have contributed to our understanding of this phenomenon. Suicidal behaviors may fit into one of three categories:

- Suicidal ideation: Thinking about suicide. This may range from thinking briefly about what it might mean to kill oneself to making a detailed plan of how to do it. No action is taken, but the person is thinking about it.
- Suicide attempt: Taking action to kill oneself.
- Suicide completion: Making a successful suicide attempt.

Many people will think about suicide at some point in their lives. Far fewer will make an attempt and only a small percentage of those who attempt will be successful. A national survey of college undergraduates found 14% had contemplated suicide (Eisenberg & Lipson, 2019). Nearly 20% of high-school students participating in the Youth Risk Behavior Survey reported engaging in some form of suicidal behavior, from ideation to attempted suicide (Kann et al., 2017; see Table 38.1). Females are more likely to make a suicide attempt (Bommersbach et al., 2022), but males are much more likely to succeed (National Institute of Mental Health [NIMH], 2024)—in part because they opt for more lethal methods, such as guns.

Rooted in the works of Stillion and McDowell (suicide trajectory model; 1996), Shneidman (*psychache* or intolerable psychological pain; 1993), White (functional classifications; 2016), and Joiner (interpersonal-psychological theory of suicidal behavior; 2005, 2012), our spiral model of suicidal behavior (Cross & Cross, 2018, 2021a) describes the path from normal, healthy functioning to imminent danger or death by suicide (Figure 13.1). Most people who die by suicide suffer from depression (Cukrowicz & Poindexter, 2014). Therefore, the model offers an explanation of depression as well.

Most people go about their day-to-day activities without distress, moving along the top plane as they work, play, interact, or enjoy solitude (Figure 13.1). Life events, however, can trip them up, causing a dip down into the spiral. In most cases, this will be a short trip, with some discomfort and stress that are manageable. With appropriate coping skills and perhaps some external supports, this person will soon make their way back up the spiral, returning to the plane of normal functioning. Some experiences are not so easily dealt with, however, and some individuals will have greater difficulties than others in responding. A person may find themselves unable to cope or without supports and will face increasing suffering. This may be a bout of depression that requires more intense support or intervention to help them back to the plane of normal functioning. Those who struggle to get back up the spiral may find themselves on a downward trajectory,

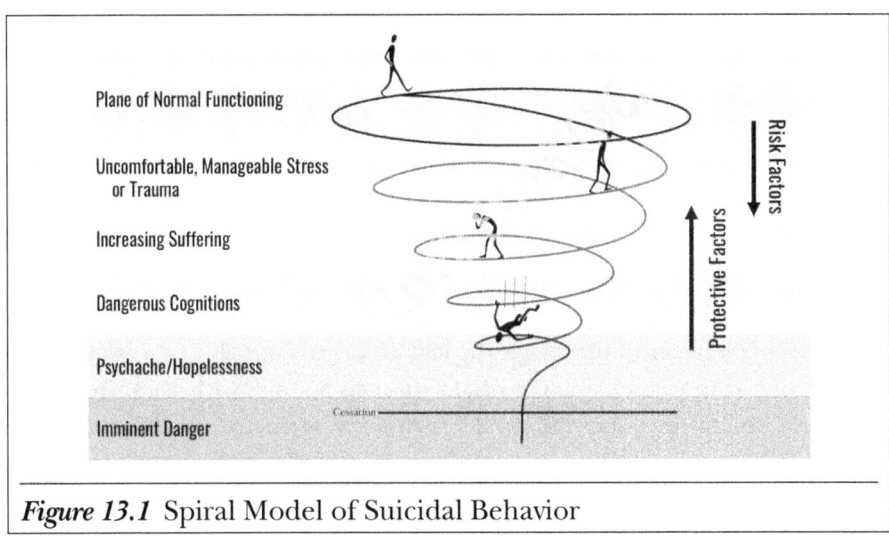

*Figure 13.1* Spiral Model of Suicidal Behavior

thinking dangerous thoughts, becoming hopeless, and possibly taking harmful action to eliminate their intolerable psychological pain.

Three components are key to understanding movement through the spiral: risk factors, protective factors, and lived experience. Risk factors may be biological, psychological, cognitive, and environmental (categories from Stillion & McDowell's suicide trajectory model). In her description of functional characteristics presenting risk or protective factors, White (2016) describes four categories: *predisposing*, *contributing*, *precipitating*, and *protective*. A person may be predisposed to suicidal behaviors (White, 2016) by a previous bout of depression or a history of childhood neglect, for example. A rigid cognitive style and poor coping skills are further examples of contributing factors to ultimate suicidal behavior. A precipitating event, such as a loss or a health crisis, may cause significant distress. These risk factors can accumulate, weighing a person down as they sink lower in the spiral. Protective factors can lift them upwards, back to normal functioning. These factors may be personal, such as positive coping skills or a history of success and optimism. They may also be external, such as a loving, supportive family or ready access to positive role models. You can be a protective factor.

One's lived experience is the backdrop for the spiral model. Lived experience (van Manen, 2016) is an intrapersonal phenomenon and cannot be known by an outside observer. What a person thinks about their experiences is idiosyncratic, shaped through the lens of their personal history and beliefs; "A person's experience is what the world is to that person" (Coleman & Cross, 2000, p. 211). What a person has experienced and how they interpret those experiences play an important role in their mental health.

Daniel's example includes both risk and protective factors. He came from a loving and economically stable family, with a mother who advocated strongly for both his exceptional needs. The risk factors of twice exceptionality, including failures in school and rejection by teachers, were ameliorated for many years by a persistent parent who found a school that satisfied his 2e needs. Medications were a protective factor, except at times of transition when they sometimes caused unpleasant side effects. Daniel's growing need for autonomy led to a shedding of protective factors, as he became more isolated from his family and stopped taking the medication that allowed him to focus in school. His risk factors increased as he spent time with friends who encouraged his substance abuse and non-academic pursuits, which included target shooting. The precipitating factors of school failure and a possible pregnancy led to new, dangerous cognitions. His comfort with guns was a risk factor in the end, as he had an easily accessible means of ending his suffering. The accumulation of risk factors was not met with adequate protective factors to lift him out of the spiral. His story is instructive for those who wish to ensure such a terrible outcome does not repeat itself. Greater attention to his needs as a 2e student could have provided life-saving protection.

# The Risk of Multiple Exceptionalities

There is no evidence that giftedness is associated with a higher risk of depression (Duplenne et al., 2024; Martin et al., 2010) or suicidal behaviors (Cross & Cross, 2017). Among the few studies that compare ideation in gifted and nongifted samples, there were no statistically significant differences in the rates of ideation (Baker, 1995; Cross et al., 2006). This does not suggest an invulnerability among gifted adolescents, but a level of vulnerability similar to their peers. The experiences of these students can contribute to their frustration and can be a risk factor for depression. For example, Irish gifted secondary students reported frequently being pressured by others to "always be right" and this pressure received the most negative rating in terms of how bad it felt to them (J. Cross et al., 2022). The mixed messages gifted students receive to perform their best and to conform to their typically developing peers present a dilemma that can also be a risk factor for depression (Cross, 2015; Gross, 1989). Risk factors such as these are not present in the lives of their peers. They may not result in a greater vulnerability among gifted students than that of their peers, but there are likely to be different potential sources of risk.

In contrast, adolescents with disabilities appear to have an increased risk of depression compared to their typically developing peers (e.g., Bitsika & Sharpley, 2015; Bron et al., 2016; Brunelle et al., 2020). Common features of the disability, such as social inadequacy among children with autism spectrum disorder (ASD) or hyperactivity among those with ADHD, can inhibit the development of positive social relationships, affecting a sense of belonging in one's environment. Belongingness is a critical human need (Baumeister & Leary, 1995; Deci & Ryan, 2000). Wellbeing suffers among those who cannot adequately fulfill the need for social connection, which can be a challenge for students with disabilities of all kinds.

# Twice-Exceptional Risk Factors

Students with gifts and talents who also have disabilities experience challenges that are unique to this diverse population. Learning disabilities, ASD and ADHD are the most common disabilities emphasized in the twice-exceptional literature (e.g., Carpenter, 2012; Foley-Nicpon & Assouline, 2015; Foley Nicpon et al., 2011; Reis et al., 2014). Amend and Peters (2021) reported that ASD and ADHD are the most commonly misdiagnosed or overlooked disorders in clinical practice. In the case of any disability, when left undiagnosed, the student may not receive necessary services for success in school. Daniel, the subject of our vignette, received no services for his giftedness in early elementary school, then no services for his disability while in the gifted magnet school. In high school, he was channeled into a rigorous International Baccalaureate program but received no attention to his disability. This neglect of his twice exceptionality was a contributing risk factor to his depression and suicidal behaviors. Many 2e students may be experiencing similar neglect.

---

**Potential Risk Factors for Depression or Suicidal Behaviors Unique to 2e Adolescents**

- Undiagnosed gifted abilities.
- Undiagnosed disability.
- Misdiagnosis because combination presents atypically.
- Being misunderstood/not socially accepted due to exceptional intellectual ability.
- Being misunderstood/not socially accepted due to manifestations of disability.
- Frustration due to limitations of disability.
- Frustration due to inability to perform/achieve at a level commensurate with intellectual ability.
- Conscious or unconscious strain of masking disability through compensatory strategies.
- Bullying for differentness (of both disability and giftedness).

---

In a study of adult Mensa members, who must test in the top 2% of intellectual ability to be eligible for membership, 7% reported ADHD as a concomitant condition (J. Cross et al., 2024). Multiple participants described the challenge of being recognized only for their giftedness, mislabeled as "lazy," or expected to conform, when what they really needed was support for their undiagnosed disabilities. After years of struggling once the challenges became more than his giftedness could overcome, first in college and then in the workplace, one participant lamented the lack of attention to his ADHD: "We late-diagnosed people have to mourn the loss [of what] we might have had" (p. 163). This participant and many others in the study had experienced depression due to their unmet needs.

The timing of identification of either exceptionality is important. By secondary school, students will have had ample opportunity to develop habits or missed learning that will impact their ability to apply themselves at an advanced level. The late-diagnosed Mensan was identified early for his giftedness, which allowed him to achieve early. Without attention to his ADHD, however, he was unable to be successful as the challenges increased. The opposite problem occurs when a disability is diagnosed early and all attention goes to remediation, and the student's giftedness is not recognized. Self-concept is affected by either diagnosis. 2e students may face the double risk of stigmatization for their giftedness (Coleman & Cross, 1988) and their disability (Wang et al., 2019).

Some 2e students may be less vulnerable than the adults in their lives believe them to be, at least from a mental health perspective. Foley-Nicpon and colleagues (2015) found the 2e students in their study had average self-concepts, despite their disabilities. This *positive illusory bias* is found in other populations of students with disabilities, not only among 2e students, suggesting it is unrelated to their high cognitive ability. This belief, however, may serve as a protective factor, keeping them positive when they experience challenges related to their disability.

Bullying is a risk factor that can affect people of any age (including adults; Kotleras, 2007), but it is a particular issue for students with disabilities (Chen et al., 2015), who are more frequently reported for victimization. In a national study of US high schools, 19% of students reported having been victimized on school property (Kann et al., 2017). Gifted students were among these (Peterson & Ray, 2006), but there is no evidence that they are more likely to be victimized than their peers (J. Cross et al., 2016). Being victimized can knock a 2e student off their plane of normal functioning, leading to depression and, potentially, suicidal behavior.

## Giftedness as a Risk Factor

Despite their ability to engage in advanced academics given appropriate supports, research indicates that many twice-exceptional students do not receive an education appropriate for their high abilities (Crim et al., 2022; Willard-Holt et al., 2013). With a focus only on remediating their weaknesses, there is certain to be frustration due to the lack of challenge. An unacknowledged or unaddressed strength can become a risk factor for depression.

One of the confounding effects of twice exceptionality is the potential for one exceptionality to hide the other. Through their exceptional intellectual ability, a student with a disability may be able to compensate for difficulties, either consciously or without their awareness. This cognitive masking (Atmaca & Baloğlu, 2022) can complicate diagnoses (Amend & Peters, 2021; Foley Nicpon et al., 2011), confusing clinicians when problems do not manifest in the typical manner. Diagnostic criteria can be too rigid in one direction to make a satisfactory diagnosis for the child or adolescent who is not underperforming, for example. The 2e student may not even get a referral.

What is known or believed about giftedness can complicate identification of a disability. Gifted education literature is replete with examples of *overexcitabilities*, an offshoot of Dabrowski's theory of positive disintegration, which is offered as an explanation of extreme sensitivities or behaviors among gifted individuals (Piechowski & Wells, 2021). *Psychomotor* overexcitability is characterized by hyperactivity and impulsiveness, which are also characteristics of ADHD. The twice-exceptional child with giftedness and ADHD may surprise parents and teachers with what they are absorbing from their environment. When they consistently give a correct answer, despite seeming inattentive, it may not seem necessary to report a potential disability. With the explanation of overexcitability as a function of their giftedness, the child's needs may be overlooked.

Educators are likely to have a mental model of a gifted student that can affect their ability to recognize a 2e student. Golle and colleagues (2023) found that the 1,304 Dutch teachers in their study expected students:

> to be gifted when, in comparison with their peers, students were superior in cognitive domains, especially with respect to academic achievement, scored higher on openness to experience and lower on agreeableness, were male, were younger, and came from families with higher parental education.
>
> (p. 64)

Research on nominations of gifted students has found that teachers will select students who meet their sometimes-biased expectations for who is gifted and are more likely to refer those who are emotionally stable (Golle et al., 2018; Hunsaker, 1997) and not from economically disadvantaged families (McBee, 2006, 2010; Ricciardi et al., 2020). The gifted student with attention or learning deficits is less likely to be recognized for their strengths by teachers whose mental models do not include a conception of multiple exceptionalities. Professional development on gifted students may not include information on 2e. For teachers with little experience of such diversity, a 2e student's abilities may go unrecognized. Schultz (2012) found that even when 2e students were placed in gifted programs, some teachers resisted making accommodations for their disability.

Students with exceptional intellectual ability are different from their peers, at least in that one aspect. Particularly in secondary school, being different can be a reason for exclusion (Horn, 2003; Mikami et al., 2010). In a cross-cultural study of the social experiences of gifted students, peer rejection due to their exceptional abilities was reported in all five countries among students at the elementary, middle, and high-school levels (J. Cross et al., 2019). A general dislike of exceptional intellectual ability is common (Howley et al., 2017) and evidence of the stigma of giftedness has been found in numerous studies (e.g., J. Cross et al., 2019; T. Cross et al., 1991; Swiatek, 1995). Gifted children with exceptional verbal abilities may be more likely to experience peer rejection (Dauber & Benbow, 1990; Lee et al., 2012). When their exceptional abilities are cause for rejection, the 2e student may choose to hide them or deflect attention in other ways (Coleman & Cross, 1988). The inability to be one's authentic self in interactions presents a mental health risk and can lead to depression (T. Cross, 2021).

## Giftedness as a Protective Factor

Students' exceptional intellectual ability can serve as a protective factor, especially when paired with an appropriate education. Achievements can be a source of pride and enhanced self-efficacy. A large knowledge base can be called on to respond in class, to support group work, and to help peers. Gifted students experiencing depression were able to support their own therapy through their cognitive abilities (Peterson, 2014; Sedillo, 2013). Those who participate in gifted education programming may find intellectual peers and an opportunity for social acceptance. When they can avail of opportunities for talent development, there is a greater possibility for realizing their potential. These positive outcomes depend, however, on the severity of their disability and the environmental supports they receive.

## Recognizing Signs of Distress

A 2e adolescent may be adept at hiding the distress caused by their exceptionalities. There may be few indications to an outside observer of the intrapersonal experience of sliding down the spiral into depression. One significant barrier to help-seeking in times of distress is the belief that one should be self-reliant and able to resolve one's own problems (Radez et al., 2021). It is important to be aware of the risk factors that may contribute to the descent. Predisposing risks (White, 2016) include prior experience with suicide, which could be the death of a family member or classmate by suicide or a previous suicide attempt. In light of the risk factors posed by 2e, such as misdiagnoses or missed diagnoses (Amend et al., 2021), twice exceptionality is also a predisposing factor. A rigid cognitive style and poor coping skills are contributing factors of which one should be aware (T. Cross et al., 1996, 2002). Perfectionism and persistent academic pressure are examples of further contributing factors that can specifically affect gifted youth (T. Cross & Cross, 2021a). Perhaps most important to those who wish to support a 2e adolescent is to be aware of precipitating factors. Has something particularly stressful occurred in the 2e adolescent's life? This could be a loss of a family member or breakup, a personal failure, or victimization. Even a health crisis can lead to negative cognitions and depression. Transitions, such as entry to a new school, may precipitate distress. Risk factors could be related to the adolescent's 2e status, as frustration over academic or social experiences that might not be problematic for others could accumulate to a breaking point. Being aware of predisposing, contributing, and precipitating factors in the life of an adolescent with multiple exceptionalities is a useful step in recognizing warning signs of greater distress. In Daniel's case, his girlfriend's announcement and his intense dissatisfaction with his transition to college were two precipitating factors to his suicidal thinking. These combined with his other risk factors to deadly effect.

A working group of the American Association of Suicidology provided a two-tiered description of suicide warning signs based on theory, research, and clinical experience (Rudd et al., 2006). The first tier of warning signs includes those that require immediate, urgent response from a mental health professional. Signs such as the following warrant a 911 emergency call:

- someone threatening to hurt or kill themselves;
- someone looking for ways to kill themselves—seeking access to pills, weapons, or other means; or
- someone talking or writing about death, dying, or suicide (Rudd et al., 2006, p. 259).

These behaviors are evidence of descent down the spiral beyond dangerous cognitions, psychache, or hopelessness, and into imminent danger (see Figure 13.1). A caring peer or adult can serve as a protective factor at this point in the spiral by encouraging, possibly even forcing, the depressed adolescent into treatment. Daniel had told his friends many times that he was considering suicide, but none believed he would carry out his threats. Action is necessary to avoid a tragic outcome.

The warning signs in the second tier are symbolic of behaviors that precede the level of imminent danger. There is a greater possibility that friends, family, or other caring persons can play a protective role at an earlier point in the spiral. Signs of increasing suffering or dangerous cognitions include:

- hopelessness;
- rage, anger, vengefulness;
- acting recklessly or engaging in risky activities, seemingly without thinking;
- feeling trapped—like there's no way out;
- increasing alcohol or drug use;
- withdrawing from friends, family, or society;

- anxiety, agitation, inability to sleep, or sleeping all the time;
- dramatic changes in mood; and
- no reason for living; no sense of purpose in life (Rudd et al., 2006, p. 259).

When one or more of these signs are present, it is imperative to seek more information or professional help for the adolescent. Daniel was full of rage against a useless system that expected him to conform. He felt trapped by his girlfriend's announcement that she might be pregnant. He had recklessly run away from home in the days before his suicide and was agitated and withdrawn from others on the day he killed himself. The signs were there, but they were couched in a history of frustration and demands to be left alone. His parents sought professional help, but Daniel refused to go. His parents' protective effect was limited when his dangerous cognitions increased, in part by their desire to respect his autonomy.

The national 988 Suicide & Crisis Lifeline provides support and resources 24 hours a day, seven days a week to those experiencing a mental health crisis. It is also available to help those witnessing signs or concerned about another's distress. As the spiral model (Figure 13.1) makes clear, the path from the plane of normal functioning to increased suffering can turn quickly into danger if there are not adequate protective factors to help lift the individual upwards.

## What You Can Do

Even when help is available to an adolescent in distress, *any* adolescent in distress, there are social and personal barriers to access. In a review of 53 studies on help-seeking among children and adolescents, Radez and colleagues (2021) found the stigma associated with mental health difficulties and embarrassment about sharing such personal vulnerabilities, along with a lack of knowledge about resources and concerns about how to access them (e.g., logistics, affordability), were the most common barriers to seeking help when in distress. 2e students may be particularly affected by the stigma, having previously been exposed to the stigmas associated with their disability, their giftedness, or both. Reducing barriers to access should be a key goal of any effort to support the mental health needs of 2e students. Of course, the resources must also be present in the first place.

Mental health professionals should be aware of the challenges presented by dual exceptionality. Providing them with resources such as reading material (e.g., Carpenter, 2021; T. Cross & Cross, 2018, 2021a, 2021b; Foley-Nicpon & Assouline, 2015; Foley-Nicpon et al., 2011, Reis et al., 2014) or professional development on 2e will provide them with insight into the potential problems faced by this population. Any professional development on the topic of gifted students should include information on the twice-exceptional subpopulation. Greater recognition of 2e concerns and attention to the needs of these students for academic challenge and remediation can reduce their frustration—a significant risk factor for depression and worse.

In addition to expanding the knowledge base of educators and mental health providers to include 2e, the students themselves need information and should be considered in plans for training. While it is important not to assign responsibility to the students to find the help they need, it is also important for them to learn to recognize their own needs and to develop strategies for dealing with distress that may occur as a result. Understanding the nuances of their disability and the wide range of its effects may enable them to apply their intellectual abilities for self-advocacy.

## Building a Resilient Community

It is not inevitable that depression will lead to suicidal behaviors, including ideation, but actions taken to prevent suicide will also impact 2e students who may be suffering from depression. Fostering a supportive environment by bolstering protective factors will help anyone who has fallen off the plane of normal functioning move upwards. The protective community provides varying levels of support (J. Cross & Cross, 2017). Friends, classmates, or siblings can provide a sympathetic ear and offer advice. Adults such as parents, teachers, counselors, and psychologists can additionally offer guidance. Trained professional counselors, psychologists, and psychiatrists can engage in psychological counseling. Psychologists and psychiatrists can provide therapy. Physicians and psychiatrists can also prescribe medications. Just having information like this about who can be a resource for different levels of need can increase the 2e students' ability to access support (Radez et al., 2021). It is critical to prepare providers of support, from friends and siblings to psychiatrists and physicians, with information about both 2e and behaviors that strengthen mental health.

Students, including those with multiple exceptionalities, spend a large proportion of their waking hours in schools. Many of an adolescent's social interactions will occur in school or during extracurricular activities. Academics should not be the only focus of schools or teachers. Teachers can be trained to recognize the features of their students' social interactions, with the goal of creating an inclusive environment for students with disabilities (Farmer et al., 2011, 2016, 2018). Schools can implement programs to develop students' psychosocial skills.

One study found that students who participated in a program to develop coping, problem-solving, and other life skills—the Good Behavior Game—in the first and second grade were half as likely to experience suicide ideation or attempt suicide in high school than students in the control group (Katz et al., 2013). Another effective program, CARE (Care, Assess, Respond, Empower)/CAST (Coping and Support Training), targets high-risk youth with motivational counseling that fosters positive coping and help-seeking behaviors (Katz et al., 2013). Students participating in the CAST group sessions receive lessons on topics such as goal-setting, decision-making, self-esteem, and academic ability. A number of studies have found the CARE/CAST programs to be effective in reducing depression, suicidal behaviors, and family distress, and enhancing self-esteem.

Help-seeking behaviors can be fostered by programs that attempt to reduce the stigma of mental health concerns, normalizing help-seeking behaviors. Education about depression or suicide and resources can address students' concerns about what to do when facing a crisis. Students also need to learn how to respond to peers who are experiencing distress. Gatekeeper universal programs are those that offer training to everyone in a school community, from students to teachers and staff, about depression or suicidal behaviors and how to respond. In a meta-analysis of 49 studies of suicide prevention interventions, gatekeeper universal programs were found to be most effective at increasing participants' knowledge and reducing suicidal thoughts and behaviors (Kiran et al., 2024). Programs such as Youth Aware of Mental Health (https://www.y-a-m.org/) have been found to be very effective in reducing suicidal behaviors (Kiran et al., 2024). Help-seeking behaviors were facilitated when students' social contacts were positive and encouraging about seeking help (Radez et al., 2021). Trained peer leaders were four times more likely than others to involve adults when they were concerned about a classmate (Katz et al., 2013)—possibly because they believed after training that adults would take their concerns seriously.

The Jed Foundation (https://jedfoundation.org/) has been a leader in suicide prevention on college campuses and high schools. This nonprofit organization offers specific advice and guidance on how to design environments that support students' mental health. Jed Campus and Jed High School partners receive detailed evaluations of the mental health climate, highlighting specific risks and providing recommendations. The foundation offers a wealth of information and resources for those interested in developing programs of their own. For example, the Set to Go program (Jed Foundation, 2024) provides resources for students, families, and educators, designed to ease the transition to life after high school. Jed Foundation-sponsored marketing campaigns target the stigma of mental health with relatable videos and other materials. For example, their Seize the Awkward campaign (Ad Council, 2020) encourages students to have difficult discussions about mental health.

## Building a Caring Community

Efforts to promote protective factors are most effective when they are holistic, addressing the needs of all students in an environment that supports their thriving. 2e students are best served in a community that is concerned about the needs of each person. Cross and Cross (2018) provide guidelines for creating a caring community that supports the mental health of all its members:

- Create an operational definition of "thriving" that allows for targeted actions that can be measured to ensure improvement is happening.
- Measure change in members as they compare with others in the community (normative) and determine change in themselves (idiosyncratic), to establish a focus on both community and individual change.
- Emphasize the development of both social and academic protective factors, such as skill-building in coping strategies and academic self-regulation.
- Institute ongoing training for members at all levels (e.g., children, teachers, staff, parents) that helps them identify individual needs for mental health support and fosters strategies for responding to their own needs and those of others.
- Develop trust among members of the community through open communication and power-sharing in decision-making.
- Dispel myths about mental health and suicide (e.g., that talking about suicide will encourage suicidal ideation and behaviors. Research evidence supports a positive effect from asking directly if one has considered suicide [Decou et al., 2018; Polihronis et al., 2022]).
- Utilize the curriculum, making adaptations to support the development of protective factors.
- Support the development of positive social relationships that emphasize individuals' strengths and interests.

A strengths-based approach is also key to Baum and colleagues' (2014) recommendations for developing a program that best supports 2e students. Based on their research of an effective program, they advise the following:

- Collect data about students' strengths, interests, and talents to be used in planning and differentiation in the classroom.
- Address 2e students' deficits within an enriched curriculum that allows for the authentic application and transfer of skills.
- Evaluate individual growth over time, as opposed to comparisons with grade-level expectations.

In her analysis of the failings that contributed to the death of a suicidal gifted student, Hyatt (2010) recommended that attention be paid to developing trusting relationships among adolescents and adults, training adults in the social-emotional needs of gifted students, and challenging perfectionistic attitudes among adolescents.

## Final Thoughts

Students with multiple exceptionalities are multiply at risk of depression and its potential sequelae. Adults who care about their wellbeing must take action to promote an environment that supports their strengths while addressing their disabilities. Training is a necessity for educators, parents, and 2e students themselves. Building an educated, caring community will support the mental health needs of all students, including its 2e students.

Daniel's is a tragic story of unfulfilled potential, likely repeated many times. Only one school in his 13 years was prepared for his dual exceptionality. He received no services to support his ADHD in elementary school. The magnet school for gifted students he attended in his late elementary years was unprepared for either his high ability or his ADHD. He was lost in high school, disinterested in an inflexible curriculum, with no special education services. A middle school attuned to his interests and needs made an important difference in his life, but when it ended after the eighth grade, he was thrown back into a negative environment. In Daniel's example, we see both depression and suicidal behaviors. Schools must be ready for all their students, including those with concomitant high abilities and disabilities.

### Things to Consider

- Twice-exceptional students often face challenges due to unrecognized or misunderstood exceptionalities. Giftedness can mask disabilities (and vice versa), leading to inappropriate educational placement and lack of support—major risk factors for depression and suicidal ideation.
- 2e students may experience a "double stigma," being misunderstood for both their giftedness and their disabilities. This often results in social isolation, bullying, and internalized frustration over unmet potential, contributing to mental health challenges.

- The spiral model of suicidal behavior (Figure 13.1) highlights how risk and protective factors interact with an individual's personal history and perceptions. Supportive family, teachers, peers, and mental health professionals can lift students out of psychological spirals—but only if these protective elements are present and accessible.
- Schools must be prepared to recognize and support 2e students' social-emotional and academic needs. This includes training in recognizing mental health risk factors, addressing perfectionism, and implementing strength-based, inclusive strategies. A single supportive teacher or well-matched educational environment can be a turning point.

## For Discussion

- How can individuals best support 2e adolescents experiencing depression?
- What risk factors are unique to 2e adolescents?
- How should schools be prepared to support the mental health of 2e adolescents?

## Note

1 A pseudonym.

## References

Ad Council (2020) *Seize the Awkward*. https://seizetheawkward.org/

Amend, E. R. & Peters, D. B. (2021) The importance of accurate assessment of gifted students: Issues with misdiagnosis, missed diagnoses, and twice-exceptionality. In T. L. Cross & J. R. Cross (eds.) *Handbook for counselors serving students with gifts and talents*, 2nd ed. (pp. 713-731). Prufrock Academic Press. https://doi.org/10.4324/9781003235415-44

Atmaca, F. & Baloğlu, M. (2022) The two sides of cognitive masking: A three-level Bayesian meta-analysis on twice-exceptionality. *Gifted Child Quarterly*, 66(4), 277-295. https://doi.org/10.1177/00169862221110875

Baker, J. A. (1995) Depression and suicidal ideation among academically talented adolescents. *Gifted Child Quarterly, 39,* 218-223. https://doi.org/10.1177/0016986295039004

Baum, S. M., Schader, R. M., & Hébert, T. P. (2014) Through a different lens: Reflecting on a strengths-based, talent-focused approach for twice-exceptional learners. *Gifted Child Quarterly, 58*(4), 311-327. https://doi.org/10.1177/0016986214547632

Baumeister, R. F. & Leary, M. R. (1995) The need to belong: Desire for interpersonal attachments as a fundamental human motivation. *Psychological Bulletin, 117,* 497-529. https://doi.org/10.1037/0033-2909.117.3.497

Bitsika, V. & Sharpley, C. F. (2015) Differences in the prevalence, severity and symptom profiles of depression in boys and adolescents with an autism spectrum disorder versus normally developing controls. *International Journal of Disability, Development & Education, 62*(2), 158-167. https://doi.org/10.1080/1034912X.2014.998179

Bommersbach, T. J., Rosenheck, R. A., Petrakis, I. L., & Rhee, T. G. (2022) Why are women more likely to attempt suicide than men? Analysis of lifetime suicide attempts among US adults in a nationally representative sample. *Journal of Affective Disorders, 311,* 157-164. https://doi.org/10.1016/j.jad.2022.05.096.

Bron, T. I., Bijlenga, D., Verduijn, J., Penninx, B. W. J. H., Beekman, A. T. F., & Kooij, J. J. S. (2016) Prevalence of ADHD symptoms across clinical stages of major depressive disorder. *Journal of Affective Disorders, 197,* 29-35. https://doi.org/10.1016/j.jad.2016.02.053

Brunelle, K., Abdulle, S. & Gorey, K. M. (2020) Anxiety and depression among socioeconomically vulnerable students with learning disabilities: Exploratory meta-analysis. *Child Adolescent Social Work Journal, 37,* 359-367. https://doi.org/10.1007/s10560-019-00631-w

Carpenter, A. Y. (2021) Twice-Exceptional students. In T. L. Cross & J. R. Cross (eds.) *Handbook for counselors serving students with gifts and talents,* 2nd ed. (pp. 305-323). Prufrock Academic Press. https://doi.org/10.4324/9781003235415-19

Chen, C.-C., Hamm, J. V., Farmer, T. W., Lambert, K., & Mehtaji, M. (2015) Exceptionality and peer victimization involvement in late childhood: Subtypes, stability, and social marginalization. *Remedial and Special Education, 36*(5), 312-324. https://doi.org/10.1177/0741932515579242

Coleman, L. J. & Cross, T. L. (1988) Is being gifted a social handicap? *Journal for the Education of the Gifted, 11*(4), 41-56. https://doi.org/10.1177/016235328801100406

Coleman, L. J. & Cross, T. L. (2000) Social-emotional development and personal experience. In K. Heller, F. J. Mönks, R. J. Sternberg, & R. S. Subotnik (eds.) *International handbook of giftedness and talent*, 2nd ed. (pp. 203-212). Pergamon.

Crim, C., Hawkins, J., Ruban, L., & Johnson, S. (2008) Curricular modifications for elementary students with learning disabilities in high-, average-, and low-IQ groups. *Journal of Research in Childhood Education, 22*(3), 233-245. https://doi.org/10.1080/02568540809594624

Cross, J. R., Bugaj, S. J., & Mammadov, S. (2016) Accepting a scholarly identity: Gifted students, academic crowd membership, and identification with school. *Journal for the Education of the Gifted, 39*(1), 23-48. https://doi.org/10.1177/0162353215624162

Cross, J. R., & Cross, T. L. (2017) Providing for the positive psychological development of students with gifts and talents. In J. R. Cross, C. O'Reilly, & T. L. Cross (eds.) *Providing for the special needs of students with gifts and talents* (pp. 199-233). CTYI Press.

Cross, J. R., Cross, T. L., O'Reilly, C. (2022) *Irish gifted students: Self, social, and academic explorations: Full Report*. Report prepared for Centre for Talented Youth – Ireland. https://doi.org/10.25774/ny41-t831

Cross, J. R., Cross, T. L., & Mishra, A. (2024) *A study of unmet needs among highly intelligent individuals*. Report prepared for the Mensa Foundation.

Cross, J. R., Vaughn, C. T., Mammadov, S., Cross, T. L., Kim, M., O'Reilly, C., Spielhagen, F., Pereira Da Costa, M., & Hymer, B. (2019) A cross-cultural study of the social experience of giftedness. *Roeper Review, 41*(4), 224-242. 10.1080/02783193.2019.1661052

Cross, T. L. (2018) *On the social and emotional lives of gifted children: Factors and issues in their psychological development* (5th ed.). Prufrock Press.

Cross, T.L. (2021) The role of authenticity in the psychosocial development of students with gifts and talents. *Gifted Child Today, 44* (2), 111-114. https://doi.org/10.1177/1076217520988777

Cross, T. L., Cassady, J. C., & Miller, K. A. (2006) Suicide ideation and personality characteristics among gifted adolescents. *Gifted Child Quarterly, 50*, 295-306. doi:10.1177/001698620605000403

Cross, T. L., Coleman, L. J., & Terhaar-Yonkers, M. (1991) The social cognition of gifted adolescents in schools: Managing the stigma of giftedness. *Journal for the Education of the Gifted, 15*(1), 44-55. https://doi.org/10.1177/016235329101500106

Cross, T. L., Cook, R. S., & Dixon, D. N. (1996) Psychological autopsies of three academically talented adolescents who committed suicide. *Journal of Secondary Gifted Education, 7*(3), 403-409. https://doi.org/10.1177/1932202x9600700305

Cross, T. L. & Cross, J. R. (2018) *Suicide among gifted children and adolescents*, 2nd ed. Prufrock Press.

Cross, T. L. & Cross, J. R. (2021a) An ecological model of suicidal behavior among students with gifts and talents. *High Ability Studies, 32,* 105-123. https://doi.org/10.1080/13598139.2020.1733391

Cross, T. L. & Cross, J. R. (eds.) (2021b) *Handbook for counselors serving students with gifts and talents,* 2nd ed. Prufrock Academic Press.

Cross, T. L., Cross, J. R., & Andersen, L. (2021) Suicide and students with gifts and talents: Advice for counselors. In T. L. Cross & J. R. Cross (eds.) *Handbook for counselors serving students with gifts and talents,* 2nd ed. (pp. 775-800). Prufrock Academic Press. https://doi.org/10.4324/9781003235415-47

Cross, T. L., Cross, J. R., Dudnytska, N., Kim, M., & Vaughn, C. T. (2020) A psychological autopsy of an intellectually gifted student with Attention Deficit Disorder. *Roeper Review, 42*(1), 6-24. https://doi.org/10.1080/02783193.2019.1690081

Cross, T. L., Gust-Brey, K., & Ball, P. B. (2002). A psychological autopsy of the suicide of an academically gifted student: Researchers' and parents' perspectives. *Gifted Child Quarterly, 46*(4), 247-264. https://doi.org/10.1177/001698620204600402

Cukrowicz, K. C. & Poindexter, E. K. (2014) Suicide. In C. S. Richards & M. W. O'Hara (eds.) *The Oxford handbook of depression and comorbidity* (pp. 254–267). Oxford University Press.

Dauber, S. L. & Benbow, C. P. (1990) Aspects of personality and peer relations of extremely talented adolescents. *Gifted Child Quarterly, 34,* 10-15. https://doi.org/10.1177/001698629003400103

Deci, E. L. & Ryan, R. M. (2000) The "what" and "why" of goal pursuits: Human needs and the self-determination of behavior. *Psychological Inquiry, 11,* 227-268.

DeCou, C. R. & Schumann, M. E. (2018) On the iatrogenic risk of assessing suicidality: A meta-analysis. *Suicide and Life-Threatening Behavior, 48*(5), 531-543. https://doi.org/10.1111/sltb.12368

Duplenne, L., Bourdin, B., Fernandez, D. N., Blondelle, G., & Aubry, A. (2024) Anxiety and depression in gifted individuals: A systematic and meta-analytic review. *Gifted Child Quarterly, 68*(1), 65-83. https://doi.org/10.1177/00169862231208922

Eisenberg, D. & Lipson, S. K. (2019) The Healthy Minds Study 2018-2019 data report. University of Michigan Healthy Minds Network. https://healthymindsnetwork.org/wp-content/uploads/2019/09/HMS_national-2018-19.pdf

Farmer, T. W., Chen, C.-C., Hamm, J. V., Moates, M. M., Mehtaji, M., Lee, D., & Huneke, M. R. (2016) Supporting teachers' management of middle school social dynamics. *Intervention in School & Clinic, 52*(2), 67-76. https://doi.org/10.1177/1053451216636073

Farmer, T. W., Hamm, J. V., Dawes, M., Barko-Alva, K., & Cross, J. R. (2019) Promoting inclusive communities in diverse classrooms: Teacher attunement and social dynamics management. *Educational Psychologist, 54*(4), 286-305. https://doi.org/10.1080/00461520.2019.1635020

Farmer, T. W., Lines, M. M., & Hamm, J. V. (2011) Revealing the invisible hand: The role of teachers in children's peer experiences. *Journal of Applied Developmental Psychology, 32*(5), 247-256. https://doi.org/10.1016/j.appdev.2011.04.006

Foley Nicpon, M., Allmon, A., Sieck, B., & Stinson, R. D. (2011) Empirical investigation of twice-exceptionality: Where have we been and where are we going? *Gifted Child Quarterly, 55*(1), 3-17. https://doi.org/10.1177/0016986210382575

Foley-Nicpon, M. & Assouline, S. G. (2015) Counseling considerations for the twice-exceptional client. *Journal of Counseling & Development, 93*(2), 202-211. https://doi.org/10.1002/j.1556-6676.2015.00196.x

Foley-Nicpon, M., Assouline, S. G., & Fosenburg, S. (2015) The relationship between self-concept, ability, and academic programming among twice-exceptional youth. *Journal of Advanced Academics, 26*(4), 256-273. https://doi.org/10.1177/1932202X15603364

Gross, M. U. M. (1989) The pursuit of excellence or the search for intimacy? The forced-choice dilemma of gifted youth. *Roeper Review, 11,* 189-194. http://dx.doi.org/10.1080/02783198909553207

Horn, S. S. (2003) Adolescents' reasoning about exclusion from social groups. *Developmental Psychology, 39*(1), 71-84. https://doi.org/10.1037/0012-1649.39.1.71

Howley, C. B., Howley, A., & Pendarvis, E. D. (2017) *Out of our minds: Anti-intellectualism and talent development in American schooling*, 2nd ed. Prufrock Press.

Hunsaker, S. L., Finley, V. S., & Frank, E. L. (1997) An analysis of teacher nominations and student performance in gifted programs. *Gifted Child Quarterly, 41*(2), 19-24. https://doi.org/10.1177/001698629704100203

Hyatt, L. (2010) A case study of the suicide of a gifted female adolescent: Implications for prediction and prevention. *Journal for the Education of the Gifted, 33,* 514-535. https://doi.org/10.1177/016235321003300404

Jed Foundation (2024) Set to Go: A Jed program. https://jedfoundation.org/set2go-jed-program/

Joiner, T. E. (2005) *Why people die by suicide.* Harvard University Press.

Joiner, T. E. & Silva, C. (2012) Why people die by suicide: Further development and tests of the Interpersonal-Psychological theory of suicidal behavior. In P. R. Shaver & M. Mikulincer (eds.) *Meaning, mortality, and choice: The social psychology of existential concerns* (pp. 325–336). American Psychological Association. DOI:10.1037/13748-000

Kann, L., McManus, T., Harris, W. A., et al. (2017) Youth risk behavior surveillance—United States, 2017. *MMWR Surveill Summ, 67*(SS–8), 1-114. http://dx.doi.org/10.15585/mmwr.ss6708a1

Katz, C., Bolton, S.-L., Katz, L. Y., Isaak, C., Tilston-Jones, T., Sareen, J., & Swampy Cree Suicide Prevention Team. (2013) A systematic review of school-based suicide prevention pro- grams. *Depression and Anxiety, 30,* 1030-1045. https://doi.org/10.1002/da.22114

Kiran, T., Angelakis, I., Panagioti, M., Irshad, S., Sattar, R., Hidayatullah, S., Tyler, N., Tofique, S., Bukhsh, A., Eylem-van Bergeijk, O., Özen-Dursun, B., Husain, N., Chaudhry, N., & Hodkinson, A. (2024) Controlled interventions to improve suicide prevention in educational settings: A systematic review and network meta-analysis. *Clinical Psychology: Science and Practice, 31*(1), 85-93. https://doi.org/10.1037/cps0000179

Kotleras, R. (2007) The workplace mobbing of highly gifted adults: An unremarked barbarism. *Advanced Development, 11,* 130-148. https://www.proquest.com/scholarly-journals/workplace-mobbing-highly-gifted-adults-unremarked/docview/197464408/se-2

Lee, S-Y., Olszewski-Kubilius, P., & Thomson, D. T. (2012) Academically gifted students' perceived interpersonal competence and peer relationships. *Gifted Child Quarterly, 56,* 90-104. https://doi.org/10.1177/0016986212442568

Martin, L. T., Burns, R. M., & Schonlau, M. (2010) Mental disorders among gifted and nongifted youth: A selected review of the epidemiologic literature. *Gifted Child Quarterly, 54,* 31-41. https://doi.org/10.1177/0016986209352684 (Note corrigendum here: https://doi.org/10.1177/00169862231199745)

McBee, M. T. (2006) A descriptive analysis of referral sources for gifted identification screening by race and socioeconomic status. *Journal of Secondary Gifted Education, 17,* 103-111. https://doi.org/10.4219/jsge-2006-686

McBee, M. T. (2010) Examining the probability of identification for gifted programs for students in Georgia elementary schools: A multilevel path analysis study. *Gifted Child Quarterly, 54,* 283-297. https://doi.org/10.1177/0016986210377927

Mikami, A. Y., Lerner, M. D., & Lun, J. (2010) Social context influences on children's rejection by their peers. *Child Development Perspectives, 4,* 123-130. https://doi.org/10.1111/j.1750-8606.2010.00130.x

National Institute of Mental Health (2024) Suicide. US Department of Health and Human Services. https://www.nimh.nih.gov/health/statistics/suicide#part_154969

Peterson, J. S. (2014) Giftedness, trauma, and development: A qualitative, longitudinal case study. *Journal for the Education of the Gifted, 37,* 295-318. http://dx.doi.org/10.1177/0162353214552564

Peterson, J. S. & Ray, K. E. (2006) Bullying and the gifted: Victims, perpetrators, prevalence, and effects. *Gifted Child Quarterly, 50*(2), 148-168. https://doi.org/10.1177/001698620605000206

Piechowski, M. M. & Wells, C. (2021) Re-examining overexcitability: A framework for understanding intense experience. In T. L. Cross & J. R. Cross (eds.) *Handbook for counselors serving students with gifts and talents*, 2nd ed. (pp. 63-83). Prufrock Academic Press. https://doi.org/ 0.4324/9781003235415-6

Polihronis, C., Cloutier, P., Kaur, J., Skinner, R., & Cappelli, M. (2022) What's the harm in asking? A systematic review and meta-analysis on the risks of asking about suicide-related behaviors and self-harm with quality appraisal. *Archives of Suicide Research, 26*(2), 325-347. https://doi.org/10.1080/13811118.2020.1793857

Radez, J., Reardon, T., Creswell, C., Lawrence, P. J., Evdoka-Burton, G., & Waite, P. (2021) Why do children and adolescents (not) seek and access professional help for their mental health problems? A systematic review of quantitative and qualitative studies. *European Child & Adolescent Psychiatry, 30*(2), 183-211. https://doi.org/10.1007/s00787-019-01469-4

Reis, S. M., Baum, S. M., & Burke, E. (2014) An operational definition of twice-exceptional learners: Implications and applications. *Gifted Child Quarterly, 58*(3), 217-230. https://doi.org/10.1177/0016986214534976

Ricciardi, C., Haag-Wolf, A., & Winsler, A. (2020) Factors associated with gifted identification for ethnically diverse children in poverty. *Gifted Child Quarterly, 64*(4), 243-258. https://doi.org/10.1177/0016986220937685

Schultz, J. (2012) *Nowhere to hide: Why kids with ADHD and LD hate school and what we can do about it.* Wiley.

Sedillo, P. J. (2013) *A retrospective study of gay gifted, young adult males' perceptions of giftedness and suicide* (Doctoral dissertation). ProQuest Dissertations and Theses Database (UMI No. 3601219).

Shneidman, E. S. (1993) *Suicide as psychache: A clinical approach to self-destructive behavior.* Jason Aronson.

Stillion, J. M., & McDowell, E. E. (1996) *Suicide across the life span.* Taylor & Francis.

Swiatek, M. A. (1995) An empirical investigation of the social coping strategies used by gifted adolescents. *Gifted Child Quarterly, 39,* 154-161. https://doi.org/10.1177/001698629503900305

Vaivre-Douret, L. & Hamdioui, S. (2021) Understanding of the prevalence of depression in a sample of gifted children by identifying the developmental trajectory of risk and protective factors. *European Psychiatry, 64*(Suppl 1), S86-S87. https://doi.org/10.1192/j.eurpsy.2021.257

van Manen, M. (2016) *Researching lived experience: Human science for an action sensitive pedagogy.* Routledge.

Wang, K. & Ashburn-Nardo, L. (2019) Disability stigma: Causes, consequences, and strategies for change. In D. S. Dunn (ed.) *Understanding the experience of disability: Perspectives from social and rehabilitation psychology* (pp. 11-23). Oxford University Press.

White, J. (2016). *Preventing youth suicide: A guide for practitioners.* Ministry of Children and Family Development. https://www2.gov.bc.ca/assets/gov/health/managing-your-health/mental-health-substance-use /child-teen-mental-health/preventing_youth_suicide_practitioners_guide.pdf

Willard-Holt, C., Weber, J., Morrison, K. L., & Horgan, J. (2013) Twice-exceptional learners' perspectives on effective learning strategies. *Gifted Child Quarterly, 57*(4), 247-262. https://doi.org/10.1177/0016986213501076

# Final Thoughts from the Editors

As we reach the close of this book, we are reminded that the stories, insights, and research shared throughout these chapters are more than academic considerations—they are reflections of real people navigating the complexities of twice-exceptionality at the intersection of multiple, often marginalized, identities. Whether our focus was on the identity formation of 2e adolescents, the distinct cognitive and emotional profiles they present, or the profound challenges faced by students of color, transgender students, those from military families, and those experiencing homelessness, one truth has consistently emerged: these learners are navigating a world that too often misunderstands or overlooks them.

We also examined the internal terrain of 2e students—the emotional intensity, anxiety, and the quiet, sometimes invisible, burden of depression and suicidal ideation. These realities demand that we, as educators, advocates, and allies, cultivate learning environments rooted in understanding and trust. Classrooms must be safe spaces where stereotypes, stigma, bias, and judgment are actively dismantled, not passively ignored. Only then can 2e students be seen not through a lens of deficiency or disorder, but through the richness of their complexity and the strength of their resilience.

Twice-exceptional students who navigate intersecting marginalized identities bring invaluable perspectives to the learning community. Their lived experiences deepen conversations, challenge assumptions, and expand what we believe is possible in both teaching and learning. These students are not simply recipients of education—they are contributors, creators, and changemakers in their own right.

We now invite you—educators, administrators, counselors, parents, and community allies—to take this knowledge forward. Begin with reflection: examine your own biases, the policies in your schools, and the assumptions embedded in your curriculum. Engage in ongoing professional development focused on equity, neurodiversity, and trauma-informed care. Advocate for systems that recognize and support the whole child. Most importantly, listen deeply to the voices of 2e students and their families. Their truths must shape the path ahead.

This work is urgent. It is personal. And it is possible. Together, we can create learning environments where twice-exceptional students thrive—not in spite of who they are, but because of it. At the end of the day, diversity is not a challenge to be managed; it is an asset to be celebrated.

*Matt and Wendy*

# Appendix A

# Social Identity Wheel

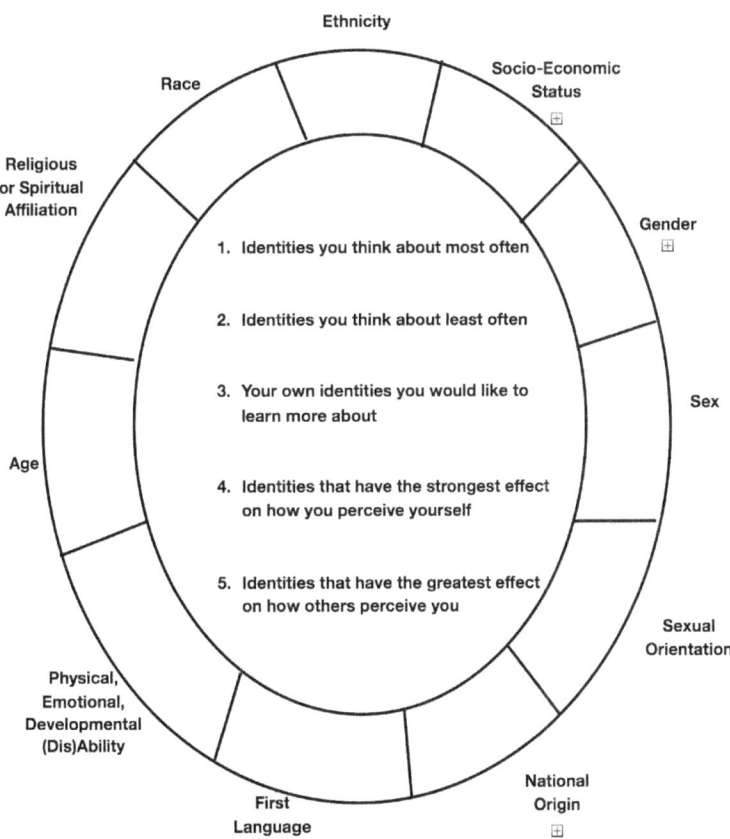

Retrieved from https://ppl-co.com/wp-content/uploads/2020/06/social-identity-wheel-1347x1500.png

# Appendix B

# Selected Intersectionality Resources

Baraka, A. (2021). *Undiagnosed: The ugly side of dyslexia*. Simple Words Books.

Brissett-Bailey, M. (2023). *Black, brilliant & dyslexic: Neurodivergent heroes tell their stores*. Jessica Kingsley Publishers.

Galbraith J. & Delisle J. (2022). *The gifted teen survival guide (5th Ed)*. Free Spirit Press.

## Podcasts

*Sheldon Gay is BUG'N* (https://sheldongayisbugn.com): Sheldon Gay discusses varied topic on the experiences of neurodivergent adolescents and adults.

*Black Girl, Lost Keys* (https://blackgirllostkeys.com/adhd/): Living as a Black woman with ADHD.

## Online Resources

Black Lives Matter at School Curriculum Resources
https://www.blacklivesmatteratschool.com/curriculum.html

Copyright material from C. Matthew Fugate and Wendy A. Behrens (2026), *Intersectional Identities of Twice-Exceptional Teens*, Routledge

Cole, F. J. (2012, April) "What I learned from my autistic brothers," TED Talent Search.

https://www.ted.com/talks/faith_jegede_cole_what_i_ve_learned_from_my_autistic_brothers?referrer=playlist-the_autism_spectrum&autoplay=true

Our Wild Minds: Online community and programs that help Black gifted adults unleash their natural gifts through community connections and learning experiences.

https://www.ourwildminds.com

W.K. Kellogg Foundation Day of Racial Healing

https://www.wkkf.org/national-day-of-racial-healing/

# Appendix C

# Cultural Recognition: Practical Tools for Educators

## Cultural Competency in Action

### Traditional View vs. Cultural Wealth Perspective

Behavior: Student calls out answers,
- Traditional: Disruptive, can't wait turn.
- Cultural wealth: Shows enthusiasm, quick processing.

Behavior: Student helps others instead of finishing own work.
- Traditional: Off-task, distracting others, cheating, plagiarism.
- Cultural wealth: Demonstrates leadership teaching ability.

### Gift Recognition Matrix

| Area of Giftedness | Traditional Signs | Non-Traditional Signs | Cultural Wealth Indicators |
|---|---|---|---|
| Mathematical | Quick computation | Creative problem-solving | Real-world applications |
| Linguistic | Advanced vocabulary | Code-switching mastery | Community storytelling |

| Area of Giftedness | Traditional Signs | Non-Traditional Signs | Cultural Wealth Indicators |
|---|---|---|---|
| Leadership | Class participation | Peer mediation | Family responsibility |
| Creative | Artistic production | Innovation in constraints | Cultural synthesis |

# Scholar Identity Model™ Implementation (Whiting, 2014)

Effective teacher preparation must address scholar identity components
- Self-efficacy development:
  - Building academic confidence.
  - Fostering resilience.
  - Developing self-advocacy.
  - Nurturing excellence.
- Cultural pride integration:
  - Celebrating heritage.
  - Acknowledging achievements.
  - Connecting to community.
  - Building cultural bridges.
- Achievement orientation:
  - Setting high expectations.
  - Providing appropriate challenge.
  - Recognizing multiple paths to success.
  - Supporting persistence.

## Practical Classroom Strategies: Classroom Implementation Guide

### Identification Practices

| Traditional Signs | Cultural Expressions | Combined Indicators |
|---|---|---|
| Rapid learning | Oral storytelling | Creative synthesis |
| Test scores | Problem-solving | Leadership skills |
| Written work | Cultural knowledge | Community impact |

## Support Systems

| Academic | Social-Emotional | Cultural |
|---|---|---|
| Acceleration options | Mentoring | Community connections |
| Enrichment activities | Counseling | Family partnerships |
| Talent development | Peer support | Cultural celebration |

## Differentiation Approaches

| Content | Process | Product |
|---|---|---|
| Multiple entry points | Learning style options | Choice in demonstration |
| Cultural relevance | Pace flexibility | Alternative formats |
| Interest-based | Group configuration | Authentic assessment |

# Urban Resource Mapping

- Community assets:
    - Cultural organizations.
    - Local businesses.
    - Religious institutions.
    - Community leaders.
    - Family networks.
- Educational partners:
    - Libraries.
    - Museums.
    - Universities.
    - Technology centers.
    - Arts organizations.
- Support systems:
    - Mental health resources.
    - Advocacy groups.
    - Mentorship programs.
    - After-school programs.

# Questions for Teacher Self-Reflection

- Perception check:
    - Am I seeing behavior through a deficit or asset lens?
    - What cultural wealth might I be missing?
    - How might learning differences mask giftedness?

- Evidence collection:
  - What alternative assessments could I use?
  - How can I document non-traditional gifts?
  - What family/community input should I seek?
- Action planning:
  - What accommodations support both gifts and challenges?
  - How can I create opportunities for strength display?
  - What resources can I provide to support growth?

# Appendix D

# Emotional and Psychological Profiles of Highly Gifted Students

## Vulnerabilities of Highly Gifted Children (Roedel, 1984)

| Trait | Description |
|---|---|
| Alienation | Communication problems with peers at early ages due to advanced abilities (i.e. abstract ideas) make it hard for very young children to find same-age playmates of like abilities. |
| Uneven development | Gap between a child's advanced intellectual capacity and more age-appropriate social and physical skills can lead to unrealistic expectations for performance. |
| Inappropriate environments | Vulnerability increases when large amounts of time are spent in inappropriate educational environments. |
| Role conflict | Conflict between society's stereotyped expectations for certain age, gender, and racial groups and the highly gifted child's need to fulfill extraordinary individual potential can be severe. |
| Perfectionism | Inner push toward perfection that drives gifted children to set impossible goals for themselves. |
| Adult expectations | Perfection is exaggerated by adults who constantly urge their children to live up to their potential. |

Copyright material from C. Matthew Fugate and Wendy A. Behrens (2026), *Intersectional Identities of Twice-Exceptional Teens*, Routledge

Intersectional Identities of 2e Teens

| Trait | Description |
|---|---|
| Intensity/sensitivity | Heightened sensitivity and internal responsiveness can intensify reactions to ordinary problems of growing up. |
| Self-definition | Classic adolescent crisis may occur earlier for gifted children due to intense analytical approach which leads to early analysis of self. |

## Intensity in Gifted Individuals (Overexcitabilities) (Silverman, 1993)

| Psychomotor | • Heightened excitability of the neuromuscular system.<br>• Capacity for being active and energetic; love of movement for its own sake.<br>• Organic surplus of energy [rapid speech; marked excitation; intense physical activity; need for action].<br>• Psychomotor expression of emotional tension [compulsive talking and chattering; impulsive actions; acting out; nervous habits (tics, nail biting); drive; workaholism; organizing; competitiveness]. |
|---|---|
| Sensual | • Heightened experience of sensual pleasure or displeasure [seeing; smelling; tasting; touching; hearing].<br>• Intense sexuality.<br>• Sensual expression and outlets for emotional tension [overeating; buying sprees; wanting to be in the limelight].<br>• Aesthetic pleasures [appreciation of beautiful objects, words, music, form, color, balance]. |
| Intellectual | • Heightened need to seek understanding and truth; to gain knowledge, analyze and synthesize.<br>• Intensified activity of the mind [curiosity; concentration; capacity for sustained intellectual effort; avid reading; keen observation; detailed planning; detailed visual recall].<br>• Penchant for probing questions; problem solving [search for truth, understanding; tenacity in problem solving].<br>• Preoccupation with logic and theoretical thinking [love of theory and analysis; thinking about thinking; non-judgmental introspection; moral thinking; conceptual and intuitive integration; independence of thought (sometimes criticism)].<br>• Development of new concepts. |

| Imaginational | - Heightened play of the imagination.
- Rich association of images and impressions (real and imagined) [frequent use of image and metaphor; facility for invention and fantasy; detailed visualization; poetic and dramatic perception; animistic thinking; magical thinking].
- Spontaneous imagery as an expression of emotional tension [animistic imagery; mixing truth with fiction; elaborate dreams; illusions].
- Capacity for living in a world of fantasy [predilection for fairy and magic tales; creation of private worlds, imaginary companions; dramatization]. |
|---|---|
| Emotional | - Heightened, intense positive and negative feelings [extremes of emotion; complex emotions and feelings; identification with others' feelings; high degree of differentiation of interpersonal feeling; awareness of range and intensity of feelings].
- Somatic expressions [tense stomach; sinking heart, blushing/flushing, pounding heart, sweaty palms].
- Strong affective expressions [inhibition, timidity, shyness); ecstasy, euphoria, pride; strong affective memory; feelings of unreality, fears and anxieties; feelings of guilt; concern with death; depressive and suicidal moods].
- Capacity for strong attachments and deep relationships [strong emotional ties and attachments to persons, living things, places; compassion, responsiveness to others; empathy; sensitivity in relationships; difficulty adjusting to new environments; loneliness; conflicts with others over depth of relationship; intense desire to offer love].
- Well-differentiated feelings toward self [awareness of one's real self; inner dialogue and self-judgment]. |

# Emotional Coping Strategies of the Gifted (Roeper, 1982)

| Perfectionist | • Cannot fail at anything.<br>• Places unrealistic demands upon themselves.<br>• Feels omnipotent beyond normal stage.<br>• Depersonalization; believes negative emotions are impossible and imperfect and should be suppressed; relegates negative emotions to unconscious resulting in guilt, fear, worries, phobias; can lead to total separation of affective domain when positive and negative emotions are suppressed; lack of affect in evident in behavior.<br>• Considers failure if unable to achieve unrealistic expectations; personal fault instead of realistic age and ability limitation.<br>• Unusually early superego development due to sensitivity and awareness.<br>• Continuation of omnipotence combines with early conscience development, creating enormous obligations.<br>• Method of suppressing emotions underdeveloped and explosive.<br>• Suppressed aggression expressed against oneself; masochist; becomes scapegoat; in extreme cases, leads to suicide. |
|---|---|
| Child/adult | • Sees themselves as an adult; feels in complete control of themselves; interference threatens self-image.<br>• Observes and reacts to adult weaknesses and insecurities; feels they can only trust themselves and are alone in the world.<br>• Paranoia arises due to having two antagonists: (a) dangers of unknown problems in the world they cannot solve; and (b) continued thread to their unrealistic positions and self-image by environment which treats them as the child they are.<br>• Becomes dependent child; doesn't battle with environment when confronted with limits of abilities; knows it is impossible to be an adult.<br>• Defends infantile selves against the world. |

| Winner of the competition | • Experiences psychosexual developmental phases differently.<br>• Becomes winner of the competition when parents are in awe of them; feels smarter, more capable than one parent and sees themselves as the partner of the other; feels like they are the adult.<br>• Forced to maintain this position, which results in carrying this competitiveness everywhere; believes they must do better than peers to show their preferred parent how great they are; relegate their need for the other parent's support to unconscious.<br>• Well-established, realistic self-concept; feels parental support. Experiences greater conflict during passage through Oedipal stage, resulting in later resolution of this stage when it is inappropriate and unexpected.<br>• Fights for imagined right. |
|---|---|
| The exception | • Omnipotence interferes with conscience development.<br>• High ability leads to great personal power which is never reconciled with needs of others; does not develop feelings for others; uses abilities to fulfill their own wishes and needs.<br>• Giftedness leads to impairment in normal development of identification; empathy and conscience remain fixed in period of infantile self-centeredness. Maintains illusion of being outside rules and regulations governing levels of normal people because it is this difference that their self-esteem is based on.<br>• Like perfectionists—unrealistic expectations but instead underestimate responsibilities. Like child/adult; superiority to adults sees themselves beyond the system. Fixation on feeling omnipotent.<br>• Like winner of the competition—feels superior to parent of opposite sex, but that competitor is not required because normal expectations do not apply to them. |

| Self-critic | • Views themselves as wanting; their emotions, actions, thoughts, behaviors do not live up to their expectations. Can separate from themselves and evaluate themselves objectively.<br>• Compulsively compelled to complete tasks over and over again; then feels overwhelmed with obligation due to double-checking process.<br>• Fails at tasks due to difficulty in carrying out their intentions. Feels obligated to straighten the world out and simultaneously feels incapable of doing so.<br>• Gives up feeling of omnipotence early but overextends their conscience.<br>• Possesses insights, deep awareness; self-criticism originates from giftedness.<br>• Does not believe in their giftedness; only their responsibilities. |
|---|---|
| Well-integrated child | • Develops more realistic conscience at proper developmental phase.<br>• Is aware of differences from other children and the consequences of their giftedness.<br>• More aware of world's problems; feels compelled to stand up for their convictions while suffering loneliness and isolation for this risk-taking.<br>• Realizes rights to their own feelings as well as their giftedness, developing empathy with feelings of others. Needs support for the resulting feelings created by reactions to their surroundings.<br>• Passes through developmental stages in normal manner.<br>• Feels parental support and sees themselves as autonomous beings who own their giftedness.<br>• Views themselves realistically; understands failure is a part of life. Positive and negative emotions are normal and basic to life.<br>• Overcomes omnipotence in normal manner. |

# Editor Bios

**C. Matthew Fugate**, Ph.D., is Provost and Chief Academic Officer at the Bridges Graduate School of Cognitive Diversity in Education. He received his doctorate in gifted, creative, and talented studies from Purdue University. Prior to this, Dr. Fugate worked as an elementary teacher in the Houston Independent School District, where he also served as a Gifted Coordinator. During this time, he received his Master of Arts in educational psychology, gifted education from the University of Connecticut. His primary area of research has focused on students who are gifted with attention deficit hyperactivity disorder (ADHD), including an examination of the relationship between working memory and levels of creative thinking in gifted students with ADHD. Additionally, he has looked at the coping mechanisms of twice-exceptional girls in secondary education as they navigate both their academic studies and interpersonal relationships. Dr. Fugate also served on a team that looked at the benefits of the Total School Cluster Grouping model, a Javits Grant funded project. He has presented to parents, teachers, and schools across the United States and internationally on topics such as creativity, culturally responsive teaching practices in gifted education, curriculum compacting, identification, twice exceptionality, underserved populations, and Total School Cluster Grouping. Dr. Fugate currently serves as President of the Texas Association for Gifted and Talented and is an active member of the National Association for Gifted Children (NAGC), having served as Chair of the Special Populations Network and on several organizational and network committees. Additionally, he serves on the editorial board for the *Journal for Education of the Gifted* and is the associate editor of *Teaching for High Potential*. Dr. Fugate was named one of "22 People to Watch in the Neurodiversity Movement" by

## Editor Bios

*Variations Magazine* and has received the NAGC Early Leader Award, as well as the Dr. Marcia L. Gentry Special Populations Early Career Award from the NAGC Special Populations Network. He has published numerous articles, book chapters, and books related to his work.

**Wendy A. Behrens,** M.A., is the Gifted and Talented Education Consultant for the Minnesota Department of Education. She is a recognized leader in building equitable systems for gifted learners, focusing on underserved populations, acceleration, service design, and inclusive policies. During her tenure, Wendy has developed procedures for student identification and acceleration, worked with districts to optimize funding, and supported impactful services.

Ms. Behrens founded the Hormel Gifted and Talented Education Symposium and developed enduring professional learning modules through two Jacob K. Javits grants. She also contributed to tools for identifying talent in computer science as part of the Universal Plus grant. She has held leadership roles with the NAGC, the Council of State Directors of Programs for the Gifted, and the Council for Exceptional Children/The Association for the Gifted.

Ms. Behrens is an accomplished author, whose recent works include *Understanding Twice-Exceptional Learners* and *Culturally Responsive Teaching in Gifted Education and Twice-exceptional Education: Connecting Gifted and Special Education*.

# Guest Author Bios

**Susan Baum**, Ph.D., is the Chancellor of Bridges Graduate School for Cognitive Diversity in Education and the Co-Director of the 2e Center for Research and Professional Development at Bridges Academy, a school for twice-exceptional students. She is the recipient of numerous awards for her research and experiences with these students. Dr. Baum's many publications including the award-winning third edition of her seminal work *To be Gifted and Learning Disabled*, which has earned her worldwide recognition.

**Cecelia Boswell**, Ed.D., has been a teacher of migrant and gifted students in a rural district, an advanced academics consultant for Texas, and the Executive Director of Advanced Academics for an urban district. She is an independent consultant working in district evaluation of gifted services and professional learning in gifted education and leadership nationally and throughout Texas. Dr. Boswell has served on the Texas Association for the Gifted & Talented Board of Directors and as President. She also served as President of Council for the Exceptional Children/The Association for the Gifted (CEC-TAG). She has co-authored seven books. Her areas of interest are program evaluation, rural gifted, 2e/3e, and migrant gifted learners.

**Tiffany Chaiko**, M.Ed., is a twice-exceptional doctoral student at Bridges Graduate School of Cognitive Diversity in Education. She is a non-practicing accredited public relations professional and a former independent sales representative. Tiffany has more than ten years of volunteer leadership experience in educational settings. She holds an M.Ed. in educational leadership from Hawaii

Pacific University and a Bachelor of Arts in English with minors in sociology and art history from the University of Denver. She is married with children. Her research interests are twice exceptionality; visual-spatial strengths; talent-focused and strength-based approaches with positive psychology; self-determination theory; supportive environments for twice-exceptional learners; and creativity.

**Carlita R. B. Cotton**, Ph.D., is committed to gifted education identification, equity, and designing culturally relevant pedagogy. Carlita's career began as a Russian translator and combat interrogator in the United States Air Force for 20 years. Upon honorable retirement from active-duty service, Carlita completed a Master's of Divinity degree at Howard University and taught eighth-grade language arts in a suburban Maryland town. She completed dual-concentration doctoral studies at the University of Connecticut and was conferred the degree of Doctor of Philosophy in 2008. Dr. Cotton has since worked as an intensive outpatient therapist, a community-based clinician and a pastoral counselor; she is currently a Professor of Psychology and mentor/advocate for fellow veterans. She is proud to represent the people of Mansfield, Connecticut (CT), as a town councilor and was appointed by Governor Ned Lamont to the CT Department of Veterans Affairs Board of Trustees.

**Tracy L. Cross**, Ph.D., is Dean of the College of Education & Human Development at the University of Louisiana at Lafayette. He served for 15 years as the William & Mary Jody and Layton Smith Professor of Psychology and Gifted Education, and Executive Director of the W&M Center for Gifted Education and the Institute for Research on the Suicide of Gifted Students. He has published more than 200 articles, book chapters, and columns; made hundreds of presentations at conferences; and written several books. He is past editor of numerous journals, including *Gifted Child Quarterly*, *The Roeper Review*, and the *Journal for the Education of the Gifted*.

**Jennifer Riedl Cross**, Ph.D., is Director of Research at the William & Mary Center for Gifted Education. She is the editor of the National Association for Gifted Children's research journal, the *Gifted Child Quarterly*. She co-edited, with Tracy L. Cross, the *Handbook for Counselors Serving Students with Gifts and Talents*, now in its second edition; and co-authored the second edition of *Suicide among Gifted Children and Adolescents*. Her research in the field emphasizes the social and psychological aspects of gifted education.

**Joy Lawson Davis**, Ed.D., is core faculty at Bridges Graduate School for Cognitive Diversity in Education and an award-winning equity activist, author, trainer, and keynote speaker with a distinguished record of scholarship in the field of gifted education. Her specific expertise is in increasing access and equity in gifted education programming for culturally diverse students. Recently, Dr. Davis' profile was featured in *The Roeper Review* as part of its "Eminent Scholar" series. In 2024, Dr. Davis received the Diversity Award from CEC-TAG.

**Kathryn Davis**, Ed.D., is an American Speech-Language-Hearing Association certified speech-language pathologist with a doctorate in cognitive diversity in education. She has focused on neurodiversity, language development, and individualized learning strategies throughout her career. As a military spouse and parent to two twice-exceptional autistic children, she brings both professional expertise and personal experience to her work. Dr. Davis is dedicated to advocating for inclusive education, effective communication strategies, and a strengths-based approach to supporting neurodivergent individuals. Through her scholarship and practice, she empowers educators and families to better understand and support diverse learners in academic and everyday settings.

**Orla Dunne**, Ed.D., is based at Dublin City University in Ireland, where she is an Assistant Professor in the School of Inclusive and Special Education and Academic Programme Manager for the Centre for Talented Youth, Ireland. Dr. Dunne holds a doctorate in educational leadership, with a focus on the experiences of gifted LGBTQ students. She has published in multiple journals and gifted education textbooks, has presented at conferences globally, and is a regular guest speaker for gifted education organizations in Europe and the United States. Currently, she is working on a cross-department project to create graduate programs on gifted education.

**Anne Gray**, Ph.D., is Bilagáana, married to Táchii'nii, with four Diné children. Dr. Gray is an Assistant Professor Elementary Education in the Department of Teacher Education at Northern New Mexico College. She graduated from the Gifted Education Research and Resource Institute, Purdue University; co-authored *Access Denied/System Failure: Gifted Education in the United States - Laws, Access, Equity, and Missingness Across the Country by Locale, Title I School Status, and Race*; is a board member for the New Mexico Association for the Gifted; and serves as co-Chair of the Diversity and Equity Committee for the National Association for Gifted Children.

**Enyi Jen**, Ph.D., is Associate Dean of Graduate Studies at Bridges Graduate School of Cognitive Diversity in Education. Through her teaching and publications, she has collaborated with children, adolescents, and educational professionals from across the globe. Previously, she served as a lecturer at Radboud University in the Netherlands, where she developed and implemented its international professional development blended program. Dr. Jen holds a doctorate from Purdue University and has extensive experience in K-12 education. Her research has shed light on the positive impact of well-designed affective interventions for gifted students, while also exploring the pressing topics that gifted adolescents are keen to discuss with supportive adults. Collaborating with Dr. Jean Peterson, she developed the Peterson Proactive Developmental Attention Model, advocating for the adoption of a developmental perspective to address the social and emotional needs of gifted students.

**Lisa Jobe**, J.D., is an educational consultant and advocate specializing in providing support for profoundly gifted 2e learners and their families. Lisa is co-founder of Sequoia Gifted and Creative, LLC, which serves gifted 2e families with strength-based learning, advocacy support, and homeschooling. She holds a Juris Doctorate from the George Washington University School of Law and is a doctoral student at Bridges Graduate School for Cognitive Diversity in Education.

**Shana Lusk**, Ph.D., graduated from the University of Connecticut in 2025. She is a member of the Catawba Nation, and her dissertation focused on preserving Indigenous stories about school integration and comparing generational experiences. Shana received her M.A. in curriculum and instruction with a concentration in English as a second language from Arizona State University. She is a former classroom teacher with experience meeting the diverse needs of general education, multilingual learners, and gifted students. She works to ensure that the strengths of multicultural learners are accounted for.

**Georgia McKown**, Ph.D., is a learning scientist who currently works as the Program Manager for Effective Data Systems and Professional Learning with the Behavior Alliance of South Carolina at Clemson University. In this work, she supports statewide efforts to help every child experience belonging at school. Her research interests include improving teacher education, leveraging educational technologies, and supporting the needs of military-connected children and families. All of this work is informed by her foundational experiences as an elementary school teacher in Virginia Beach, Virginia.

**Maureen Montanía**, MSc, is the Lab Coordinator at Aikumby, Paraguay's first center for giftedness and creativity, and a researcher on three national projects funded by the Paraguayan National Council of Science and Technology. Additionally, she lectures at Universidad Católica and Universidad Comunera in Paraguay; serves as a peer reviewer for the *Gifted & Talented International Journal*; and is an associate editor for the *Journal of the Faculty of Medical Sciences* at the National University of Asunción. A co-founder of R-Ladies Asunción and the Association of Gifted Professionals of Paraguay, Ms. Montanía received the Princess Diana Award in 2022 for her scientific-humanitarian efforts and was honored as an Illustrious Citizen of Fernando de la Mora in 2023, alongside a tribute from the Paraguayan National Congress for her contributions to scientific research.

**Angela Novak**, Ph.D., is an equity advocate, associate professor, and gifted coordinator at East Carolina University. For more than 25 years, she has engaged collectively with learners, families, communities, and staff in K-22 education as an inclusion co-teacher; in a variety of gifted classroom, support, and administrative roles; and in the non-profit sector. Multilingualism, equity, and belongingness have been deeply embedded in her professional work and personal lived experiences, contributing to her research and writing projects in equity, giftedness, professional learning, collegians, and play. Angela is an author, editor, and speaker and is the current editor of the *Journal of Advanced Academics.*

**Yvette Robinson**, M.A. Ed., is the chief executive officer and founder of Xavier House Unlimited, Inc., the nation's first foster group home for gifted and talented children. With over 25 years of experience, she specializes in supporting at-risk youth, including those involved in the juvenile justice system, human trafficking, and teenage parents. She holds a B.S. in social work and an M.A. in education, focusing on at-risk and alternative education. Yvette has served with state and national gifted advocacy associations and was honored with the 2024 President's Award from the National Association for Gifted Children for her work with Xavier House.

**Debbie Troxclair,** Ph.D., is Associate Professor at Lamar University, where she developed and teaches in the online graduate programs in special and gifted education. Active in professional organizations of both fields, in 2024, she received the CEC-TAG Service Award, was recognized by Phi Delta Beta Honor Society as an international scholar and was elected president of the Association for Gifted and Talented Students in Louisiana. Throughout her 20 years as a K-12 teacher and in her current role, she has advocated for children with exceptionalities—especially those who are twice exceptional and gifted. She has publications in gifted education journals and books and presents at conferences about twice-exceptional learners, attitudes toward giftedness, and social-emotional issues.

**Eleonoor van Gerven**, Ph.D., is director of Slim! Educatief BV, a private institute for teacher education in the Netherlands. She specializes in gifted education and a systemic change and solution-focused approach. She has developed a competency matrix for specialists in gifted education. She has also developed the postgraduate courses Specialist in Gifted Education and Specialist in Educating Twice-Exceptional Learners, both of which are accredited by the Dutch Society for Higher Education. She has written 17 books and almost 100 articles on gifted education. In 2014, she won the Dutch Mensa Award for her lifelong contribution to gifted education. In 2018, she was made an honorary member of the Dutch Professional Association of Specialists in Gifted Education. Dr. van Gerven is also program manager of the Dutch National Knowledge Center on Gifted Education. Together with a team of experts, she developed the Dutch national curriculum for teacher education, focusing on educating gifted learners in primary and secondary schools.

**M. Alexandra Vuyk**, Ph.D., is a researcher at the National Council for Science and Technology in Paraguay, her home country, where she is ranked in a selective government program for researchers. She applies her quantitative and statistical expertise to study the social and emotional development of intellectually and creatively gifted individuals. She has a doctorate in counseling psychology with a specialty in quantitative psychology from the University of Kansas, USA, and an M.S. in special education with a concentration in gifted, talented, and creative from Emporia State University in Kansas, USA. Dr. Vuyk hopes to advance gifted education in her native Paraguay.

**Gilman Whiting,** Ph.D., is Professor in the African American and Diaspora Studies Department at Vanderbilt University. He is the creator of the Scholar Identity Model™ and directs the Scholar Identity Institute. He researches sociology of race, underperformance in special and gifted education, and summer programming. His research has been implemented across five continents. Dr. Gilman has received numerous honors, including 2018 Purdue University Distinguished Alumnus and 2021 Palmarium Awardee. He is a former world-class athlete and a retired US Army combat officer and was inducted into the Black Belt Hall of Fame in 2018. Dr. Whiting considers assisting students, teachers, families, and administrators to actualize their highest potential as his raison d'être.

For Product Safety Concerns and Information please contact our EU
representative GPSR@taylorandfrancis.com
Taylor & Francis Verlag GmbH, Kaufingerstraße 24, 80331 München, Germany

www.ingramcontent.com/pod-product-compliance
Lightning Source LLC
Chambersburg PA
CBHW060509300426
44112CB00017B/2595